Brain-Savvy Business

8 principles from neuroscience and how to apply them

Copyright © Jan Hills 2016

The right of Jan Hills to be identified as the author of this work has been asserted by her in accordance with the Copyright, Design and Patents Act 1988

First published by Head Heart + Brain 2016
157, 41 Millharbour, London E14 9ND. United Kingdom
www.headheartbrain.com

info@hhab.co.uk

British Library Cataloguing in Publication Data

A CIP catalogue record for this book is available from the British library

ISBN 978-0992900748

You could dip in and out of this book, though I think you'll more likely be hooked from cover to cover as Jan serves up the latest neuroscience to explain why people behave the way they do. Providing more than just fascinating insight, the brain-savvy tools set out in the context of common workplace challenges make this an indispensable field guide for the modern leader.

David Perks
CEO, Pay Compliment - 1 place for all your feedback

A one stop shop for business leaders that navigates, distils and busts some myths in the ever advancing field of Neuroscience. With an unswerving focus on practical application Jan's book shows how using the right amount of science can help you master the art of leading the modern organisation where old rules don't apply and new norms continue to emerge"

Paul Lemon
CEO Managing Partners Forum

Brain-savvy Business translates complex science into eight key principles that you can easily apply to a range of business challenges. It's a great read for those new to the topic, and keen to expand their mind with the latest neuroscience insight in an easily digestible format.

Ruth Stuart
Lead Consultant, Strategic Projects – CIPD

Jan Hills has done it again. In Brain-Savvy Business she demonstrates her depth of knowledge and understanding of the human side of the workplace. Insightful, comprehensive and laid out in an easy to follow format, the eight principles provide the essential who's who for the practical application of the neuroscience and business today. This is a book that can be dipped into time and again - highly recommended for all brains in business.

Dr Jenny Brockis
Brain and organisational health specialist, and author of Future Brain

Neuroscience is increasing our understanding of how people really do learn, what drives our decision making, and the relationship between the emotional and the rational brain. Brain-savvy Business brings it in to the realm of the practical and pragmatic, giving us actionable insights to help develop our people and our leaders to create lasting change, and to drive better and more sustainable businesses for the future.

Peter Cheese
Chief Executive, CIPD - the professional body for HR and people development

All businesses are looking for a competitive edge. They must be looking to obtain the best from their people and improve the relationships they have with their clients. This is particularly true of the legal profession who are often accused of being too slow to embrace change and innovation. This is a fascinating insight into how an understanding of neuroscience can give you an edge, as by understanding the science we can challenge the more traditional ways in which we have managed our people and client relationships. The neuroscience is cleverly backed up by practical application with insightful and very business relevant case studies with the chapters addressing areas such as adapting the mind-set of your people to be high achievers and how we connect and engage with clients to build a lasting relationships so that they stay loyal to you, being incredibly relevant to any one in business service sector.

David North
Partner for Osborne Clarke LLP

This and Jan's previous book are written in an easy to consume way that can help frame strategic approaches to people management, such as performance ratings and reward processes with how the brain operates and how we each see the world. This enables two significant things: 1) a greater chance of encouraging the right behaviours for organisational performance than unintentionally promoting less effective ones and b) people being more self-aware and aware of others which tends to result in greater quality of life. Both have a profound impact on the success of any company.

James Rule
Director, Culture & Effectiveness Thomson Reuters

Brilliantly organized and user friendly, the Brain Savvy Business harnesses the most up to date insights from Neuroscience and delivers them to the reader in a clear and compelling manner. Written with clear explanations, examples and tools, there isn't an organization in the world that wouldn't benefit from the insights in this book!

Tricia Naddaff
President, Management Research Group

Jan Hills in her new book creates an insightful link between the fascinating world of neuroscience and everyday business life. An understanding of how the brain works under specific circumstances becomes extremely relevant when the business leaders have to take important decisions that affect both the business and other people's lives.

The book brings the science behind the key business situations, the application and concrete case studies. Jan writes in a language easy to read and with practical application for the workplace, making it an essential operation tool for modern organizations.

Renato Mosca
CEO, Training Luxury

This book is thought-provoking and insightful - I have already used its principles in discussing leadership development with our partners. The case studies provide really valuable examples of how the science has been applied by others. A great tool to have.

Caroline Rawes
Chief Talent Officer, Ashurst

Thank you

The findings from neuroscience suggest we are social animals, we need each other to thrive. This has certainly been true in the work to get this book written. After publishing Brain-savvy HR I said 'that's it' but then the itch started drawing me to write another book. This was mainly because I saw how much people struggled to apply the interesting insights from neuroscience to their everyday work in business. My aim was to address this in Brain-savvy Business by covering the science but also the practical application.

I want to thank our clients who have inspired our application of neuroscience to business and helped us test many of the ideas in this book.

Thanks also to my colleagues Sarah North and Lindsay Hanson who have supported me in this effort.

Finally thanks to all the people who helped with editing, type setting, illustrations proofing and printing.

And thanks to the neuroscientist who are doing such great work. Those who have been an inspiration include. Matt Lieberman, Dean Mobbs, Kevin Ochsner and Josh Davis.

Finally, thanks for taking an interest in this book. I look forward to hearing how you apply the ideas and the success you achieve. You can always reach me at janhills@hhab.co.uk

Jan

Contents

Foreword p.1

What's Challenging Your Business? p.3

Principle 1:
Minimise Threat & Maximise Reward p.17

Principle 2:
Social Connection – A Super Power p.71

Principle 3:
Mind-set Matters p.117

Principle 7:
Create Brain-Savvy Working Habits p.307

Principle 8:
Manage Energy p.333

The Brain-Savvy Leader p.389

Foreword

It weighs around 1.5 kilos, has the appearance of a giant, rotten chestnut on the rare occasions it is available to view, and is transformed under trauma to a shocking mess of bloody matter. The human brain is a source of endless prurient fascination for crime writers and Hollywood script-writers. At one moment a psychological mystery of character motivation, at the next an audience shocker tipping the hand of the censors into an 18 certificate. Part matter, part something ephemeral. How is it wired? And is mine wired differently from yours? Or his? Or hers?

"What are you thinking?" The cri de coeur question of insecure lovers the world over. And no closer to an honest answer than it has ever been. "What are you thinking?" The anxious enquiry of the commission-dependent salesman fishing for an insight into his likelihood of success. And open to exploitation by the putative client convinced the question reveals much of the inquisitor's own mental and emotional wiring. "What are you thinking?" The desperate hope-against-hope enquiry to the specialist in whose diagnosis the patient's future resides. And as much an invitation to benevolent dishonesty as a frank appraisal of the facts.

As we get older we like to think we get wiser. But that wisdom may simply be the recognition that there is much that is unknowable, and that to rail against this ignorance is futile. I'll never truly know what you are thinking. Where once I asked in hope of pure knowledge, now I'll do so to gain some contextual understanding of the situation you and I now find ourselves in. As elite sports coaches strive for the aggregation of small marginal gains, so in business and socially perhaps the best I can hope for is the accumulation of small pieces of insight. I take what you tell me you are thinking - if you deign to give me an answer - and weigh it on the scales of my life's experience, assessing the accuracy of your reply as best I can, secure in the knowledge that all is guesswork.

Management is a continuous process of such guesswork. Colleagues are endlessly mysterious and capable of surprise, each with their own wiring as unique as their fingerprints. Generalisations are possible, indeed can take you a long way, but are ultimately dangerous. How to make sense of this mass of seemingly irreconcilable interpersonal data? This book purports to provide answers, to make you more savvy - of brains, your own and of others. Not their blood and gore, though therein lies their mystery, but their unseen and unseeable wiring.

In my advancing years I may not be richer in true understanding, but I hope to be wiser - savvier - in how I approach the world's challenge of human co-existence. Jan Hills demystifies this challenge for our business interactions. Read her. I feel sure I know what she is thinking. That's a start, and a reassuring one at that.

Ed Warner, chairman of investment bank Panmure Gordon and of UK Athletics

What's challenging your business?

We wrote this book for one very simple reason - to bring together the latest advances in neuroscience and lay out how they can be applied to help businesses. We wanted to help businessmen and women understand how the brain works and the impact this has on how others work, connect and lead. We wanted to enable them to run more efficient, more effective, more successful organisations – organisations that we like to call brain-savvy.

We've been helping our clients apply the findings from neuroscience to a wide variety of businesses since 2009. One thing we've learned since then is that though our discipline isn't the only approach to getting the best out of people and organisations, mixed with the right tools and a sound business strategy it can make a big difference.

Neuroscience is often counter-intuitive. The findings often contradict established opinion, particularly when they relate to what helps and what hinders performance at work. So whilst the challenge can feel uncomfortable, we've found that they get results where other approaches don't. Neuroscience can give you great insight into why a policy, practice or way of leading may not be working, or explain why it is working.

And this insight is good to have but, without the right tools to go on and harness its potential, it's of little practical use. So we've provided a range of these tools and indicated where they may be used and the types of problems they will help you solve. The tools are the same ones we've used to great effect with our clients. Many are simple and we usually find that it's these that can have the biggest impact.

How this book is structured

We have drawn together the neuroscience findings and their implications for business, and grouped them into a number of principles. Each Principle chapter has six main types of information and you can dip in and out - it is not necessary to work through in a linear fashion. The sections are:

The science: A description of what neuroscience and other behavioural sciences are saying about how our brains work.

The application: Here's where we summarise how this knowledge can help you improve policy, practice, leadership or processes. This section gives more details about how the science helps or hinders typical ways of working.

Case study: Theory is all very well, but sometimes it's hard to see how to apply it. So we've used real-world examples from our experience helping clients solve a business issue or improve how they manage and lead their organisation.

Tools: These are the best and often incredibly simple methods we recommend for applying insights to your own business. All the tools have been tried and tested with our own clients so we know they work and are consistent with a brain-savvy approach to business.

Principle summary: Each section ends with a summary of how the Principle applies to business. This can be a very useful starting point for discussing the ideas with others.

References: At the end of each chapter we've listed the major papers that cover the main scientific principles discussed so that if you want to dig a little deeper, you can. If you want a less scientific explanation, one that's simpler or shorter, then we've also supplied a number of accessible videos and books on the subject.

A guide to the types of business challenges each Principle helps

Sometimes an issue doesn't fit neatly into one particular Principle so you may want to investigate more than one. So before jumping straight in, take a look at the scenarios below. They're designed to give you some guidance as to which principles to focus on.

Business challenges and the Principles

Change

However positive the changes you're facing, from past experience you know it can be a struggle to implement them effectively. Sometimes people simply and instinctively resist, or perhaps the budget escalates, all but eliminating the reasons for making the change in the first place. Other times, the people leading the change take their foot off the gas too early, and good initial results quickly dissipate. Alongside that, change is usually very process-oriented, the 'people stuff' gets overlooked and it's this that's probably going to make the biggest difference. You have a sneaking suspicion the emphasis is on processes rather than people because the people stuff can be harder to pin down and nobody is really confident that they know how to tackle it.

Go to:

Principle 1:
Minimise Threat & Maximise Reward

Principle 6:
Change = New Behavioural Habits

Principle 8:
Manage Energy

My team need new skills

There's nothing wrong with your team - but though they're all highly technically skilled the market is changing and clients are demanding a different type of service. That means people need new skills. They - and you - need to understand the client's business strategy, the developments in the sector and how to provide a more commercial service. There are a number of learning programmes but you want more than a couple of days in a classroom. Also, you know the team need to be helped to apply these skills to the job and some of them need convincing they have to change how they work.

Go to:

 Principle 6:
Change = New Behavioural Habits

 Principle 3:
Mind-set Matters

Our leadership development isn't making much difference

Leadership has been a focus for the company for a while now and there's been considerable investment of time and effort into getting it right. However not much has actually changed: There's still no convincing pipeline of people for the key jobs, and those leaders who have received development continue pretty much to do what they've always done. The money spent on training seems to be wasted but it's not acceptable to say so. You've taken part in some of the programmes yourself and they're really interesting but you're finding it hard to apply what you learnt when you are back in the office and dealing with the day-to-day work load.

Go to:

 Principle 3:
Mind-set Matters

 Principle 5:
Create Brain-Savvy Learning

 Principle 6:
Change = New Behavioural Habits

Can people really change?

The leadership team are considering a new leadership development programme. You've been asked for your views. You know there is pressure on budgets and you want a better approach to training and development. You also hear people saying they don't have time to attend the programmes which are on offer, and as a manager of a team you tend to agree. You don't really have the resources to send people off site for three or four days, and you definitely can't afford to keep flying people around the world to attend programmes.

It might be worth it if they actually did something different when they came back. You've seen attempts to use learning technology but the results haven't been very good. Your younger team members seem to use the internet and lots of resources which are freely available, and then there are a handful of people who seem to get their development from watching others and applying the best of what they do.

Why some people use the learning available better than others is a bit of a mystery, and it would be worth understanding more.

Go to:

 Principle 3:
Mind-set Matters

 Principle 5:
Create Brain-Savvy Learning

Principle 6:
Change = New Behavioural Habits

Diversity and inclusion

You are a member of the diversity and inclusion committee. The company is very committed to creating opportunities for a more diverse leadership team and to create a culture where people with different skills, backgrounds and ideas can thrive. You've been at it for a while but the data suggests not much progress is being made. Privately you think the issue has 'gone underground' - people say all the right things but don't follow through.

Go to:

Principle 4:
Emotions Win the Day

We just have to make better decisions

You've just had a major project end in failure because the decision to start it was based on the wrong assumptions. It's easy to see in hindsight, but why couldn't it have been seen before? People seemed to be in too much of a rush to really connect the dots. Also, as clever as the team are, they never seem to stop and think; it's just one decision after another. You're determined to find a way of improving the quality of decision-making in your team because you don't want another project post-mortem like this last one.

Go to:

 Principle 4:
Emotions Win the Day

 Principle 6:
Change = New Behavioural Habits

People just aren't that engaged

You're on the company working party that oversees engagement. (Somehow you drew the short straw!) The engagement survey is showing people don't trust the leadership and don't much like the company. They definitely wouldn't recommend working there to a friend, according to the results. The scores have been sliding for a couple of years but everyone always blamed the economic climate. But that can't be the excuse any longer - business results are good and the market is doing better. Somehow you and the working party need to come up with some solutions that will get people connected to the company, believing in it and trusting the leaders.

Go to:

 Principle 2:
Social Connection – A Super Power

 Principle 1:
Minimise Threat & Maximise Reward

 Principle 8:
Manage Energy

Performance management isn't helping performance

You're fed up with struggling through the annual performance management process and you know something needs to change. The root of the issue is the process just isn't working for staff or managers. Some people say it's because the emphasis is too much on managing and not enough on getting people performing better. Others say it's just too bureaucratic and that there are simply too many forms to fill out. The employees in particular say it's just looking back at all the mistakes they made and rehashing them. Whatever the real issue - and maybe it's a bit of all of these - it's not working. But what can you do to make it better?

Go to:

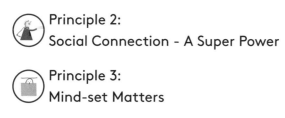 **Principle 1:**
Minimise Threat & Maximise Reward

Principle 3:
Mind-set Matters

Principle 6:
Change = New Behavioural Habits

Principle 8:
Manage Energy

It takes more than smarts

You've always been one of the cleverest people in your group, whether it's at school, university or work. But now you're beginning to realise being simply bright and talented isn't enough. After many years the profession is changing. Clients want more. And the old adage that people buy the person not the technical knowhow has never been truer. You know you need to be doing something different. How do you connect with clients and build a relationship that means they don't want to go to the competition?

Go to:

Principle 2:
Social Connection - A Super Power

Principle 3:
Mind-set Matters

Principle 8:
Manage Energy

Just too busy

You're under enormous pressure to get more done but there just aren't enough hours in the day. Also, the issues are getting more complex and you don't have the head space to make the connections. Rationally, you know that if you slowed down a bit you would be able to think better but you just can't seem to make that happen. You're also exhausted from always checking emails and responding to the 24/7 demands of the job.

Go to:

Principle 7:
Brain-Savvy Working Habits

Principle 6:
Change = New Behavioural Habits

Principle 8:
Manage Energy

Applying the Principles

Although there's plenty of advice in each chapter about how to put specific insights into practice, it can still be difficult to go from sit-ting-and-reading-a-book to not-just-thinking-that-this-might-be-a-good-idea-for-some-other-time-but-actually-doing-something-about-it.

We see this all the time when we're working with clients. They're very curious about the science and most of the insights make sense, but it's daunting to move from an intellectual understanding to changing a major policy, leadership style or approach throughout the company or just within a particular team.

And let's be honest - our brain is actually working against us taking what is new and unfamiliar and introducing it. The brain likes novelty but it also likes to be able to predict the future, to be certain. You can't be certain exactly what will happen in your company or your team if you introduce these ideas. What you can be certain of is this: If you follow the following steps, you will be working in a way that works with the brain, not against it.

If what you are doing isn't working...

The trick is to start with the current issue which is taking up energy and focus, and try something different.

The following steps are designed to get the ball rolling. We're not suggesting you follow them to the letter - just use them as a guide. Use your own judgement about the speed at which you can intro-duce change and, depending on your culture and the beliefs and preferences of your stakeholders, how much of the science you need to reveal. We often use the science with our clients 'behind the cur-tain'. That is, the science informs the design and structure of what we are doing and it may even be the basis of the policy and process we develop - but it's not always explicitly mentioned. The change is framed as right for the goals the company is trying to achieve. The advantage of this approach is that people have less to think about and therefore less potential worry, too.

On the other hand, some clients are seeking the scientific under-standing because they like to know why something works or why it is being proposed. Having this evidence helps them accept the change. You will know which way's right for your business.

Our advice is to take one step at a time, review the results and then move on to the next step.

Step 1: Getting yourself up to speed

Whether you skip straight to the case studies, the science or how it plays out in business doesn't matter. Start where it feels right for you - with the issue you're trying to solve or the business policy you want to make even better. Obviously any given case study is just one way of dealing with an issue but each one will give you an idea of what a company did and the results they were seeking.

It's also worth bearing in mind: You don't have to become an expert in the science. The summary of the Principle might be all you need to get started. The details are there to give you a sense of how the science plays out in different business situations.

We recommend you start with the most pressing issue or the one that promises the greatest potential reward. If that feels high-risk, then think about running a pilot or experiment where you can introduce the ideas in one area where you can monitor the results, and then learn about how the Principle works in your culture.

Step 2: Identifying the real issue

First things first: Think about the root cause of the issue you have. It can be easy to jump to the conclusion that everything's about there being too much threat and not enough reward, or everyone having a fixed mind-set. Both of these may be true but are they what's causing the issue?

The other trap it's easy to fall into, is solving the myths in an organisation - the stories that people tell about why the organisation or a department or function is not as successful as it could be. You'll have heard the stories: "Finance can't work with HR because they just don't talk the same language." Or, "The CFO and the HRD don't talk to each other." Or, "Marketing has never really understood the potential for the product." These stories are often based on past truths or historical problems but may not be relevant now.

There will almost certainly be many contributing factors and that can mean you get a bit stuck, perhaps because you have too much data or because you're giving too much weight to the views of one particular set of stakeholders. There are two potential approaches to overcoming these obstacles and getting the ball rolling:

> The first is to talk to a number of people who experience the issue from different perspectives. The most senior to the most junior; the experienced to the novice; those inside the company and those who interact with the company but are not employees, like your customers or suppliers. Gather the data and then reflect on the patterns you're seeing. The brain is an excellent pattern recognition machine so you should quickly identify what's reoccurring, what is only seen by one group of stakeholders, or what you notice but no one else has mentioned. Look also at people's beliefs rather than just the facts. Beliefs will be what drive behaviour and people will filter the facts to meet their own beliefs.

> The second approach is to pinpoint the teams, departments, leaders or professionals who are working in such a way that they are successful despite the issue. Understanding the difference that makes a difference in their success can point you in the direction of transferring those successful elements to others. We do this through our Success Profile methodology and you can read more about it on our web site. Again, talk to a range of successful people, collect the data and use your brain's natural love of patterns to help you analyse it. The resulting model will tell you how those successful people are successful - the things they do which make the most difference. Remember, you don't need to know everything to help others be successful, just the beliefs and behaviours that really matter.

Step 3: Planting seeds and creating insight

Once you have a good idea about the root cause (or the success factors of those that are successful despite the issue) turn to the section above on the scenarios and the Principle or principles linked to them. Start talking to the people you'll need to influence and who'll need to agree with your approach - your stakeholders. Take it gently, as some of the science contradicts strongly held views in management, leadership, business and people processes.

Also bear in mind (it's a recurring theme, this one!) that the brain tends to create a feeling of discomfort when it is faced with something new. It will be worth getting people familiar with the ideas before jumping in with both feet. It generally works best to let people have the insight for themselves rather than telling them what they should do or think, so consider the best way to help people get familiar with the Principle and the application of it to your business. Could you send them an extract from the chapter or a link to one of the videos or maybe start with one of our shorter articles or blogs on the topic, perhaps? There are also videos of webinars we have run on some of the principles covered in the book. Once your stakeholders are familiar with the ideas you're introducing, you can start discussing how they might apply in your situation. Asking powerful questions can work well here. These are questions that get people thinking differently, shifting their perceptions and beliefs. For example, 'What one thing could we change to create a high performing culture' or 'If we had no constraints what would we do differently?'

The other thing to think about is how the ideas might create a sense of threat or reward. Principle 1 will be helpful in planning your tactics to influence stakeholders. Another thing to consider is whether people really want to solve the issue or is their mind-set that it is just the way the business works? Take a look at Principle 3 and check if mind-set might be a contributing factor. And finally consider the energy to solve the problem - Principle 8 will be helpful with that.

Step 4: Getting people focused

Once people begin to see the value of the Principle, you should map out how you might apply it and what people will need to be able to do. How big a change is this? Will they need training? Or will you need a formal change plan? What do you anticipate the challenges will be? How can you create a plan to overcome the challenges? What are your measures of success and how will you monitor them in real time to check you are getting the results you desire? What will you do if you face resistance? There are resources and tools in the book that can help you to do this stage in a brain-savvy way. In particular, look at the tools section in Principles 1, 5, 6 and 8.

Also decide if you are going to use the science 'behind the curtain' or in front of it. Are you going to follow the Principle but not explicitly discuss the science?

Whichever method you use, getting people involved in the change is what's important. Not only do you harness the collective wisdom of the business but you also reduce feelings of threat. You can use the CORE tool (see Principle 1) to design and monitor the results of your change plan, and also look at the case study in the same Principle as well as the section about threat and change.

Step 5: Keep going long enough to establish new ways of working

Many change efforts, be they big or small, fail because the change team stop too soon. This also happens to individuals: You think you're in the habit of going to the gym or connecting with the team or taking more time to listen - and then things get tough and you forget to do it. Most of what we do is habit rather than intentional behaviour. This is because our brain seeks to operate in the most energy efficient way. Helping people to understand how habits are formed and supporting and celebrating the new behaviour for long enough to make it a habit is what creates real change. No one knows how long it takes to form a habit but it is longer than a week or even a month. So keep going and give people the support necessary to embed the new behaviour. The information in Principle 6 on habits will be helpful.

Further reading and viewing

Brain Basics video. Head Heart + Brain http://www.headheart-brain.com/brain-basics/

Principle 1:
Minimise Threat
& Maximise Reward

Before you plunge headlong into this section, take a few moments to consider the following questions. Your answers should reveal something about the balance of threat and reward in your organisation's culture:

Do people know what's expected of them in their role?

Are they given the opportunity to organise their own work and choose how they achieve their goals?

Are they praised for their achievements?

Are leaders aware of individuals' ambitions?

Are people given positive feedback on their progress towards goals?

Would people say the culture is fair and honest?

Is communication transparent?

Do people feel energised at work? Are they open to new ideas?

How easy is it to implement changes in the organisation? From the leadership on down, how is everybody involved in making these changes?

How do people manage when there are changes? How much resistance is there?

colleague and realise that her off-putting manner is just the result of feeling ill at ease in a new company. We'll find that she's actually quite likeable as well as very useful.

Are your professional relationships creating threat or reward?

The threat response

Neuroscience sheds new light on how people react in social situations. We can use these insights to form better relationships and be more effective at influencing other people. For example, the brain is highly evolved to work in a social environment, and if the environment doesn't provide the social support we need, our brains can interpret this as a threat. There are a number of things that we look for in terms of social support, like when we feel included in a group, when we know what's happening, when we feel a connection with others, or we have another person support us.

Without the social support we need, older parts of our brain - the parts that govern fight-or-flight - are activated. And that takes resources away from the newer parts of the brain - the prefrontal cortex - that deals with lateral thinking, connection-making, creativity, and the regulation of emotions.

This is because our brain evolved to ensure we survived and our ancestors didn't need those parts to protect themselves in a threatening environment. This prefrontal cortex may be powerful but it's slow compared to the more primitive parts of the brain. Taking the time to analyse whether the movement in the bush was an animal about to pounce or just a breeze would have made them easy targets.

In modern business, these older, instinctive reactions impact on our ability to engage with others and perform well.[2] If we can get better at understanding this reaction in ourselves and our colleagues, we can build more productive relationships and be more influential.

Reward response

Not surprisingly, the reward response often operates as the mirror-opposite of threat. We feel good about a situation or a person so we look forward to seeing them. We're more willing to engage, we're more open to ideas, and we're probably more creative, too. Again, most of this happens unconsciously, but it still influences what we do and how well we do it.

When people learn about these threat and reward responses in the brain and apply this knowledge to their own situation, very often they have a light-bulb moment. Their insight helps them formulate new strategies to overcome unconscious responses and do what's best for the organisation and their own career. Sometimes it's enough just to understand the science and recognise why they've been responding in a particular way. At other times, people may need tools or coaching to put together new strategies.

Threat areas

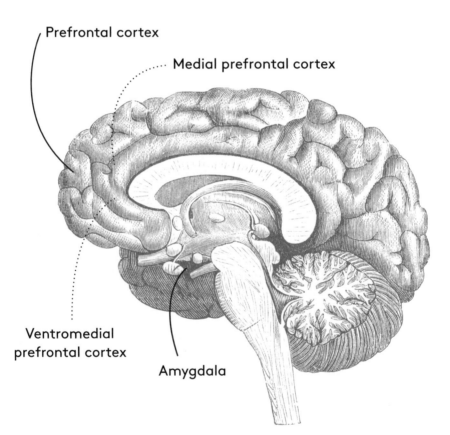

Prefrontal cortex

Medial prefrontal cortex

Ventromedial prefrontal cortex

Amygdala

Tolerance to change and stress

Stress activates similar areas of the brain that threat does. Some people seem to handle change and stressful situations better than others, and there are a couple of useful theories about why. One theory suggests this is related to the degree of stimulation or arousal they experience.

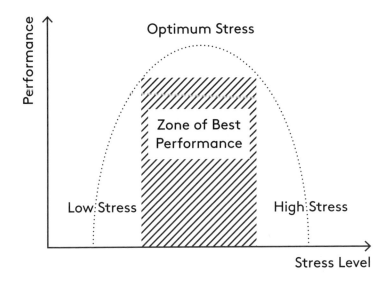

The Inverted U Model

Ever since 1908, the Inverted U model[3] (also known as the Yerkes-Dodson Law after the psychologists that discovered it) has been used to demonstrate the relationship between stress (or extreme threat) and performance. The model illustrates that performance peaks when people experience a moderate level of stress, but when they experience too little or too much, performance drops off.

Those to the left of the graph's peak are being under-challenged. Not enough stress, and you just can't get round to writing that report, making that phone call or clearing those emails.

At the midpoint we're in what's called 'flow', a state defined by psychologist Mihaly Csikszentmihalyi[4]. He devised a formula to help people achieve the flow state. In essence, it involves striking a balance between how difficult you believe a task to be and how capable you think you are of carrying it out. If the challenge is too low you go into the so-called 'drone zone', and never engage. If you think the task is beyond you, you go into the 'panic zone' and go to pieces.

Those to the right of the peak are being overly challenged. They're stressed. When we find ourselves in this state we're likely to react emotionally, we may lose sleep, be forgetful and find that we're not making the connection between bits of information. It's that feeling any of us can get when we say something to someone and then realise we haven't made the connection with what we already knew about that person - like asking a colleague if they know a new member of the project team when actually we know they used to work in the same department, or asking them if they know a prospective client when they have already told us about their experience in a previous meeting.

How stress hormones work

Stress can cause our bodies to secrete a number of different hormones. It's important to recognise though, that they're not in themselves 'bad' – they can actually be very useful. It's an excess of them that causes the problems.

Adrenaline, noradrenaline and cortisol are part of the group of hormones called glucocorticoids. They help us function properly in the face of danger. They trigger the stress (or threat) response that our bodies have developed to keep us safe - the fight-or-flight response - and also help us with learning and forming new memories. When we get *too* stressed, however, we can enter a state called cortisol dominance, which negatively affects learning, attention span and memory.

What is experienced as stress varies hugely from person to person. It may stress you if there's a backlog of work waiting to be done. But to a team member it may be super stressful always having you two steps ahead of them.

In other words, what matters most is not *what* happens to you, but how you *react* to what happens to you.

What happens to our brains under stress?

According to neuroendocrinologist Bruce McEwen, stress is 'all in our head', since our brain is responsible for recognising and responding to stressors.[5] The areas that are mainly involved are the amygdalae, the hippocampus, and the prefrontal cortex, which work the hypothalamus to flip on or shut down the production of stress hormones and other automatic responses to over-arousal, such as increased heart rate. Researchers are learning more and more about how stressors can physically alter the brain, possibly affecting how we learn, form memories and even make decisions. Stress, it seems, can do some nasty things to our brain. Luckily most are temporary and can be remedied with exercise and lifestyle.

For example, neurobiologist Tallie Baram looked at how short-term but acute stress like making a very difficult presentation to the board affects the adult brain.[6] She found that the brain produces a very specific type of stress hormone in response to short-term stressors called corticotrophin (CRH). Just a few hours of CRH exposure was enough to destroy the delicate balance between the parts of the brain that transmit and receive messages.

The effects of stress on your body

The fight-or-flight response isn't only manifested in the brain: Our bodies are physically affected as well. Blood flow is directed away from extremities and towards the heart, lungs, legs and spine.

Historically this was a big help. When something with big teeth and razor sharp claws jumped out at one of our ancestors, her body was gearing up for action before her conscious mind had even finished weighing up the pros and cons of either standing her ground or hightailing it out of there. However, this response reduces fine motor skills dramatically. And because the body wants to use all of the available energy for fighting or running away, it puts other processes like digestion on the back burner - which is why we often feel sick during or after high-stress situations. It's also why we often can't remember peripheral details after a stressful situation, only the ones directly related to the event.

You've probably noticed how your heartbeat automatically speeds up during stressful situations. This in turn sends a signal to the brain's prefrontal cortex, the parts of your brain that handle planning, analytical thinking and decision-making, and shuts them down temporarily, allowing the limbic kill-or-be-killed brain networks to take over. When we're in this state, instinct takes over from rational thought and reasoning. Kill-or-be-killed is a commendable precept when confronted with a hungry tiger but it's less helpful during a performance review or a board meeting.

Stress has also been implicated in various health issues, particularly chronic stress. It can impair our immune system, making us more susceptible to illness, high blood pressure and heart disease, as well as causing everyday aches and pains, weight gain, sleep loss, a reduced sex drive and skin conditions such as hives or eczema.

Change isn't necessarily stressful

Different people need different amounts of arousal to achieve optimum performance, and it may be that the base level of arousal of people who generally welcome change is lower than those who find change difficult. Their lower arousal gives them a greater tolerance of the stimulus created in the brain when confronted with change. On the other hand, people who already have a high natural state of arousal are pushed over the edge when they encounter the same level of change and uncertainty.

An individual's response will also vary under different circumstances. An employee who is moving house, whose parent is ill or whose teenager is leaving home may be less tolerant of change in their workplace. The solution is to understand what is going on for individuals. Instead of labeling people as 'difficult' if they react strongly to change, it makes more sense to work to reduce their arousal. Using the CORE tool described below is one way of doing this.

Threat and reward preference

The second theory about why people react differently to change is called the 'avoid response preference' model.[7] This model maintains that people who have dominant activity in the left prefrontal cortex tend to experience reward more frequently and to seek it out more. Those with dominant activity in the right prefrontal cortex, however, are more likely to be experiencing those inhibiting avoidance responses.

These two dominant states create personality traits or what we might call 'preferred behavioural habits'. Individual differences in these preferences and how they are triggered will depend on many factors including the level of threat and the sensitivity of the individual. So when it comes to change, it can be useful to think about which preferences may be dominant in an individual or group of individuals, and how actions by certain people or the organisation as a whole may activate these preferences.

We've discovered from neuroscientific research that describing the change using language that mirrors the preference can activate different brain regions. Some language patterns tend to be linked to a preference to move towards change, while other patterns are linked to avoiding problems. The former patterns talk about the rewards to be gained by the change, for example: 'Changing the company operating model gives us an opportunity to grow the customer base, increase market share and treble the business.'

Avoidance language patterns, conversely, describe the threats to be moved away from: 'Continuing with the current operating model is losing us market share, customers and opportunities to grow.'

Drawing from work in Neurolinguistic Programming (NLP) we have been able to teach clients to understand people's preferences by carefully listening to the language they use. Noticing and matching the pattern enhances understanding, communication and goal setting. Neuroscientist Elliot Berkman uses avoid/approach to structure goals using the different language structures.[8]

We have provided the tool below and described how we used this in the case study.

The application

Whether they mean to or not, some companies evolve a culture that's more threatening than rewarding. Although people can get accustomed to working in this environment, it comes at a cost. Employees need more energy to stay focused, they're likely to be less creative and they're more easily pushed over the edge into stress.

There are three areas in particular where we frequently see threat and reward responses play out in business - change, influence and performance management. All three have a number of common features. People are required to do something new or to adopt a new methodology. They might also be asked to stop doing something in which they've invested their time, energy and skills.

Because of the way the brain works, these things can be a challenge. We'll deal with how to help people change behaviour in the Principle on habit, and concern ourselves here on reducing resistance to change, being more influential and making performance management more effective, whether that's the formal process or how it's used by managers. We will also consider how it is our attitude rather than events themselves that seem to determine stress levels.

Change can be a threat

Leaders often tell us that people don't resist change deliberately. Someone may agree in theory with a proposed change, but fail to adopt that change in practice. They may fail to shift at all. They may shift very slowly, and only after productivity and engagement have dropped. Or they may revert to their old ways of working after an initial shift. Incentives and threats have little effect, and serve only to drive resistance underground so that people might continue to work in the old way whenever the boss's back is turned, or keep going back to using the old system.

Why do they do this, even when there's no logical reason for people to continue working in the old way?

When scientists look at this question on a neurobiological level, the studies show that individuals' responses to change are remarkably similar. Change, they discovered, can prompt the same sort of painful experience in the brain that being punched on the nose or breaking a bone does.

Change is pain

We find it so hard to change because our brain responds well to patterns and actively looks for them. Patterns are short cuts that reduce uncertainty and save energy. Routines or regular activities are run by the basal ganglia, which is an energy-efficient part of the brain - that's why you don't have to work out how to open a door every time you come to one. Many parts of our jobs are similarly a habit and brain efficient.

Doing something different - breaking one of these patterns - sends an 'error' message to the amygdala, the emotional centre of our brain - and it's the amygdala that creates a fight-or-flight response.[9] Our prefrontal cortex can override this more primitive emotional response, which is why we don't always run away whenever someone suggests we do something differently. But this override process can take up a lot of energy.

So set up a reward response

Traditional change management doesn't take into account this understanding of the brain's functioning. Bonuses, incentives or coercion don't overcome this biological reaction, and nor will simply selling the change programme more persuasively. Appealing to people's intellect won't help them circumvent their instincts.

The way to get past the threat response is to help people decide for themselves that the new approach is what they want. Getting them involved in the change, giving them some control over how the change is introduced and letting them decide for themselves how they structure their job to incorporate the change all create reward responses in the brain. This can go a long way to offsetting the threat created when people are experiencing change. We've created a Leaders' Change Charter to help people remember the steps to take and have included the tool below.

The CORE model

We've developed something called the CORE model as a quick and easy way to help understand and manage potential responses in yourself and in other people when influencing people, suggesting change or building a relationship. It's based on research that has identified that people experience threat or reward in four key social situations (such as are found in day-to-day office life). Understanding when a threat response might be triggered and how it could be avoided or minimised, and when a sense of reward can be created in each of these areas is essential for managing areas like change, performance management, learning - and of course communications.

Social experience can be broken down into four areas where we experience the threat or reward responses, and it's these that give the model its name:

Certainty: our confidence that we know what the future holds.[10]

Options: the extent to which we feel we have choices.[11]

Reputation: our relative importance to others (our social ranking).[12]

Equity: our sense of fairness.[13]

These four elements can activate either the reward or threat circuits in our brains. For example, a perceived threat to our sense of equity activates similar brain networks that a physical threat would. Similarly, a perceived increase to our reputation or social standing gives us the same buzz as a monetary reward might. The reaction happens automatically and instantaneously, before we've even had a chance to consider it rationally.

You'll find that threats are flagged up more often than rewards as we apply the CORE model. This is because our brains evolved to prioritise responding to threats because they're critical to our survival. In a work environment, that means we need to offer many more or greater rewards than you might expect in order provoke a feel-good response to a new initiative. It also means that just one threat can negate the benefits of a number of reward offerings.

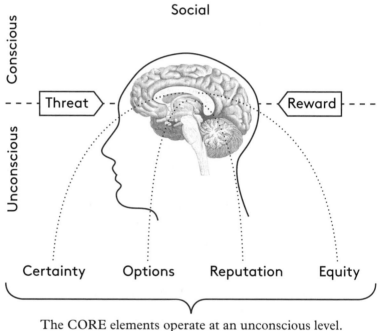

The CORE elements operate at an unconscious level.
Once triggered by a perceived **threat** or **reward** take
the following steps:

1 **Sense** what has happened

2 **Explore** which element has been triggered

3 **Take action** by mitigating, compensating or removing (**threat**) or maximising or magnifying (**reward**)

Using the CORE model to facilitate change

Let's imagine you're looking at restructuring a department. This will require staff applying for the newly structured positions, and as a result they may experience the changes as threats or rewards in any or all of those four CORE areas.

Moving to a new job can threaten someone's sense of **certainty** for a variety or a combination of reasons. Perhaps they don't have any experience of the new role, and they may not have worked under that line manager before. Maybe they're just not confident of their abilities in that area.

On the other hand, if they're given some **options** about the roles they can apply for, the location they might be working in, or their job structure or title, they may well perceive a reward in that other CORE area.

Given that the workplace is a social environment, it's clear that **reputation** and hence social standing matter a lot. How they perceive their standing relative to others affects how they react to their colleagues, how they're motivated and how they perform. So having got the job they applied for, they may feel their reputation and their responsibilities within the team have been enhanced.

Finally, at the end of the process, even if everyone didn't get a job in the restructure, if the process was robust and transparent their sense of **equity** may be satisfied, so there are potential rewards there, too.

Why do CORE responses matter?

Whether people feel a threat or a reward will have a significant impact on their ability to solve problems and make decisions, the amount of stress they experience, their ability to collaborate and their motivation more generally. Knowing the drivers that cause a threat response makes it possible to devise ways to minimise them, and understanding those that can activate a reward response makes it easier to motivate people more effectively.

In a stable environment there's clearly a big advantage in being able to recognise these many responses, for example by using them to light up reward pathways using methods other than the conventional ones like pay rises or promotions.

In times of change, however, understanding these responses is even more important. When the status quo is disrupted people will be constantly and unconsciously scanning for ways in which they are threatened in all of these CORE areas; they'll be the subtext of every team meeting and the subject of every informal conversation. Scanning for and analysing these perceived threats will, on a physiological level, divert resources from people's prefrontal cortex, that part of their brain responsible for planning, analysing and driving goals. And the result of this is as you might expect: Performance and productivity will suffer, decreasing morale and maximising disruption at a critical time.

However, if we can shift a perceived threat from an unconscious level to a conscious one, it can be addressed. This could be as simple as giving an explicit, categorical assurance of security or continuity, or devising alternative rewards that will compensate for threats.

Overcoming threats

Below are some of the typical threat triggers produced by a change scenario in each of the CORE areas, and the initiatives that may limit the threat or offer compensatory rewards.

Area where threat or response may be experienced	Common threat triggers	Actions to decrease threat /increase rewards
Certainty	Lack of information about future plans and impending change.	Publicise agendas and timetables
	Postponed staff meetings or monthly updates, a sense that only a few people 'in the know'	Tell people when they will know about the changes
		Create new routines
	Unpredictable behaviour, especially by those in leadership roles. Unexplained meetings, off-sites or visitors to the offices	Explain the strategy and new plans
		Break down large changes into chunks
	Job insecurity	Help people see why the change is good for them personally
Options	Telling people what to do (the command and control model)	Give people choices
		Create flexible work patterns
	Excluding people from shaping plans	Develop high-level policy allowing for discretion and judgement
	Dictating detailed processes	
	Micro-managing	Leaders set the overall direction, teams define the details
		Individuals design the detailed changes to their own role
Reputation	Giving detailed instructions, especially in public	Ask for self-assessment of performance
	Leaving people out of activities and briefings	Give positive feedback, especially publicly
	Reducing the responsibility attached to a role	Provide opportunities for learning and enhanced responsibility
	Giving critical feedback	
		Ask for input and expertise
Equity	Perceived favouritism	Clearly explain reasons and context
	Uneven workloads	
	Unclear expectations	Ensure decision-making is transparent
	Lack of transparency	Stick to agreed policies

You can use the CORE model to plan the change: Where might the threats be and what are the possible ways of mitigating them? It's also useful to diagnose issues in the change programme: Why are people behaving in this way what may be causing a threat?

Using the CORE model to exert influence

Relationships are of primary importance to all of us - and that's as true in the workplace as it is at home. And if we find stepping back to analyse our own threat or reward responses can provide some helpful insights, it is even more useful to understand other people's reactions. Our ability to anticipate their responses and take steps to mitigate them is crucial to our success in negotiating with other people and influencing them.

When you think about influencing someone - a colleague or maybe your boss - what's your goal? To get them to think you're smart? Or are you trying to get them to think that **they're** the smart one for supporting your idea? Throughout all our research into successful leaders, we've found that one common trait is their ability to achieve the latter or, better still, to get someone to think that they thought of the idea for themselves.

That's because people naturally have a mild threat response to changing their mind. More accurately, they have one if they think they'll be **seen** to change their mind. Ideas and opinions are hard to dislodge when they've taken root, and the secret to getting people to change their minds is to get them to think they were right all along by doing what you're suggesting. So influencing is all about the goal of minimising the threat response and maximising the reward response.

When you're planning to exert influence, there are three things you need to take into account:

1. The change itself and your relationship with the other person: Are you feeling confident or scared? What would be the best way to be feeling when you start the meeting? How can you shift your state?

2. What you know about the thoughts and feelings of your key stakeholders - those people who you need to change their minds.

3. The culture or commercial environment: How important is this change to the company achieving its business goals? How will it support or challenge the values and the way things get done in the company?

Context
When and where to use the skill

Others
The skills needed to achieve
goals with other people

Self
Understand the skills needed
internally to be successful

As we said above, CORE is a quick and easy way to remember the
key neuroscientific principles of relationships.

For example, a perceived threat to our sense of equity ("My boss has
favourites," or "Some people get more information than others,")
activates similar brain networks to those that would be activated if
we walked into a store and found a stranger waving a gun.

Likewise, a perceived increase to our reputation ("They used a
quote from my Twitter account,") activates the same reward circuitry in the brain as getting a pay rise does. Our reaction is completely
automatic and happens in a nanosecond, driving our behaviour before we've even had a chance to consider our response.
The model can be applied in three main ways:

+ To better understand your feelings about a relationship.
This is especially useful for particularly difficult relationships

or when you're concerned about a new initiative.

+ To understand a stakeholder better.

+ To plan how to position an idea when you need to gain agreement.

When we first meet someone we unconsciously categorise them as friend or foe. Foe is the default setting: it's safer to assume someone is a threat until we have a reason to think otherwise.

That's why our brains are constantly scanning for threat or reward signals. In the workplace, that can mean we react to things strongly and quickly before we've had a chance to let our rational brains assess the situation: a new team member may be perceived as a threat, or a frown on someone's face may be mistaken for dissatisfaction or disapproval.

How CORE works when it comes to influencing people

Imagine you're giving a presentation to your boss about a new project and you want to enlist their support.

To manage their sense of **certainty** it's important to include in your presentation how this initiative links to existing business practices, reducing the threat of the unknown.

Give them some **options** so that they don't feel corralled in one direction but feel they have control over the decision.

Create a sense of reward to their **reputation** by indicating how the idea will enhance their standing within the organisation. Avoid any suggestion that current work methods they're associated with are not working.

Finally, position your idea **equitably**, making sure the way it's implemented will be fair to the them and their team.

Whether they perceive a threat or a reward will have a significant impact on their problem-solving, decision-making, stress management, collaboration and motivation. It's going to make the difference between whether they say yes or no.

Sometimes, though, it's not within your power for you to create a reward for your key decision-makers. But it's still important to think about the specific person you're trying to influence: Which of the

CORE elements are most important to them in this situation, and what might trigger their sense of threat? How might they find this initiative rewarding for themselves? Just ask yourself, "What's in it for them?"

Here's a situation many professionals will recognise. You believe you have the solution to a long-standing problem within the team. Or you've got a creative idea for developing more sales. But the person you need to persuade has said no to the suggestion once already. They've asked for more evidence, and you feel apprehensive about going back to them.

Reducing threat

Look at your proposal from all angles, and use the CORE model to analyse what might be a threat to your stakeholder:

> **Certainty:** Are you giving them information about how this solution will impact on their work or their role? Have you painted a clear picture of the outcome?

> **Options:** Do they have some control over how the solution will be rolled out or communicated?

> **Reputation:** Could they suffer any fallout from adopting this solution?

> **Equity:** Is there any way your proposal might be seen as unfair? For example, does it result in more work for particular teams or individuals? Might it reduce their access to resources?

Creating reward

You can also build in opportunities to create a sense of reward. These might not always be obvious, so it's a useful checklist to run through:

> **Certainty:** Can you make links to existing activities or information that will explain how the solution will work? In what ways can you make the reality of your idea more intelligible?

> **Options:** What kind of choices can you present to give your stakeholder a greater sense of choice?

> **Reputation:** How might this idea be seen positively by the

rest of the organisation? Could it enhance the reputation of the stakeholder and their team? How can you highlight the way they will benefit from the outcome?

Equity: How can you ensure the proposal is fairly implmented and has an equitable outcome?

Running through the CORE model quickly becomes second nature. Once you begin to think about relationships more scientifically - through the lens of how the brain works - and you get into the habit of considering threat and reward responses, you'll find you can easily adjust your approach to give you the best chance of meeting your goals.

Threat and performance management

We recently ran a webinar on this topic. We asked our participants a few questions about their performance management policies and practices. 53% of participants reported that the level of threat in their PM process was high, with a further 41% saying it was medium.

As described above, the CORE model identifies the common factors that activate both reward and threat responses. For example when thinking about performance management, threat responses may be activated in the following ways:

+ If there's a lack of **certainty** about the views of the manager with regard to job performance standards.

+ If there's a demand to carry out the role in the way the manager judges is correct, this reduces the element of choice and therefore the rewards for **options**.

+ Offering negative feedback impacts the sense of **reputation**, which would lead to reduced connection with the group and potentially create a sense of shame.

+ If the power in the process, including rating, is all with the line manager, it's likely to affect an individual's sense of **equity**.

Some of the ways in which you can reduce threat responses include giving more control to employees, creating more of a culture of feedback, initiating conversations more regularly, setting clear expectations on the role of the manager and the employee, and following a strengths-based approach in performance management that focuses on what the employee can do well and how they can maximise that in their job rather than on what went wrong or the weaknesses they may have shown.

The pros and cons of feedback

Maybe one of the most threatening elements of performance management is the whole notion that feedback will improve performance, especially negative or 'constructive' feedback. A meta-analysis of psychological research in 1996 found that 38% of feedback actually made performance worse.[14] In fact, it's hard to see how the idea ever became so pivotal in management practice, given the lack of evidence of its effective impact on performance.

Neuroscience is adding to these concerns by pointing out that feedback creates threat in all of the CORE social domains. In addition, people create a mental model to cope with the volume of information coming in through their senses, and these mental models also pop up at work. They create shortcuts to help them get the job done. People are highly unlikely to have similar mental models, and therefore feedback rarely fits with the mental model held by any one employee. What's more, shifting mental models is hard to do, particularly when there's little or no obvious reward for the brain.

The good news is that social neuroscience suggests we have a primary need to be connected to others and that we get social rewards through signs that others like, admire and love us. Lieberman tells us about this research in his book *Social: Why Our Brains are Wired to Connect*.[15] He asked people close to the participants to write two letters, one that contained unemotional statements of fact such as 'You have long hair' and one that expressed their positive emotional feelings for the participant like 'You are the only person who has ever cared for me more than for yourself'. In the study participants were scanned while reading these letters written about them by the people they cared about.

In a follow up study, Lieberman and his colleagues looked at how rewarding these touching statements really were. They asked people to pay money for the statements. Many were willing to give their whole payment for participating in the study to obtain the positive letters. We often assume that money is the biggest motivator but it seems positive recognition is more powerful.

But what happens when the feedback is from someone we don't know? This is what Lieberman's team looked at next. Participants watched a series of strangers' faces appear on a screen and were told after seeing each face whether that person wanted to have an online discussion with them. Participants showed increased activity in the brain's reward system when the strangers wanted to talk to them online.

These findings were interesting for two reasons. First, the feedback was from strangers who had only seen a participant's picture and knew very little else about him or her. Second, the positive feedback led to reward activity even when the participants had no interest in having the talk with the other person. So even strangers we don't want to interact with can activate the brain's reward system when they tell us they like us.

Imagine how powerful more positive feedback, praise and recognition could be in business. The trouble is we get out of the habit of noticing the behaviour of others that deserves praise and so we also get out of the habit of giving that praise. One simple way to address this is to set a target and keep a log. Note down behaviour worthy of praise, even little things, and check that you let the person know. Oh - and saying it in public can be doubly rewarding by also increasing the person's sense of reputation, of course!

Creating a culture of reward through feedback

In our work with clients over the years we've been helping them to focus on brain-savvy positive feedback. We've also helped them to teach employees how to understand the performance standards and to seek feedback that helps them optimise their performance. Asking for feedback reduces - and in many cases eliminates - the threat response and can increase rewards for options and certainty. We also find managers like this method, not least because it makes their job easier. Most employees are very well aware of their shortcomings and happy to discuss them in a culture of support that's geared to helping rather than catching people out.

Rating scales

Rating scales tend to create in-groups and out-groups across the business. Whilst this may not be all bad, it can heighten tensions and reduce collaboration. They can also create a sense of threat. One study found that even those who were rated at the top of the scale experienced threat.[16]

Many leaders say they heartily wished ratings would be eliminated. However, these same leaders also recognise that for many companies eliminating them would lead to difficulties in talent and reward policy. The companies we talk to still have ratings and are trying to mitigate some of the associated threat through more frequent, better-quality feedback conversations and by getting the employee more involved in the process rather than simply being on the receiving end of it.

reported helping others, even if they dealt with additional stresses.

"The harmful effects of stress on health are not inevitable," McGonigal says. "How you think and how you act can transform your experience of stress. When you choose to view your stress response as helpful, you create the biology of courage. And when you choose to connect with others under stress, you can create resilience."

The implications for business are important. On a personal level, what are your beliefs about stress? For your organisation, how are you talking about stress and responding to it? And when it comes to people's performance at work, how are you helping people re-frame their experience to be a more positive one?

Case study:
Brain-savvy change

An Australian-based bank was undergoing significant change across most areas of the business and all the major functional areas. Over the course of a year, we worked with them to support the change programme to create a super-regional growth strategy in the business.

The challenge

Like many organisations making multiple changes, the leadership team fell into different camps. The old guard were deeply cynical about many of the changes that hit them right in the CORE. They were experiencing a major threat response as the definition of success had changed, they were being told that their old approach to business was no longer valid, threatening their certainty and their reputation. They definitely felt it was unfair that their past successes would largely no longer be valued.

More recent recruits, on the other hand, were being hired from banks where the culture was much more aggressive and were mainly focused on proving their worth and meeting the reputational expectations of their new bosses. In addition, many leaders and the HR senior team in particular had comparatively limited change-management skills, and many of the senior HR team, like the business leaders, were ambivalent about the change.

The HR team were suffering from threats across the CORE elements, too. There were threats to their certainty over what was required of HR in this new business strategy and also their options - how could they do their job in a way that met their values and made the most of their skills. They were suffering threats to their reputations since many of the new leaders did not come from companies that had strong HR functions, and many of the old guard felt that HR was not taking a sufficiently strong leadership role in the change. Finally their sense of equity mirrored the business leaders' feelings of resentment and ambivalence about the business direction.

Our challenge was to engage them all in the change, increase their commitment, and give them skills to manage themselves and their clients through the changes, thus reducing some of the threats and creating more rewards in the CORE elements.

After investigating the difficulties that the leaders were experiencing and consulting them on how they were used to managing strategy and change, we designed a three-pronged approach to their change programme.

Stage 1: Apply some brain-based understanding

The first stage was a change leadership programme for their top 200 HR people, based around a three-day workshop. The workshop encouraged these senior people to take responsibility for the change personally, with their HR team and also with their business clients. We designed the programme based on our brain-savvy learning model (see Principle 5), and integrated neuroscientific insights to help them understand how people commonly react to change and how to manage their own levels of threat and reward.

Secure your own mask...

We got leaders analysing their own CORE threats and rewards based on the change they had experienced. They then contracted with colleagues to help them mitigate the threats and find where they could increase the rewards. We also helped people to understand their mind-set and the specific ways they thought about the change, and how these might be keeping them stuck. (You can see this tool in Principle 4).

We helped the team determine who was on board with the change, who was on the cusp and could be shifted either way depending on events, and who was definitely not on board. We observed that in most change situations the energy goes into those who are actively resisting. With this analysis, leaders came up with plans to put energy into keeping the group who were positive as advocates. Research has shown it *is* possible to change opinions. Passionate believers attract more believers.

Scientists have used computer modelling to measure when a minority belief becomes the prevailing belief in three different types of social networks:

> A small company or business unit where each person is connected to every other person.

> A large company where everyone has roughly the same number of connections.

> A small number of individuals who are opinion leaders and who each have a large number of connections.

Each model had a mass of people who held a traditional belief, but were open to listening to other ideas. A 'true believer' minority who were unshakable in their belief proved able to convince others to change their views in all three types of networks. The threshold was ten per cent. Once ten per cent of a group holds an unshakable belief that an idea is right, it tends to be taken up by the majority. If that figure remains below ten per cent, nothing is likely to change.

This research has significant implications for leading change and allowed our leaders to plan around these questions:

> Are we measuring the number of people who are on board with the change?
>
> Do they really believe in the idea?
>
> Are the majority of people open to listening?
>
> How do we ensure 'true believers' are sharing their views?
>
> Are we keeping up the effort until we've passed that critical ten per cent mark?

This formed the basis of their plan for their team and provided a useful tool to use with their business groups.

...before helping others

Part of the HR leaders' role was to lead change in the business, to educate other leaders and to plan how they could work together to get teams on board. We wanted leaders to make sure the people throughout the business held shared beliefs about the purpose and relevance of the change.

This idea comes from author and business advisor Simon Sinek, but it's based on an understanding of brain structure and how we make decisions.

People need to understand *why* a change is important to them personally. In Sinek's phrase - they need to believe what you believe. Much of change management is focused on *what* must happen: What do people need to do differently? What are the measures? What governance is in place?

But for change to actually work you need to focus on the question of *why*. *Why* is this change important to the business? *Why* is the change important to me personally? Why will the team benefit?

The work on the programme made clear that this is more than making a good pitch. You need to facilitate understanding so that people create the belief for themselves. Why? Because research indicates people will only be motivated to adhere to change when they create a clear vision of the outcome for themselves. Scientists in Germany have found that people are more able to resist the temptations to go back to old ways of working or behaving - and more likely to stick to their goal - if they have a clear picture of what the future will be like once the change has happened. This activates the hippocampus, the part of our brain responsible for memory and for imagining the future, and *also* the anterior cingulated cortex (the ACC), which is involved in reward-based decision-making.

The language you use is vital

It was in this part of the programme we also introduced the idea of 'towards' and 'away from' language. How change is talked about makes a significant difference to the ease of making the change happen.

In a paper that attracted a lot of media attention, Ruud Custer and others showed that many factors that facilitate change or a new way of working are unconscious.[21] We're affected by peripheral things such as the language used or our physical environment: People are warmer and friendlier when they're holding a hot cup of coffee; they're tougher in a negotiation when they're sitting on a hard chair.

In a change situation, don't neglect the impact of a word of praise. Custer's study showed that a group given positive cue words worked harder and were more persistent when solving a problem than a control group given neutral words. No one ever left home to follow a leader who said simply 'I've got a plan.' It's 'I have a dream' that gets people motivated.

That's why we asked managers to assess whether they're threatening or encouraging their people to change. We asked them to reflect on how inspiring they made the future appear. We soon discovered that they'd been using threat-based language in their communication. The session quickly enabled leaders to write about the change, in emails and more generally, using a more balanced vocabulary. See Tool *'towards'* and *'away from'* language

We also made the programme experiential, requiring leaders to come away with a clear plan for the habits and behaviours they would adopt as a result of our findings. Again we covered the three perspectives - themselves, their team and their business.

Stage 2: Taking the change to the team

The second stage involved working with the company's most senior HR leaders to design change interventions based on our CORE model. This enabled them to diagnose, plan and monitor communication and activities based on the potential threats or rewards. All communications were written to maximise reward and minimise threat responses. It sounds obvious, but they quickly realised that their habitual way of communicating created more threat than reward. For example, they might say that 'employees who fail to complete expense reports by the 15th of the month will be reported to the division leader' rather than 'to ensure timely payment please ensure you submit expense by the 15th of the month.'

Where it wasn't possible to eliminate a threat response entirely, efforts were made to mitigate it. So for example, the threat of uncertainty about the outcomes of the proposed change was mitigated by training people in facilitating neuroscience-based change workshops, increasing their sense of options and improving their reputation within the business.

Stage 3: The right tools for the job

The third and final stage gave the HR leadership the tools - the CORE model and our Leaders' Change Charter - to engage their business clients in the organisational change. They took part in a two-day workshop learning how to use the tools in practice and how to pass on the skills to their teams, so that the HR leaders then led the next stage of the change process in the business. This gave them options over how they lead the change so they could be flexible depending on the CORE analysis for their business.

For some it was more about working 'behind the curtain', coaching leaders to behave differently and to lead their teams toward greater certainty. For others it was about designing and rolling out similar workshops to these we had designed. In these scenarios leaders were actively involved in using the CORE tools in diagnosing and introducing changes. We knew things were taking root when the head of the biggest business told us he was using CORE to roll out his new business strategy.

The results

There was increased take-up of the responsibilities for change across the business and especially amongst HR leaders, and the CORE model was widely used by business leaders in managing their own change efforts. During this turbulent time, when there was also downsizing across the business including in the HR department, the results in HR's own staff-engagement survey improved significantly. We also tracked the share piece for the bank which rose during the period and continued to outperform its competitors for six months after the project. We know it wasn't all down to our work but getting people through the change and being productive was a contributing factor.

The client said, "What impressed me most about the work was the facilitation, interactive activities and reinforcement of concepts. Most importantly it provided us with tools and concepts we can apply to any change."

Where else does threat and reward matter?

Threats create suboptimal brain functioning in the individual, and therefore affect the effectiveness of your team as a whole. Policies that create a sense of threat will drive people to avoid or ignore certain issues they face, they'll reduce productivity and creativity, and potentially reduce engagement, too. Look for threat in policies and practices like:

Budgeting.

Planning reviews.

Assessment centres and your recruitment process.

Selection for training, especially where training implies the employee needs to perform differently.

Interventions about leadership style, especially where there is limited involvement and collaboration, and also a lot of instruction.

You can use the template on the next page as a general guide to analysing the balance of threat and reward.

Tools

CORE Checklist

Think about actions or processes that could be perceived as a threat and then consider those that could be perceived as a reward.

Element	Threat Triggers	Reward Trigger
Certainty		
Options		
Reputation		
Equity		

Where there is no reward response, what could you do to create one?

Where there is a threat response, what could you do differently to create a more positive response?

Where this is not possible, how can a reward response be created in this element or, if not in this element, another?

The tools below suggest a few different ways of managing each of the CORE elements.

The person on side A gives their perspective on the issue.

The person on side B gives the perspective of the customer or another person you are seeking to understand better.

The person on side C listens carefully to both A and B then identifies the complementary aspects that can be combined into a new perspective.

The person on the last side D listens to the three previous speakers, then offers something totally different - a thought, point of view, a perspective that has not been considered and that will shed a completely different light on the subject.

Change tolerance

As we've seen, whilst biologically people's brains reacts to change in similar ways, there are differences in how change tolerant people are. Rather than see those who react strongly to change as difficult or performing poorly, try to understand what might be happening to them and consider how you can reduce their stress levels. Again, one way is to use the CORE model. Consider how each of the four elements of human social experience may be being threatened and how you can mitigate that or create a reward reaction.

The language of change

We often hear change described in emotional terms - 'the burning platform', 'do or die', 'sink or swim', 'the end of an era'. The language we use may be descriptive but it also sends subliminal messages to the brain impacting levels of threat, motivation and creativity.

So when you're describing change it pays to watch your language. Review formal communications and identify words that generate fear. Also bear in mind that some people are motivated by moving towards a vision of the future, whilst others are more motivated by getting away from current problems. Ensure your language and communications appeal to both preferences. The first step is to understand your language preferences. So for example:

'This change will create more flexibility for shift workers and give employees more control over work schedules.' ('Towards' language) 'This change will solve our problems with more efficient work schedules and shifts.' ('Away from' language)

Finally, think about the person you need to influence - your key stakeholder. What is their preferred way of talking - do they talk about moving away from the problem or towards a vision of the future? Whichever it is, try to talk to them in the same manner.

The Leaders' Change Charter

We know that helping people to feel less threatened, setting clear goals and maintaining motivation are all desirable. We've brought them together under what we call the **Leaders' Change Charter**.

The Charter encourages leaders to help people recognise the benefits of the change for themselves, reinforcing their ideas and helping people stay on track. The Leaders' Change Charter checklist:

> + Involve people in the design of the strategy and new ways of working

> + Encourage people to generate their own ways of working within the broad strategy

> + Encourage personal insight by asking the right questions

> + Provide training and workshops that allow people to build on their existing skills and to develop new ones

> + Encourage people to create symbols, triggers or cues that prompt them to work in the new way. For example, change the time and your location of management meeting, call the project team by a new name, move office location or mix up the seating plan

> + Create multiple ways of reinforcing the new behaviours such as telling stories about the results you're getting, praising people working in the new way and celebrating successes - no matter how small.

For many leaders we work with, this is a new way of working. They may feel as though they've handed over control, that it's all a bit time consuming and undirected. That's possibly their threat response talking. We have to overcome this and give it a try. The results will be seen in better take-up of the change, with less personal pain and organisational resistance.

Principle summary

Threat and reward are triggered in the brain in social environments such as a workplace.

The brain registers something like 3-5 times as many threats as rewards.

A sense of threat reduces attention, creativity and increases the likelihood of stress.

Feeling threat takes up a lot of the brain's energy, reducing our willpower and ability to think logically.

People sensing threat avoid or move away from that threat.

People sensing reward move towards that situation or person.

A sense of reward is associated with learning, being open and engagement.

Use the CORE tool to understand threat and reward.

Check your leadership style and policies for threat, and seek to increase opportunities for reward.

References

1   Evian Gordon, *Integrative Neuroscience: Bringing together Biological, Psychological and Clinical Models of the Human Brain*, Singapore Harwood Academic Publications, 2000

2   Matthew Lieberman & Naomi Eisenberger, 'The Pains and Pleasures of Social Life: A Social Cognitive Neuroscience Approach', *NeuroLeadership Journal*, vol. 1, 2008

3   Robert Yerkes & John Dodson, 'The Relation of Strength of Stimulus to Rapidity of Habit-formation', *Journal of Comparative Neurology and Psychology*, vol.18, 1908

4   Mihaly Csikzentmihalyi, *Finding Flow: The Psychology of Engagement with Everyday Life*, Basic Books, 1997

5   Bruce McEwan, 'The Brain on Stress: Toward an Integrative Approach to Brain, Body, and Behavior', *Perspectives on Psychological Science*, vol. 8(6), 2013

6   Pamela Maras & Tallie Baram, 'Sculpting the Hippocampus from Within: Stress, Spines, and CRH', *Trends in Neurosciences*, vol. 35, 2012

7   Trey Hedden & John Gabrieli, 'The Ebb and Flow of Attention in the Human Brain', *Natural Neuroscience*, vol. 9, 2006

8   E Berkman & M D Lieberman, *The Neuroscience of Goal Pursuit: Bridging the Gap between Theory and Data*: http://www.scn.ucla.edu/pdf/Berkman&LiebermanGoals2009.pdf

9   Matthew Lieberman & Naomi Eisenberger, *'The Pains and Pleasures of Social Life: A Social Cognitive Neuroscience Approach'*, *NeuroLeadership Journal*, vol. 1, 2008

10   Trey Hedden & John Gabrieli, 'The Ebb and Flow of Attention in the Human Brain', *Natural Neuroscience*, vol. 9, 2006

11   Susan Mineka & Robert Hendersen, 'Controllability and Predictability in Acquiring Motivation', *Annual Review of Psychology*, vol. 36, 1985

12   Caroline Zink, Yunxia Tong, Qiang Chen, Danielle Bassett, Jason Stein & Andreas Meyer-Lindenberg, 'Know Your Place: Neural

Processing of Social Hierarchy in Humans', *Neuron*, vol. 58(2), 2008

13   Golnaz Tabibnia and Matthew Lieberman, 'Fairness and Cooperation Are Rewarding: Evidence from social cognitive neuroscience', *Annals of the New York Academy of Sciences*, vol. 1118, 2007

14   Avraham N Kluger & Angelo DeNisi, 'The Effects of Feedback Interventions on Performance: A Historical Review, a Meta-Analysis, and a Preliminary Feedback Intervention Theory', *Psychological Bulletin*, vol. II9(2), 1996, pp. 254-284

15   Matthew Lieberman, Social: Why Our Brains are Wired to Connect. *Oxford University Press*, 2013

16   Satoris Culbertson, Jamie Henning & Stepganie Payne, 'Performance Appraisal Satisfaction: The Role of Feedback and Goal Orientation', *Journal of Personnel Psychology*, vol. 12(4), 2013, pp. 189-195.

17   Abiola Keller, Kristin Litzelman, Lauren Wisk, Torsheika Maddox, Erika Cheng, Paul Creswell & Whitney Witt, 'Does the Perception that Stress Affects Health Matter? The Association with Health and Mortality', *Health Psychology*, vol. 31(5), 2012

18   Kelly McGonigal, How to Make Stress your Friend, TEDGlobal, 2013

19   Jeremy Jamieson, Wendy Berry Mendes & Matthew Nock, 'Improving Acute Stress Responses: The Power of Reappraisal', *Association for Psychological Science*, vol. 20, 2012

20   Michael Poulin, Stephanie Brown, Amanda Dillard & Dylan Smith, 'Giving to Others and the Association between Stress and Mortality', *American Journal of Public Health*, vol. 103(9), 2013

21   Ruud Custers and Henk Aarts (2010). The unconscious will: How the pursuit of goals operates outside of conscious awareness. Science 329

Further reading and viewing

Evian Gordon, Know your Brain: https://www.youtube.com/watch?v=fKt_toIXtAw

Head Heart + Brain, CORE for Change in Business: http://www.headheartbrain.com/core-model/

Head Heart + Brain, Reactions to Change: http://www.headheartbrain.com/reactions-to-change/

Head Heart + Brain, Brain Basics: http://www.headheartbrain.com/brain-basics/

Matthew Lieberman, Social: Why our Brains are Wired to Connect. *Oxford University Press*, 2013

Matthew Lieberman, The social brain and its superpowers, TEDxStLouis, 2013: https://www.youtube.com/watch?v=NNhk3owF7RQ

Kelly McGonigal, How to Make Stress your Friend, TEDGlobal, 2013: http://www.ted.com/talks/kelly_mcgonigal_how_to_make_stress_your_friend?language=en

Principle 2:
Social Connection –
A Super Power

Before you start this section, take a few moments to consider these questions:

Do people trust each other and give each other the benefit of the doubt?

Do you celebrate success?

Do people feel able to discuss how they feel and what is happening with them?

Are people connected and working well across the organisation?

Do people ask for help and support when they need it?

Are people kind and helpful to each other?

Do people discuss their performance and ask for feedback?

The science

There are a number of theories about precisely why humans developed an unusually large brain and a large prefrontal cortex in particular. Whatever the reason, it's to this part of the brain that we owe our gift for logical, rational processing. One such theory is all about social connection.

The Mentalizing System

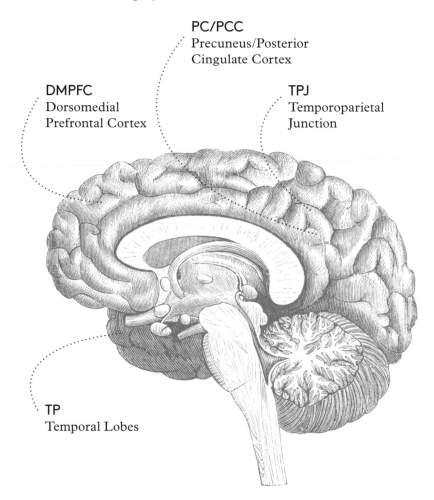

PC/PCC
Precuneus/Posterior
Cingulate Cortex

DMPFC
Dorsomedial
Prefrontal Cortex

TPJ
Temporoparietal
Junction

TP
Temporal Lobes

This theory proposes that our brain developed to help us connect with one another better - to understand each other and cooperate more effectively.[1] A larger prefrontal cortex made this possible, and as it developed, so did our ability to live together in ever larger tribes. This ability to understand one another also became a fundamental need. We're shaped by our social interactions and suffer when our social bonds are threatened or broken. Our well-being depends on connections with others. (In other words, Maslow got his hierarchy of human needs wrong: physical needs followed by safety needs, followed by social needs.[2] In fact, social relationships are as essential as food, water and shelter).

To put it very simply, we can't survive without social connections and this, of course, has an impact on the way we manage businesses in particular. So when it comes to understanding the workplace, it's important to understand a few fundamentals about brain development.

We love our in-group

One of the things our brains love doing is sorting things into different groups and categories - it's a shortcut that helps us think more efficiently.

Whenever we encounter someone for the first time, we automatically put them into a mental in-group or out-group. Our in-group consists of the people we see as similar to ourselves, and we file away the people who are somehow different in the out-group. Once we've done this, these categories become basic assumptions that are hard to shift, which is why it's not easy to think of someone as a friend if we had them marked down as an enemy when we first met them. We each have our own broad criteria for our different categories, according to David Amodio of New York University.[3]

The judgements we make happen in the blink of an eye, and it's important for businesses to try to break them down quickly. That's why things like induction, team off-sites and sharing common goals across business units are so essential. And because it's easier to break down our initial judgements person-to-person, these processes are even more important for teams that work remotely, where there may be little opportunity for the personal encounters.

How we process social pain...

Research at UCLA by social neuroscientist Matt Lieberman and his wife Naomi Eisenberger shows that the brain networks for physical pain are also used for social pain (the pain of rejection or humiliation, for example).[4] Although social pain may not feel quite the same, just as the pain of a stubbed toe feels different to a headache, the networks processing it in the brain are the same.

This seems a little less surprising when we think about how we express ourselves. People around the world, speaking myriad different languages, use the vocabulary of physical pain to express social hurt. We talk of broken hearts and hurt feelings, and it turns out that this is more than just poetic instinct. Social pain is real pain. In fact, the connections are so close that the Lieberman and Eisenberger research also found, astonishingly, that social pain can be alleviated by taking conventional painkillers. If you're feeling hurt because you haven't been invited to an off-site or the boss forgot to ask you to a meeting, it might actually help to pop an aspirin.

Lieberman says, "The things that cause us to feel pain are things that are evolutionarily recognised as threats to our survival and the existence of social pain is a sign that evolution has treated social connection like a necessity, not a luxury."[5]

This means that when it comes to the working environment, we've got to pay close attention to teamwork and to situations that might cause social pain, like giving negative feedback in public.

...and social reward

There are two theories about why we help others. The first suggests that we do what we know is considered normal or 'right'. It's not our actual *desire* to be nice to each other, but we worry that if we're not nice then there will be negative consequences, so we override our natural instinct to be selfish and instead help others.

The second and slightly more heart-warming theory is that we are wired to be nice or, in the jargon, to act 'pro-socially'. For example, Warneken and Tomasello found that children as young as 18 months will make efforts to help someone when they see that the other person, even an adult, cannot accomplish a goal on their own.[6] Helping others seems to be something we are born to do. (There's a lovely video demonstrating their research listed in the popular references at the end of this chapter).

Neuroscientific examination has shown that an area of the brain called the ventral medial prefrontal cortex (VMPFC) becomes active when we perceive something that is of value to us or, very simply, rewarding. So one way of studying pro-social behaviour is to examine and investigate this area of the brain.

For example, there's plenty of research that shows how people prefer resources to be divided fairly across the group: Elizabeth Tricomi found that the VMPFC is active when we see others sharing fairly.[7] In another study, Mitchell and Zaki found a similar result in an experiment where people had an opportunity to make money for themselves: In some cases making money was fair to others; in other cases it was unfair.[8] Getting money usually lights up the reward regions of the brain, but in cases where obtaining the money put social connections at risk, participants showed less activity in these regions. Being nice, it seems, is its own reward.

In a second experiment, Zaki looked at how people respond to delayed rewards.[9] We know people tend to want the things they want right away, and that they discount the value of these things, whether they're material goods or experiences, that are in the future. The research looked at whether this is also true when it comes to being nice to each other. For example, if you see a great gift for your daughter, do you buy it and then keep it for the three months until her birthday (delaying your pleasure of giving the gift) or do you tell her you have it because it makes you feel good right now, even though it spoils the surprise?

Zaki found people were impatient regardless of whether they were the recipient or the giver. This outcome suggests we're reluctant to wait to be nice to someone else, which is good in so far as it drives nice behaviour, but the motivation for the behaviour is really about the good feeling we get when we do something nice for another person rather than anything purely altruistic.

Failing to make the most of these findings in business means we're missing out on the power of social rewards. Connection to a social group is critically important for our emotional well-being; positive feedback lights up reward pathways in the brain. Being treated fairly by others also increases activity in the ventral striatum and ventromedial prefrontal cortex, two key components of the brain's reward system.

This research about pro-social behaviour goes a long way to explain why we're nice to each other, why people tend to form bonds at work which are based on social rather than economic gain and why people don't always act in a narrow, self-interested way.

It also explains why so many people give their time and expertise freely as volunteers and fundraisers, mentors and informal coaches. The research suggests social reward is hard-wired into us, and it's a motivational end in itself. Being connected simply makes us feel good.

How we understand other people

Another social skill our brain has developed is the ability to understand what another person is thinking. We can put ourselves in their place, think about their goals and motivations, and predict their behaviour with a fair degree of accuracy. We tend to think that mind-reading is a super-power when in fact we're all able to do it, to some extent.

We use these skills every day. For example, we make assumptions based on circumstances, gender and appearance that enable us to cooperate with one another. We might think, "You're like me, you're not a threat to me, we can work together." This ability, though, is not part of our general powers of thought and analysis. We use our prefrontal cortex network for that, but a completely different part of the brain - the default network - for understanding other people. Neuroscientist Matt Lieberman (amongst others) has found that the medial prefrontal region is the area that enables us to be influenced by others.[10] The more active the medial prefrontal region is when someone is trying to persuade us to adopt a new strategy, for example, or assign resources to a project, the more likely we are to do it.

In his book *Social: Why Our Brains are Wired to Connect*, Lieberman says that our minds are less like hermetically sealed vaults that separate each of us from one another, and more like 'Trojan horses'. We're likely to accept the beliefs of other people without our realising the extent to which we're being influenced. This has the effect of ensuring that we have the same kind of beliefs and values as people around us, creating the social harmony that we depend on.

This network for mind-reading goes quiet when we're busy with cognitive kinds of thinking like solving a question of strategy or problem solving. And when we're engaged in understanding the motives of others, the mind-reading type of thinking, we dial down the cognitive circuitry and the default or mentalizing system is activated. These two work a bit like a see-saw; one is active (up), the other is quiet (down).

The mentalizing system is active, like a reflex, whenever we're not engaged in a task or analytical thinking. And if we're primed to be thinking about the motivations of others, we will be more likely to notice and understand them.

And the more this network is activated when hearing about an idea or learning new things, the more likely you are to pass on the new information to other people. Learning with a view to helping other people activates this network. And it makes us better at learning than when we use our analytical brain. It seems we can't do both at the same time.

This has significant implications for us at work. Many leaders tend to focus on systems and processes, and this pushes people throughout the organisation to think exclusively rationally rather than socially, using the reasoning areas of the brain rather than the more instinctive areas responsible for social awareness. Over time, this rational thinking becomes a habit - it's simply the way things are done - and less and less attention is paid to social connections. People will be missing lots of vital social cues as a result, and the information and opportunities that could provide relational rather than logical, analytical solutions to problems such as 'we just need to run the numbers'. As we know, many of the toughest business challenges (like engagement, motivation and productivity to name just three) require social solutions.

The application

What's the level of trust in your workplace?

A key component of social connection is trust, and understanding how trust works at a biological level is an important element in guiding business policy and advising leaders.

The moral scientist

Neuro-economist Paul Zak at California's Claremont Graduate University is an expert on trust.[11] One of the things he's discovered is that countries characterised by high levels of trust between citizens are also the most economically successful. Zak started out looking at morality in general. He suspected that oxytocin, the neuromodulator hormone commonly associated with mother-and-child bonding, might have a part to play. He subsequently focused on trust itself as a more concrete, more defined system. The studies carried out by Zak and his colleagues investigated how the human brain determines when and when not to trust someone.

Participants took part in the Trust Game, designed to study individuals' propensity to be trusting and to be trustworthy, and their oxytocin levels were monitored throughout. It transpired that when participants felt they were trusted, their brains responded by producing oxytocin, and the more they felt they were trusted, the more oxytocin their brains produced. The most startling discovery, though, was that the rise in oxytocin levels resulted in participants actually *behaving* in a more trustworthy way. People who feel trusted actually become more trustworthy as a result of increased oxytocin levels in their brain, leading Zak to call oxytocin 'The Trust Molecule'.

Trust and emotions

When there's a breach of trust the brain's conflict detector (the anterior cingulate cortex) activates the amygdala. As one might expect, it's also the case that high levels of trust are associated with *decreased* amygdala activity and a reduced sense of threat. Trust, in fact, actually frees up the brain for other useful activities such as creativity, planning and decision-making.

The darker side of oxytocin

But what about the flip side? What about distrust? Zak and his team have discovered that when male participants are distrusted it results in a rise in levels of a hormone called dihydrotestosterone (DHT). This hormonal spike increases the desire for physical confrontation. Men, it seems, can react aggressively to not being trusted. And what about women? Women are what Zak calls 'cooler responders'; they react less aggressively (or maybe they're just waiting to get even?), although this has yet to be fully understood or verified.

It's also worth understanding that, according to other research, oxytocin can actually *increase* emotional pain.[12] It appears to be the reason that stressful situations like being bullied or experiencing extreme pressure on a project can trigger fear or anxiety long afterwards. If a social experience is stressful or negative, it activates the lateral septum, which is known as the oxytocin pathway. That in turn amplifies fear and anxiety and intensifies the memory, making people susceptible to feeling fear in similar stressful situations in the future.

We don't yet know for certain, but it's possible that oxytocin also intensifies positive social memories and therefore increases feelings of well-being.

One thing is clear however, if you want to increase trust in the workplace, the best place to start is at home, by being trustworthy and by trusting other people more.

There are various great examples of companies putting these theories to good use, such as Netflix and Virgin having no requirement for employees to have holiday time signed off, they trust their employees to 'do the right thing'. Again, it's too early to tell whether this inevitably leads to a more trustworthy culture as the research suggests we might expect.

What's the level of engagement in your work place?

Engagement isn't a fluffy extra. It leads to a real improvement on the bottom line - some research suggests by as much as 28%.[13] But before we get bogged down in stats, it's worth pointing out that there's no single definition of engagement at work. Survey companies have created definitions so that they can provide you with benchmark data but this will be dependent on the survey you use. There are often overlaps with other constructs such as happiness and motivation. We do know that employee engagement involves the interplay between three factors: cognitive commitment (purpose), emotional attachment (trust), and the resulting behavioural outcomes (discretionary effort and interest in the results).

The Conference Board found that across all the studies reviewed, and for all locations and age groups, there was agreement that the relationship with the immediate line manager is the strongest of all drivers on employee engagement. So focusing on this relationship potentially gives the best return for effort made.

There are, in our experience, five basic requirements for leaders wanting to develop an engaged workforce.

1. In-group and out-group

It takes just 200 milliseconds to categorise a new face by sex and race, and after that we organise them into other categories too. The amygdala is carrying out an unconscious quick-and-dirty assessment of whether the new person is a threat.[14]

This affects our subsequent processing. For example, we spend longer looking at the faces of people in our in-group, and how we categorise a person will affect how we interpret their bodily movements and how much empathy we have for them in a painful situation.

Once we've got someone neatly pigeon-holed, we link them to other stored information about that particular pigeon hole: How similar they are to us, what characterises them, whether these characteristics are positive or negative. These stored characteristic and category links are built up over time, through socialisation and culture.

They create the expectations we have of people - they're the lens we see them through.

The motivation to do this categorisation is sharing social understanding, getting along and controlling socially different behaviour, which all serves to build trust within the group. So categorising people into groups can be useful for our long-term safety, but it can also have negative consequences.

Under threat we turn to our in-group

The effect of in-group identification becomes even more intense when people are threatened.[15] People turn to their in-group when they feel at risk. The threat could be anything from negative feedback or redundancies to competition for budget or even just the sense that the boss favours one part of the work unit over other parts.

Researchers asked participants to complete a decision-making task while being monitored in a functional magnetic resonance imaging (fMRI) scanner.[16] During the task they were exposed to the judgements about them from both in-group and out-group members, some positive, some negative.

It quickly became clear that being part of the in-group makes you feel good and that you will be better able to understand the perspective of your in-group colleagues. But you'll also find it difficult to put yourself into the shoes of people in another group. This means that, for example, we're less receptive to feedback from people not in our group.

2. Purpose

Matt Lieberman, a neuroscientist at UCLA, has studied extensively the two systems we have for understanding others: The mirror neuron system and the medial prefrontal cortex or 'default' system.[17] He found that the two systems have slightly different jobs. Mirror neurons help us to understand what someone is doing and how they're doing it. The default system, however, helps us understand why they're doing it in the first place. We activate this latter system whenever we're not involved in a specific cognitive or task-type activity. It comes on like a reflex.

But when we're busy and in the habit of focusing on analytical, cognitive tasks, we may not notice the signals the default system is sending. These signals come as an intuition or a gentle nudge: that fleeting sense of concern about what the leader is saying, the discomfort registered on someone's face. When it comes to engagement, a clear purpose and understanding why you are doing something, sharing with an in-group provides a sense of reward in the brain and helps people to push past threat. Combining this with options about how employees meet shared goals further strengthens this sense of reward.

3. Positive mood

We have a natural bias towards noticing threat and negative emotions at the expense of more positive ones.[18] This threat or negativity bias kept our ancestors alive and even today it stops us taking too many risks or getting into fights, physical or verbal, with someone more powerful than us.

There is less agreement and less written about positive emotions. When we think about positive emotions like joy, happiness, and gratitude, they may seem to have little purpose other than to balance out the negative. But the Broaden & Build theory developed by Barbara Fredrickson is relevant to our thinking on engagement.[19]

According to Frederickson, when you experience a positive emotion it can be rather fleeting and it tends not to come with the same compulsion to take action (or 'action urge' to use her term) as a negative emotion does.

To understand what she means, take a moment to try this short exercise. Remember a time when you were angry or scared. Notice how it feels in your body and the urge you have, probably to stop thinking about the emotion or to get away and do something else. Now shake that off and think about something positive - a sunset, a holiday or whatever works for you. Again notice the physical feelings and the action urge - people feeling joy tend to find that it leads to wanting to be playful, those feeling grateful tend to want to return a favour.

Fredrickson argues that we have positive emotions because they build action urges to connect with others, and to be open to learning. Her theory also states that whilst they are indeed fleeting, the feelings build up, creating resilience to stress and tough situations, and helping us manage these things more effectively. For example, studies by Fredrickson and others have shown that people in a positive mood notice The Big Picture.[20] They're more open to new ideas and learning, and more adept at solving problems and making connections between bits of information. Fredrickson uses the metaphor that positive emotions are a bit like vegetables - you know eating greens once a month won't do much for your health. You need your five a day.

It's the same with positive emotions. You need to have a regular dose and you need to tip the balance of the negativity bias by making sure you notice the positive and savour it. In a business context this involves going out of your way to capture and amplify the positive, like celebrating small successes, getting people to help each other and noticing what's going particularly well.

4. Trust

Trust has been shown to be a core component of employee engagement by many studies, including the Edelman Trust Barometer.[21] Alongside trust, it helps when people are connected with an in-group, when they have a clear purpose and autonomy to carry out their role and when they feel positive about what they're doing.

5. Emotional contagion

So how can you spread engagement and augment business productivity?

There's masses of research showing that emotions, both positive and negative, are contagious. And it turns out that there's a sound evolutionary reason for why someone else's grumpy or happy mood can infect you.

According to Frans de Waal, a psychologist and primate expert at Atlanta's Emory University, we initially just contracted the negatives like fear and alarm.[22] That's what's happening when one bird takes off in fright, the whole flock follows suit. This reaction meant we saved vital seconds in reacting to danger. Mood contagion also serves the function of synchronising activities. The individual who doesn't stay in tune with what everyone is doing will lose out. The contagion theory of mood explains why there's a tendency for groups of people in a training workshop or project team to share a similar experience of the emotions generated. In addition, psychologists believe another form of evolutionary development includes our instinctive tendency to unconsciously imitate other people's facial expressions, vocalisations, postures, and body movements; if some-one smiles at you, you will tend to smile back even if you don't know the person.

Happy networks

A study reported in the *British Medical Journal* in 2008 found that social networks have clusters of happy and unhappy people within them that reach out to three degrees of separation[23]. A person's happiness is related to the happiness of their friends, their friends' friends, and their friends' friends' friends - that is, to people well beyond their social horizon. The study found that happy people tend to be located in the centre of their social networks and to be located in large clusters of other happy people, and that each additional happy friend increases a person's probability of being happy by about 9%. Happiness, then, isn't just a function of personal experience, but also is a property of groups. Emotions are a collective phenomenon. Given that a positive mood is crucial to engagement we might reasonably assume this finding also applies to how engagement spreads.

This idea can be worked into your engagement policy, since it implies that to create more engagement you should gather your engaged people together and help them reach out to others until you reach a tipping point of engaged networks.

Are you maximising social connection in your workplace?

As Dan Pink notes, "There's a mismatch between what science knows and what business does."[24] To support this assertion, he describes consistent findings across many studies that financial incentives actually inhibit rather than promote creative problem-solving and motivation. In addition, a review of 51 studies by the London School of Economics showed 'overwhelming evidence' that financial incentives reduce motivation and pleasure at work.[25] Once basic needs are met, it appears, additional income does not affect job or life satisfaction.

How neuroscience views reward

Neuroscientific consensus views reward in two ways. First, we move towards something to satisfy primary needs like water, food, and social connection. Second, we move away from threats that could cause us harm. Rewards and threats provide the motivation to act.

In the first instance, the 'move towards' impulse, the dopamine system is primarily active. Dopamine is a neurotransmitter that's found all around the brain and determines how the brain processes reward and hence motivation. There is a system of three brain regions that are particularly important, the nucleus accumbens, the striatum and the ventral medial prefrontal cortex. The system is a primitive and all-purpose one that probably developed to provide motivation to find food, shelter and other basic requirements. But although it evolved to seek these very essential rewards, it adapted to process other things that people find rewarding such as an attractive face or a bar of chocolate.

The threat or 'move away' system evolved to keep us safe out in the wild and relies on a different neurotransmitter, serotonin. In modern day organisations it can be triggered by threats like a dissatisfied boss, a low performance rating or inequality of return in exchange for effort[26].

Purpose and relatedness

Relatedness refers to our need to care about others and to be cared about by them, to feel connected to others without concerns about ulterior motives, and to feel that we are contributing to something greater than ourselves. Economists, and most business people, assume that work is an economic contract whereby time and skills are given in exchange for money. But behavioural economists and neuroscientists are now suggesting that work is actually a social contract. Matt Lieberman, founder of Social Cognitive Neuroscience, says, "Social is not one of our programmes - it is our basic operating system."[27] Zink and colleagues came to a curious conclusion in 2008 that also supports this theory. When subjects were rated higher in a social hierarchy, activity increased in the ventral striatum, part of the reward circuitry.[28]

Zaki has found being like others is rewarding in and of itself.[29] In one experiment, people were asked to rate how much they liked particular foods. Participants were then scanned as they learnt whether peers agreed with them or not. When peers either liked or did not like the same foods, there was activity in nucleus accumbens, the reward system, indicating that being the same as the group was rewarding. Disagreement with peers showed no activity in the brain region for reward and, later on, those people's behaviour showed motivation to engage with the group, to be more like them and to establish greater social connection.

In related research, Mobbs conducted the Game Show study, where people were first introduced to two contestants who played a guessing game.[30] First, participants were asked to rate how similar they were to the contestants on social, ethical and personal preferences like favourite films or music. Next, participants were scanned whilst watching as the contestants played the game. Results showed that when the participants observed the contestant that they most identified with winning money, activity increased in the ventral striatum - they were getting a reward buzz. Rewards were not seen when the dissimilar contestant won money.

Relatedness is deepened when leaders ask people how they feel about an assigned project or goal and then are seen to listen to the response, taking time to understand how people's values at work align with their goals. Enhancing social contact in the workplace can also be very rewarding. Mentoring subordinates or nurturing client relationships leads to an increased sense of personal connection - as well as a better bottom line.

Social connection vs money

Research has demonstrated that if there is a choice between money and social connection then we are motivated more by the latter than the former. The brain experiences physical pleasure when we are socially rewarded - when we give, when people cooperate with us, when we believe we have a good reputation or when we receive recognition. Scientists found a similar result in an experiment where people had an opportunity to make money for themselves.[31] The methods of making money were either fair to others or unfair. Getting money usually shows a positive activity in the reward regions, but in cases where obtaining the money put at risk their social connections, participants showed less activity in these regions. The value of money was overridden by the risk to social connection.

The rewards of reputation

Because humans attach such importance to relationships, it seems clear that we should consider how reputation - our social standing compared to others - can be an effective reward. Employees usually make comparisons with others not across the whole company but within an identified peer group (in psychological terms, their 'in-group'). If you're a CEO, you will compare yourself with other CEOs. Traders will compare themselves with other traders, HR business partners with other business partners.

Research demonstrates that we feel envious if someone in our in-group receives greater reward and recognition than we do. This envy leads to reduced co-operation and empathy, and even a delight in any setbacks that may befall the other person.

But concerns about reputation can be used positively. In fact, the neuroscientific evidence points to the need for a radical overhaul of the assumptions that underpin corporate reward strategies. For example, we know that people feel rewarded when their reputation is enhanced through learning new skills, being praised publicly or having their expertise recognised, and when it comes to non-financial benefits like this, things like social media can make this kind of instant reward simple to implement.

Empathy: the ultimate social connection?

Soft skills are often seen as optional or expendable, and to date it's been hard to explain to leaders why they're important. Neuroscience is beginning to help in this regard, and it's becoming clear that empathy is far from 'soft' in terms of its power to help us to form deep relationships, influence people and engage with them.

What is empathy?

Empathy is usually defined as the emotional understanding of another person, and it enables crucial insights into their thoughts and feelings. We all feel empathy, and in a work environment it's perhaps most obvious with colleagues with whom we have a shared experience, like working on a tough project or designing a new initiative. Empathy is activated from older parts of the brain - the amygdala, the hypothalamus, the hippocampus as well as the orbitofrontal cortex - that allow us to experience feelings quickly. These areas of the brain arouse the same emotional states in our own brain as others are experiencing. Our brain patterns match up with a client's or your colleague's, and we literally *feel their pain*, or their joy.

People who can deeply understand how others are feeling create an emotional connection that makes them more persuasive and better able to make decisions that impact others and to gain their trust. People who tend to find it difficult to be empathetic are often seen as cold and unfeeling, and may underestimate the impact their decisions have on others.

Empathy can be focused on different things - being empathetic about either outcomes (the project failed for unusual reasons), or intention (the person wanted to achieve the right outcome but was distracted by a competing goal). Interaction with others hones these empathetic skills in a way that sitting in the corner office will never achieve.

When empathy can be unhelpful

But getting completely absorbed in an employee's situation can be counterproductive. Identifying too closely with them can make it hard to see different options and perspectives. For example, being empathetic when a team member is stuck dealing with a difficult client may keep our perspective on the problem too narrow; a wider perspective might help us to see alternative ways of improving the relationship. The same can be said of situations such as wage or union negotiations. Adam Galinsky has found those who were empathetic ended up with worse deals than those who took a detached perspective.[32]

Taking a perspective

Perspective-taking (or cognitive empathy to give it a more technical name) enables us to understand how someone else sees a problem or situation. This is the classic 'putting oneself in someone else's shoes' and means that we see their point of view rather than feel their emotions. Perspective-taking can be useful as it enables us to explain policy or practice in ways that are meaningful to the other person, a skill that's essential to getting the best performance from your team and also engaging clients.

It appears that different perspectives activate different brain regions. The ability to *reason* about another's mind as opposed to feeling what they're *feeling* shows a shift from frontal to posterior brain regions and from bilateral to unilateral left inferior parietal. So, from a biological point of view, emotional empathy and cognitive empathy are activating different brain regions.

In Galinsky's study,[33] the ability to see something from someone else's point of view resulted in an increased ability to discover areas of potential agreement that others might miss like, to extend the previous example, understanding that the union has to go back with some wins but not necessarily acquiescence to every single demand they're making.

Learning empathy

Research conducted by Helen Riess, director of the Empathy and Relational Science Program at Boston's Massachusetts General Hospital, suggests that empathy can be learned.[34]

Her programme taught participating doctors to focus using deep, diaphragmatic breathing and to cultivate a detachment - to watch an interaction from the ceiling, as it were. "Suspending your own involvement to observe what's going on gives you a mindful awareness of the interaction without being completely reactive," says Riess. "You can see if your own physiology is charged up or balanced. You can notice what's transpiring in the situation."

Doctors were taught to notice if they were feeling irritated, for instance, and that it might be a signal that the patient was bothered too. These are similar skills to those needed by any business professional when dealing with clients or team members.

Riess believes that acting *as if* you are empathetic can build the ability to *become* empathetic.

Similarly, if you act in a caring way, looking people in the eye and paying attention to their expressions, even when you don't particularly want to, you may start to feel more connected with them. It's an idea that's supported by Harvard research where Amy Cuddy[35] has found that trying to put yourself deliberately into a certain state of mind - like feeling confident - can generate changes in hormone levels that are associated with that state naturally.

The right response for your culture

Different organisational cultures and even different situations within the same culture will be more attuned to either empathy or perspective-taking. This means that having the skills to identify a given culture or situation can be really important. For example, being empathetic in a culture that values perspective-taking may lead to criticism of being 'soft', or having empathy when you need to discipline a staff member for poor work may not serve you well. On the other hand, being able to understand another's feelings when asking them to change a piece of work, could be very useful.

Perspective-taking can also be more useful when planning for difficult conversations, or when it's essential to influence someone else. The important thing is to hone both your empathy and perspective-taking - and to assess which to engage in a given situation.

What's the truth about teamwork?

One of the questions that leaders ask themselves more than any other is this very straightforward one: How do I improve the performance of the people who work in my team? The answer, of course, is less straightforward than the question, but neuroscience can throw some light on what works and what doesn't.

First of all, bearing in mind our natural tendency to form in-groups and out-groups, one useful tactic is to create a common goal across work groups so that people believe they have the same purpose and interests. Common goals form common in-groups of people who will work and thrive together, people who'll all receive positive brain-based rewards in the CORE categories according to the whole team's performance. (The CORE model is explained in the previous Principle, encapsulating what has been found to trigger threat or rewards in social situations; CORE stands for Certainty, Options, Reputation and Equity). So for example, if the team achieves a tough goal then the whole team's sense of reputation goes up; each team member feels a greater sense of positive reputation because they are part of the team that achieved the goal.

Second, emotional contagion is strong in a team, for good or ill.[36] If a team member is feeling positive CORE rewards then others are likely to also be feeling them too. But if dominant members of the team feel threat or uncertainty or a lack of equity this can also spread to the whole team.

Research on collective intelligence has found that teams that are high in social skills and able to read the intentions and emotions of others are stronger overall and tend to be more successful on a number of performance measures including problem-solving, moral judgements and solving cognitive puzzles.[37] Social intelligence is also related to having more women on the team. The other contributing factor is a balance in the conversations across the team. Work by Pentland at MIT has found that, alongside these factors, teams that have members who explore outside the team and bring in new ideas are more effective.[38]

Third, leaders should be looking to encourage dialogue. Open discussion and respectful disagreement are all factors in effective team performance. At a brain level this results in positive CORE.

And one more tip for every leader out there: Hold back on your own CORE rewards, giving the team members space to contribute before voicing your ideas.

Case study:
Using social connection to enhance business development

One of our clients is a professional services firm with whom we've worked on a number of projects. This case study is about defining the requirements for partner success in the future and establishing a partner leadership and business development programme. We'll examine the thinking behind the programme and also the results, though the application of the partner success profile is still on-going.

The challenges

Helping partners to understand the expectations placed on them

The firm was undergoing many changes, all driven ultimately by the changes the sector is experiencing as a whole: Pressure from clients to be more commercial; the growth of new and different types of services being developed; services being outsourced and deregulated; greater demands from clients for cost efficiency.

Alongside this, the firm realised there were different career expectations amongst employees. Not all were aspiring to partnership and different partners held different ideas about the contribution expected of them.

We worked with a sponsor group to create a success profile for partners that we then turned into a performance tool. Partners could use this to assess their own performance, identify their personal development needs and create personal practice plans which were integrated with the overall practice group plan. They could also use this tool with their practice group leader to agree their annual contribution to the firm. The success profile was used to communicate the personal and business development requirements of partnership to future partners.

One of the outcomes of the success profile exercise was a deeper understanding of the expectations of partners to support colleagues, to expand their practice and to offer clients a wider range of services. This cross selling resulted in the need to create joint business campaigns such as working on sharing market intelligence, joint events across sectors, introducing partners from different disciplines to a client and collaborating on growing key client accounts.

The model also provided the standards expected of partners in leading initiatives that went across the firm.

Developing well-rounded partners

Like many professional services firms, this one had a fantastic development and training programme to take employees from graduate-level to senior associate, but when people got to that level they had to learn many new skills and responsibilities. The most challenging of these were in the areas of leading others and winning client business. Traditionally these skills have been developed through distinctly different development experiences, even though many of the underlying skills are common. For example, we identified in the success profile that a skill like connecting deeply was as important with clients as it was in attracting the best employees to work on complex client projects, and asking the right thought-provoking questions was as important in a performance review as when understanding a client's issue. Helping future partners to see that they could learn and use these skills in multiple situations was a key feature of the approach we took.

The success profile methodology

Our unique success profile methodology identifies 'the difference that makes a difference' in the most successful people or leaders and creates a model that can then be used to design talent identification, assessment and development processes, development training and performance tools. Because the success profile identifies the ambitions and beliefs of the most successful and codifies these into a model, it works on a deeper level than most competency models and identifies the mind-set that will lead to success. In addition, the resulting profile describes success in that specific organisation rather than using more general, generic descriptions. It takes into account the culture, strategy and ambitions of the firm as a whole.

The profile is derived from interviewing the most successful individuals in an organisation - in this case partners - and therefore uses language and examples that are uniquely recognisable, relevant and believable. The success profile focuses on just those attributes associated with exceptional performance rather than covering everything a partner has to know and do. This in turn makes for greater focus in assessment and development, and a profile that is more credible to the partnership as a whole.

The success profile:

+ Explains 'the difference that makes the difference' when it comes to success.

+ Is based on the views and experience of the most successful individuals who already have a proven track record.

+ Identifies and defines the secrets of success within the firm and makes them explicit.

+ Identifies those magic ingredients in the business and culture that are unique to the firm's success.

+ Identifies what's getting in the way of success.

+ Creates a verified model of success in the organisation.

Programme design

We used our brain-savvy design principles.

The first is what we call 'behind the curtain', sharing the structure of the programme with the client but not sharing the reasoning behind it. This approach makes participants more likely to apply learning and new behaviour and thus ensures a great return on the firm's investment.

It includes:

Design based on how the brain actually works, so participants understand what's in it for them to attend the programme and adopt the new behaviours.

Generating insight rather than simply imparting information - all of us are more likely to act on personal insight.

Reinforcing insight through tools that help continued learning back in the workplace.

Pacing learning carefully to avoid overloading people and providing active reflection such as on-the-go coaching.

Partitioning content and learning into easily digestible chunks and using multiple learning methods.

The science of habit formation to instil new behaviours in the workplace.

The second design area is the use of core skills. We believe that skills which are applicable in several contexts are often developed in only one. For example, skills like those that might be developed when agreeing action with clients when someone closes a deal can also be applied with team members when agreeing performance goals and also when agreeing practice group plans with colleagues. This skill is rarely acknowledged as being the same in all of these contexts.

Developing and practicing the skills required for the complex role that a partner or executive plays helps to reinforce learning, provides multiple opportunities for practice, begins to build new behavioural habits in the development programme and ensures that people feel confident that they know how to apply the skill. It also optimises the training budget.

When introducing people to these core skills, we use a three-point model that ensures they are acquired in the relevant contexts and thus embedded and easily transferred to the work place.

Thirdly, we applied neuroscientific findings to help participants in

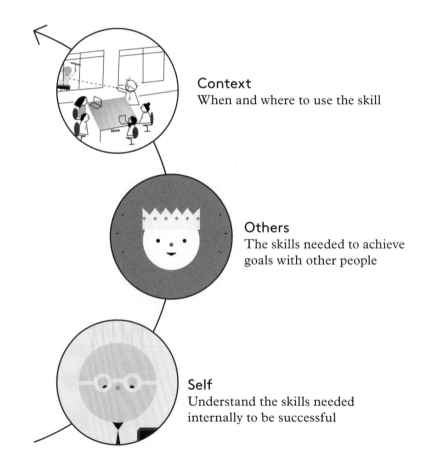

Context
When and where to use the skill

Others
The skills needed to achieve goals with other people

Self
Understand the skills needed internally to be successful

the programme understand more brain-savvy ways of leading and engaging with clients. The neuroscience was introduced where relevant and topics included:

> How clients react in a sales or pitch situation.

> How associates may experience a sense of threat or reward depending on the partner's style.

> How partners can understand the effectiveness (or ineffectiveness) of their work habits. We brought the science of behavioural change to bear on understanding how work patterns and habits are formed and how they can be changed.

One feature of the programme was the use of a brain-savvy self-assessment questionnaire that allowed participants to assess their own work habits and target areas for development.

Another feature was the use of a case study that examined an actual piece of client work all the way from the first sniff of an opportunity through pitching to putting together a team to work on the project and dealing with difficult client situations - in this case a budget overrun.

Part of what made the programme so successful was the opportunity to work with real data and take precisely the kinds of decisions they'd encounter in their day-to-day jobs. This tested their understanding and provided opportunities to practice core skills in a realistic context. From a psychological perspective, this meant that new habits were beginning to be developed even before participants left the learning programme.

A further fourth feature was that we used our understanding of changing behaviour to provide extended support to participants to help embed the learning after the face-to-face elements were completed. This included:

> The provision of a site where participants could continue to access materials.

> Group coaching with participants 3, 6 and 9 months after the workshops.

> Refresher workshops throughout the year.

> New materials supporting the theme of the programme throughout the year.

Setting up of a 'buddy' scheme - a colleague responsible for providing ongoing support and coaching.

During the workshop, participants also developed a charter for working with teams and for creating business development opportunities alongside their everyday client work. This was shared with practice group colleagues after the workshop and, in the majority of groups, became part of the practice group plans.

The results

Aside from the concrete business benefits, one of the most pleasing results of the workshop was the bond formed between the participants and the ongoing support they gave each other. This forged a cohort of people across different sectors and geographies who had a common experience, a common language and a stake in each other's success.

The client told us: "The program was different to other development events that I have attended in that it covered a number of behavioural and emotional areas and encouraged us to step away from the day-to-day routine of being an analytical, rational and logical ... We were pushed to think about our careers and dealings with clients and our teams from a different perspective with a view to encouraging deeper engagement on an emotional level. I think there is a tendency to think about these things (a) pejoratively as 'soft skills' and to say that you are either born with them or you are not and (b) as being irrelevant to day-to-day practice. The programme highlighted to me how that this is absolutely not the case and that there are small, practical steps anyone can take to improve their approach, outlook and relationships."

In answer to what element of the programme was the most useful: "The sessions that incorporated learnings from psychology and behavioural science were terrific - I will definitely be trying to apply some of them in my own career as well as outside work. It was great to hear directly from the Chief Executive Partner about his vision for the firm and the ultimate objectives of initiatives to reshape the firm and to redefine the way we work with clients. Then there was the challenge to pose a thought-provoking or 'powerful' question for the Chief Executive himself that delivered new insights for him - I think everyone enjoyed that exercise.

"The mix of learning about brain science and practical market data and applying it all to work scenarios was really powerful."

Some months later we asked which elements of the programme were still proving useful. "The opportunity to meet and get to know the others - fantastic people, without exception - still proves to be invaluable. Finally, the thought-provoking sessions about behavioural science and the subsequent practical applications to our careers, business development and the way we work together in teams are excellent."

To sum up: "It has provided me with confidence and encouragement that the firm is really keen for me to succeed and to be in a meaningful leadership role that will be important in helping us deal with the new paradigm of the shrinking and changing market."

Where else does social connection matter?

The workplace is essentially an environment where we connect socially. Failing to maximise the opportunities this gives for greater collaboration, engagement, job satisfaction and even happiness is a waste in any business.

Consider policies that could increase the amount of social connection between people when it comes to CSR, volunteering, charity, teaching others both inside and outside of the organisation, and providing rewards that are socially oriented.

It's also important to look at where policy may be undermining social rewards and opportunities to connect such as budget restrictions that prevent people meeting in person, technology that hinders connection and leadership styles that undermine helping.

Tools

Building a socially connected team

Providing a socially connected, stress free, equitable work environment creates better performance and happier people. Check your approach as a leader:

+ Do you have cliques within the team? Who's in the in-group and who's in the out-group? What would bond people across these divisions? Have you created shared goals? What else could you personally change to role model 'one team'?

+ How focused are you on the relationships between team members? How do you create co-operation, harmony, and shared pride in their work?

+ How does your leadership style contribute to a sense of reward? How might you be creating a sense of threat?

+ How do the policies and systems, culture and practices in the company manage stress and create a positive mood?

Maximising group connection

For your team to work effectively, you need to minimise in-group and out-group feelings. Sometimes just a greater awareness of such groups is enough to prompt people to modify their behaviours and realise they are treating some people differently. At other times, you need to overcome the unconscious categorisation.

+ Take time for introductions and induction of new people

+ Create a common goal across the groups

+ Make sure people get to know each other and feel able to share personal information

+ Create common goals

+ Remember to have social events from time to time

+ Look for similarities in attitudes and work practices that could help establish common ground

The qualities of successful teams

Sandy Pentland at MIT has invented a wearable electronic sensor that measures exactly and in real time what good communication involves. His 'sociometric badge' captures *how* people communicate, not *what* they say. Pentland's three most important factors for team productivity and cohesion are:

Energy: how team members contribute to the team as a whole

Engagement: how team members communicate with each other

Exploration: how team members communicate with those outside the team, bringing in new ideas.

You may not be able to use these badges but you can consider mapping the levels of each of these factors in your team. Pentland found there are usually a few people who score highly in all three areas but it's important that you have people who exhibit these attributes and that the time and the resources are available to allow people to work closely together.

Creating trust

Trust is a powerful tool in the leader's kit. It's the foundation of many factors including engagement, motivation, discretionary effort, and creativity. People will not take risks and suggest new ideas if they don't feel trust. Also, trust takes time to build but can be undone quickly, so think about how you can sustain trust as well as foster it. Trust is built when the CORE elements are attended to whereby rewards are created and threats mitigated.

Go on a walkabout: Be open and engage in conversation.

Capture vital information: Learn about each employee's life.

Find similarities: Instead of focusing on differences, look for mutual interests.

Ask for ideas and feedback: Ask what your people need to perform their jobs better and reassure them that you're taking their opinions on board.

Acknowledge progress and milestones: In many organisations, problems are solved, barriers are surmounted and tasks are completed - but progress is not noted.

Learning to teach others

The default system is active, like a reflex, whenever we're not engaged in a task or analytical thinking. The more this network is activated when you're reading, hearing about an idea, or learning new things, the more likely you are to pass on the new information to other people. Learning with a view to helping other people activates this network and it makes us better at learning than when we use our analytical brain. It seems we can't do both at the same time.

Set the team up to help and mentor each other. Help people learn new ways of working or key messages by telling them they are going to teach others. You stand to gain in two ways, firstly because your messages will get passed on more effectively and secondly because people will feel a sense of engagement and reward from helping each other.

Creating a strong virtual team

As we've evolved, our brain has developed to bond with those we see as similar to us, a friend or part of our in-group. We have a sense of threat when we encounter those we see as different, a foe or part of our out-group.

Divisions like this within organisations sap energy and reduce productivity, especially when people need to work in different physical locations. The leader needs to take extra care to create a culture where people feel they are in the same group. The best relationships at work go beyond a merely professional understanding. Real trust is developed when people know each other personally. This personal exchange is often lost when teams work remotely or the pace is fast. Practise the following yourself and encourage it in the team:

+ Reveal something personal.

+ Share some struggles and challenges.

+ Talk about common non-work interests.

+ Talk about shared values and goals.

+ Get people talking about what's important to them outside of work.

+ Use humour.

+ Look for opportunities for the team to meet face to face.

Principle summary

Social connection is a primary need in the brain, and we can't survive and thrive without the understanding and cooperation of others.

We automatically categorise new acquaintances into friend or foe based on how similar we perceive them to be.

Helping others and acting pro-socially creates a reward response in the brain. Social connection drives teamwork, empathy and trust.

Social connection and in-group identification across the business drives teamwork.

References

1   Matthew Lieberman, Social: Why our brains are wired to connect. *Oxford University Press*, 2013

2   Abraham Maslow, 'Hierarchy of needs: A theory of human motivation'. *Psychology Review*, vol. 50, 1943

3   David Amodio, 'The social neuroscience of intergroup relations', *European Review of Social Psychology, vol. 19*, 2008

4   Naomi Eisenberger, Matthew Lieberman and Kipling Williams, 'Does rejection hurt? An fMRI study of social exclusion', *Science*, vol. 302, 2003

5   Matthew Lieberman, Social: Why our brains are wired to connect. *Oxford University Press*, 2013

6   Felix Warneken & Michael Tomasello, 'Altruistic Helping in Human Infants and Young Chimpanzees', *Science* 2006, pp. 1301-1303

7   MR Delgado & E Tricomi, 'Reward processing and decision making in the human striatum', *Neuroscience of decision making*, pp.145-172

8   J Zaki, & J Mitchell, 'Equitable decision making is associated with neural markers of subjective value', *PNAS*, vol. 108(49),

9   Nook & Zaki, in prep cited at the NeuroLeadership Summit, 2014

10 Matthew Lieberman, Social: Why our brains are wired to connect. *Oxford University Press*, 2013

11 Paul Zak, 'The neuroeconomics of trust', in *Renaissance in Behavioral Economics*, ed. Roger Frantz, Routledge, 2007

12 Frank Krueger, Kevin McCabe, Jorge Moll, Nikolaus Kriegeskorte, Roland Zahn, Maren Strenziok, Armin Heinecke & Jordan Grafman, *Neural correlates of trust. Proceedings of the National Academy of Sciences*, vol. 104(50), 2007.

13 John Gibbons (2006). Employee Engagement: A Review of Current Research and Its Implications. *The Conference Board.*

14 Pascal Molenberghs (2013). 'The neuroscience of in-group bias', *Neuroscience and Biobehavioral Reviews*, vol. 37(8), 2013

15 Falk et al, 'Social comparison affects reward-related brain activity in the human ventral striatum' *Science* vol. 318, 2007

16 JJ VanBavel et al, 'Social identity shapes social perception and evaluation: using neuroimaging to look inside the social brain', *The Neuroscience of Prejudice*. Ed. B Derks, D Scheepers & N Ellemers , Psychology Press, June 7, 2013

17 Robert Spunt, Emily Falk & Matthew Lieberman, 'Dissociable Neural Systems Support Retrieval of How and Why Action Knowledge', *Psychological Science*, vol. 20(10), 2010

18 Evian Gordon, 'NeuroLeadership and integrative Neuroscience: It's about validation, stupid!' *NeuroLeadership Journal*, vol. 1, 2008

19 Barbara Frederickson, 'Positive emotions broaden and build', *Advances in Experimental Social Psychology*, vol. 47, ed. Patricia Devine & Ashby Plant, Academic Press, 2013

20 Karuna Subramaniam, John Kounios, Todd Parrish & Mark Jung-Beeman, 'A Brain Mechanism for Facilitation of Insight by Positive Affect', *Journal of Cognitive Neuroscience*, vol. 21(3), 2009

21 Edelman trust barometer, http://www.edelman.com/2015-edelman-trust-barometer/trust-around-world/

22 Fran de Waal. Moral behaviour in animals, http://www.ted.com/talks/frans_de_waal_do_animals_have_morals?language=

23 James H Fowler & Nicholas A Christakis, 'Dynamic spread of happiness in a large social network: longitudinal analysis over 20 years in the Framingham Heart Study', *British Medical Journal*, vol. 337, 2008: http://dx.doi.org/10.1136/bmj.a2338

24 Daniel Pink, Drive: the surprising truth about what motivates us, *Riverhead*, 2009

25 http://www2.lse.ac.uk/newsAndMedia/news/archives/2009/06/performancepay.aspx.]
A workshop where the research was discussed was lead by Dr Bernd Irlenbusch from the LSE's Department of Management London School of Economics and Political Science

26 Nathaniel D. Daw & Daphna Shohamy, 'The Cognitive

27 Neuroscience of Motivation and Learning', *Social Cognition*, vol. 26(5), 2008, pp. 593–620

28 Matthew Lieberman, Social: Why our brains are wired to connect. *Oxford University Press*, 2013

29 CF Zink, Y Tong, Q Chen, DS Bassett, JL Stein & A Meyer-Lindenberg, 'Know your place: neural processing of social hierarchy in humans', *Neuron*, vol. 58(2), 2008, pp.273-83: 10.1016/j.neuron.2008.01.025

30 J Zaki & J Mitchell, 'Equitable decision making is associated with neural markers of subjective value', *PNAS*, vol. 108(49), 2011,

31 O Feldman Hall, T Dalgleish, R Thompson, D Evans, S Schweizer & D Mobbs, 'Differential Neural Circuitry and Self-Interest in Real versus Hypothetical Moral Decisions', *Social, Cognitive and Affect Neuroscience.* vol. 7(7), 2012, pp.743-751

32 JJ VanBavel et al, 'Social identity shapes social perception and evaluation: using neuroimaging to look inside the social brain', *The Neuroscience of Prejudice.* Ed. B Derks, D Scheepers & N Ellemers , Psychology Press, June 7, 2013

33 Adam Galinsky, 'First offers as Anchors: The role of perspective-taking and negotiator focus', *Journal of Personality and Social Psychology*, vol. 81(4), 2001

34 Adam Galinsky (2001). First offers as Anchors: The role of perspective-taking and negotiator focus. *Journal of Personality and Social Psychology* 81(4)

35 Helen Riess, John Kelley, Robert Bailey, Emily Dunn & Margot Phillips, 'Empathy training for resident physicians: a randomized controlled trial of a neuroscience-informed curriculum', *Journal of General Internal Medicine*, vol. 26(1), 2011

36 Amy Cuddy, Caroline A. Wilmuth, and Dana R. Carney. The benefits of power posing before high stakes social evaluation. August 30, 2015. http://nrs.harvard.edu/urn-3:HUL. InstRepos:dash.current.terms-ofuse#OAP

37 Elaine Hatfield, John Cacioppo & Richard Rapson, 'Emotional contagion', *Current Directions in Psychological Science*, vol.2, 1993

38   Anita Williams Woolley,Christopher F. Chabris, Alex Pentland, Nada Hashmi, Thomas W. Malone, 'Evidence for a Collective Intelligence Factor in the Performance of Human Groups' Science, vol.330(6004), 2010 pp. 686-688: http://www. sciencemag.org/content/330/6004/686

39   Alex Pentland, *Honest Signals: how they shape our world*, MIT Press, 28 Sept. 2010

Further reading and viewing

Matthew Lieberman, Social: Why our brains are wired to connect, *Oxford University Press*, 2013

Warneken & Tomasello, Experiments with altruism in children and chimps, The Max Planck Institute for Evolutionary Anthropology: https://www.youtube.com/watch?v=Z-eU5xZW7cU

Daniel Pink, Drive: The surprising truth about what motivates us, *Riverhead*, 2009

Dan Pink, The puzzle of motivation (TED Talk): http://www.ted.com/talks/dan_pink_on_motivation?language=en

RSA Animate, summary of Dan Pink's Drive: The surprising truth about what motivates us https://www.youtube.com/watch?v=u6XAPnuFjJc

Alex Pentland, How social networks make us smarter (TED Talk): https://www.youtube.com/watch?v=XAGBBt9RNbc

Alex Pentland, Honest Signals: https://www.youtube.com/watch?v=T1iKKAA2FOw

Alex Pentland, Honest Signals: how they shape our world, *MIT Press*, 28 Sept. 2010

Principle 3:
Mind-set Matters

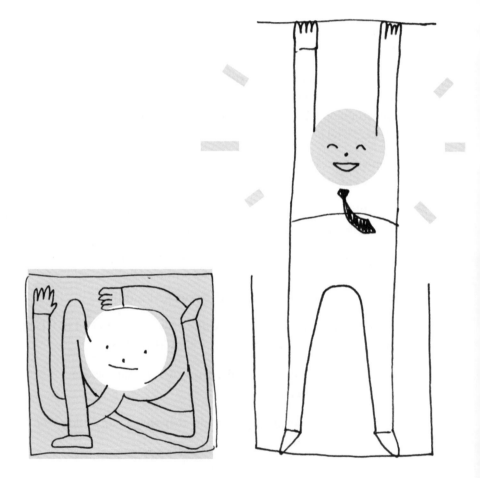

A few questions for you to turn over in your mind before you get stuck in to this chapter:

How do you - personally and as an organisation - define 'talent'?

What's your recruitment policy? Do you hire people with experience of doing a similar role in a similar company or do you look for aptitude and potential to grow with the role?

What happens when someone messes up a project? Do you take the learning and apply it to other projects or lower the employee's performance rating whilst brushing the mistakes under the carpet?

When you invite people to attend a development programme, do you help them to understand the benefits and how they will grow as a result?

What are your beliefs about your own success? Were you simply born with certain talents and abilities and fortunate enough to find roles that allow you to make the most of them? Or do you enjoy testing your abilities, looking for new challenges and learning the skills required to overcome them?

The science

Stanford psychologist Carol Dweck has spent her career researching learning, and in particular exploring the mind-set for success.[1]
She describes a mind-set as someone's entire psychological world,
where their outlook and attitudes are founded on their core beliefs.
Her studies show that people tend to have one of two belief systems
that create their mind-set about work, learning and their own abilities. (As you read on, you might find it useful to consider your own
approach to learning and challenges).

A fixed mind-set

Dweck describes people who hold a belief that talent, ability and
intelligence are things that you're born with as having a fixed mind-
set. It's extraordinary how much of our language surrounding ability
and performance is framed by this belief: 'He's very bright', 'She's
so talented', 'She's a natural leader', 'He has a gift for languages'.

People with this mind-set believe you either have it or you don't,
and there are a range of behaviours which reflect this world view.
The first rule of a fixed mind-set is look clever - at all times and at all
costs. And if you're not going to look clever, don't do it. In the face
of any setbacks, hide your mistakes and conceal your deficiencies,
because the fixed mind-set pre-supposes that mistakes and deficiencies are permanent and that's going to be a black mark against you.

In her studies, Dweck has found that people with a fixed mind-set
say, "The main thing I want when I do my work is to show how good
I am at it." If this is you, you probably change jobs when the standards or requirements change, and you're always looking for roles
that match your demonstrated abilities, where you know you can
shine. Because you're bringing what you believe to be your innate,
natural talents, you tend to tackle the new role in a similar way to
how you worked in the last one, molding the role to your strengths
and ways of working.

We frequently see these traits in senior leaders who introduce to a
new company the same strategy that worked for them in their last
company - irrespective of changes to the market, corporate climate
or the differences between the two organisations themselves. In
fact, it's not unusual for recruitment briefs to request precisely this.

Employees with this mind-set believe their performance is a result
of their talents. They're concerned about their ranking and reputation, and are quick to compare their performance with their peers'.

Dweck found that they exhibit less persistence and less ability to learn from experience than those with a growth mind-set. Their mental framework provides no mechanisms for dealing with setbacks and this can mean they're reluctant to take on tricky assignments. Their readiness to change jobs can be less about enthusiasm for a new challenge than unwillingness to persist with current problems when their performance may show up as less than excellent.

Dweck says those with a fixed mind-set hold a belief that hard work and effort are to be avoided; successful people look cool and achieve things effortlessly. Her latest thinking describes organisations with this mind-set about their people and talent processes as having 'cultures of genius.'[2] They revere, hire, promote and reward people who are great at what they do right now.

A growth mind-set

In contrast, people who have a growth mind-set believe that talent, abilities and intellect can be developed. Their primary rule is learn, learn and learn some more. They're the people leaning over your shoulder when the new software programme's being demonstrated, the first ones to sign up for an optional seminar, the person who went on a course as part of their last holiday.

People with a growth mind-set think things like, "It's much more important for me to have a challenge than to be rated the highest." They do care about ratings, of course, but they care even more about having an interesting, challenging role where they're going to be exploring new areas and working with interesting and varied people.

For these people, it's not about intelligence and talent, and even if they have these traits in abundance, they see them as simply a launch pad rather than the end point. They believe that mistakes are part of learning. They see that deficiencies are part of being human and indicate you need to work harder. They're the ones who actively seek out new things to learn, people to teach them and the next testing opportunity.

Dweck's studies show that people with a growth mind-set work harder, learn from experience and are willing to take more risks to achieve results. After a test, they're not the people celebrating their high score but the ones grabbing the paper and saying, "Hang on, which question did I get wrong?" - a trait demonstrated in Dweck's experiments.[3]

The application

Mind-set in the work place

Mind-set plays out in individuals and in the culture that grows up around talent and performance.

It's not hard to spot who's who in the workplace. The fixed mind-sets are quick to claim the plaudits, share the news of successes, and propose rolling out the same plan again. They're impatient of introspection and would tend to say, "If it isn't broke, don't fix it." You'll never hear them say, "Tell me where I went wrong." It's all, "Let's move on…"

But people with a growth mind-set are definitely the people you want on a team if clients or customers have new expectations, because to the right people this will be interpreted as a powerful learning opportunity. They're open to new roles they have no experience of and they're ready to put themselves into unfamiliar but interesting situations. They're also probably more comfortable with change and new ways of working.

Those with a growth mind-set see taking on challenges simply as part of the learning process. During her experiments, Dweck scanned participants' brains when they performed a task and made mistakes. Those with a fixed mind-set showed considerably less brain activity compared to those with a growth mind-set. The latter were actively processing errors in order to learn from them.

Before we rush to write off all those fixed mind-sets we encounter out of hand, it's important to note that the same research found that these individuals could be taught to adopt a growth mind-set and formerly fixed mind-sets started to learn from their mistakes.

Working with Heslin, Dweck undertook research which showed that very simple changes can influence the mind-sets of employees and managers.[4] In their work, they trained managers to shift their beliefs in a short workshop which included exercises like thinking of times when they learnt something new, identifying people whose performance had changed for the better and pointing to examples in the company where people had learnt from challenges or experienced initial failure and gone on to be successful.

In our own experience of running short, simple workshops (they can be as short as 90 minutes) it's possible to turn managers' beliefs from fixed to growth. Giving them exercises to do that gets them to notice growth in themselves (as well as in others) is a highly effective way of doing this. And the best news is that the evidence suggests that the changes stick.

Heslin and Dweck carried out similar training and found the managers proceeded to coach more, give more performance suggestions and also notice the efforts of their employees more often. They checked the shift in beliefs six weeks later and the growth mind-set was still in place.

So, to move beyond the fine statements in the annual report and develop a truly effective talent culture within your organisation, understand the mind-set of your managers. And to develop adaptability, learning and growth, make sure you're praising people's effort, considered risk-taking and their willingness to take on a challenge.

The mind-sets of individuals and leaders

The thing about individual managers' beliefs is that, collectively, they form an entire culture. That culture becomes the way everybody views talent and how it's managed, assessed and developed.[5]

Dweck says that when you leave mind-sets alone they're stable; people's beliefs are not challenged and so they continue to think and act like they always have. But when people learn about mind-sets and focus on times when they have had to learn something new and been successful, their beliefs can shift. Peter Heslin, who frequently collaborates with Carol Dweck, assessed managers' mind-sets in a company. The employees were then asked how much the manager helped analyse performance, gave useful feedback, acted as a sounding board, inspired confidence and supported new challenges. In addition, employees said that the managers with a growth mind-set provided better developmental coaching. The research also found a link between mind-set and the amount of coaching employees received. Managers with a fixed mind-set did little or no coaching, and nor did they give much performance feedback or help employees understand their strengths and weaknesses. The study also indicated that managers with a growth mind-set noticed improvements in their employees, whereas those with a fixed mind-set did not. After training, managers who had adopted a growth mind-set (and those who had always had one) were more willing to coach and give constructive suggestions for improvement.

How do mind-sets impact difficult conversations?

Managers with a growth mind-set are also more likely to speak up and try to solve a tricky issue. Those managers with a fixed mind-set tend to shy away from such a conversation, thinking there's little point in confronting issues if people can't change. The more difficult the problem, the less likely the manager is to deal with it.

All this has a significant impact on performance management, engagement and other business processes. It also suggests that shifting mind-sets is a prerequisite to successful training in handling difficult conversations and issues surrounding professional relationships.

Are you giving enough praise – and is it the right kind?

For managers to have an impact on an employee's performance and to help them develop a growth mind-set, they should be praising effort rather than achievement, as well as encouraging risk, debriefing learning, and noticing progress towards goals.

At work, employers speak admiringly of 'being smart'. Dweck says this doesn't work in high-change, high-challenge environments and that instead you should be giving people the tools to become more confident learners.

She found that when intelligence was praised, people in her study didn't opt for a challenge - they wanted to work on something they knew they could do. When presented with a difficult challenge they lost their confidence, and their performance on an IQ test actually declined over the course of the study.

Those praised for their effort, on the other hand, performed better and were more confident about taking on difficult tasks. Their overall performance improved.

It's clear, then, that we need to praise the efforts people make and struggles they undertake. As Dweck reports, "Someone said to me recently: 'In your culture, struggle is a bad word.' And it's true: we never say, 'Oh I had a fantastic struggle today,' but we should."

The predominant organisational culture is usually one in which it's thought that tasks should appear to be accomplished effortlessly, demonstrating that the employee is operating with ease and complete mastery of their area of expertise. Any kind of additional effort or stress usually remains well hidden, and it's the seamlessly completed project that gets singled out for commendation.

But Dweck says managers would do their staff a greater service by noticing and commenting on their efforts and the challenges they have overcome rather than just the results, and praising persistence in the face of setbacks. Similarly, recognising the thought that goes in to finding a strategy as well as the initiative to try out a new one is also a good idea.

She suggests encouraging employees to welcome a challenge, to get a kick from testing themselves, and to learn to bounce back when things don't go as planned - all of which will help them build confidence, self-esteem and resilience.

The collective mind-set

Dweck's recent work shows that organisations have mind-sets, too, and that they closely resemble individuals' fixed or growth mind-sets. They permeate everything in the business and have a particular impact on a company's ability to grow talent and drive performance. As mentioned, she calls cultures that believe in fixed abilities and talents a 'culture of genius', and those with a growth mind-set, who believe talent can be developed, she calls a 'development culture'.

In development cultures, people said they had more trust in others and more connection to the company. They more strongly endorsed risk taking and valued trying hard to achieve goals and they believed that they would be supported if they failed. What's more, managers hired with an eye for potential poured development into people.

In contrast, people who worked in a culture of genius said that, although there was talk about risk-taking, people were risk averse because they'd be penalised if they failed. Worryingly, these fixed mind-set cultures also had a tendency to hide information and keep secrets; people took shortcuts and cut corners. Dweck found that, when talent is worshipped, people fight to be seen as the superstar so employees were also in competition with each other and, in turn, were more likely to cheat. And unlike their development culture counterparts, culture-of-genius managers saw their employees as having less potential.

How mind-sets develop

Mind-sets are transmitted through the feedback that's given. When we only praise talent or ability it creates a fixed mind-set and people cease to take risks. But when we praise the process, teamwork, taking on risk and learning from errors, we create a culture of growth and creativity.

To define what kind of culture each company had, Dweck's study asked a diverse sample of employees at each organisation which culture they thought their company had - a culture of genius or a culture of development. She wanted to find out about their perception of the organisation's culture and how the most common, widely held beliefs influenced satisfaction, collaboration, innovation and ethical behaviour.

The results were:[6]

Trust: Employees in a growth mind-set culture expressed a 47% higher agreement rate when presented with statements about having more trust in their company.

Engagement: Employees in a growth mind-set culture were 34% likelier to feel a sense of ownership and commitment to the future of the company.

Innovation: Those from growth mind-set companies showed 65% agreement that their companies support risk taking and 49% agreement that their organisations foster innovation.

Ethics: Those from a growth mind-set company disagreed 41% more strongly that their organisations were rife with unethical behaviour.

Supervisors in the culture-of-development companies rated their employees as more innovative, collaborative and committed to learning and growing. They also viewed their employees as having far greater management potential - all things that make a company more agile and more likely to stay out in front.

Mind-set and organisations

The prevailing mind-set of your organisation is revealed by the language that's used about people and the processes that are used to identify, assess and develop them. For example:

+ Is talent commonly described as a select, static group? Is talent a fixed trait that some people have?

+ Do you rely on measures of intelligence and aptitude?

+ Do you offer stretch assignments or projects with measures of progress?

+ Are mistakes seen as opportunities to learn? Are people de briefed after projects to help identify what can be learned and applied for greater success next time?

In the past, talent strategy in most businesses was firmly based on a fixed mind-set: Find talented people and keep them in the company.

Managers would define potential leaders as people who were similar to themselves. They would work with a team developed in their own image, and the prevailing belief was that progression was based on intelligence and only the brightest would rise through the various grades and rites of passage.

Managers fostering this kind of culture will be heard to say things like, "She's really smart - went to a top university, got the grades, and flew through our entrance exam." Or, "He's so clever he out-thinks everyone else - he's our go-to guy for new projects."

Why fixed mind-sets need to be fixed

If the dominant mind-set is fixed, change is seen as risky, painful and hard.

One of the other disadvantages of a fixed mind-set across an organisation is that it can create fear and threat, and in extreme cases it can even be abusive. Instead of learning, growing, and moving the company forward, leaders worry about being judged, and these feelings cascade through the company making it hard for courage and innovation to thrive.

Managers who hold a fixed mind-set find it hard to see the point of development programmes, feedback and coaching. They see talent as a static trait. The implications for their talent strategy are clear: You need to find those naturally talented people and then work to hire and retain them. Anything else is a waste of money, effort and resources.

Why you should go for growth

If the collective mind-set of the organisation is a growth one, the prevailing belief is that change is an opportunity to learn and grow. The views of growth mind-set managers about the members of their teams tend to centre on how they approach their work. The ones who are viewed as high potential and worth investment will be the ones identified as hard workers who try new things, take risks and learn from their mistakes.

You'll hear them saying things like, "He messed up but he learned from it." Or, "You have to admire her guts - this is the third assignment she's accepted where the stakes were high, but she came through."

These managers will be more inclined to give feedback, provide stretch assignments and coaching. You'll see that they themselves have a readiness to be a novice again and to review their performance in the light of new standards and changing business needs. Same thing, different attitude

A single activity in a talent strategy can be creating growth or fear depending on how it's presented and judged.

For example, in a growth mind-set culture, stretch assignments are seen as recognising potential and providing an opportunity for development. But in a fixed mind-set culture they can be seen as tests of capability, or rites of passage.

To create a growth mind-set across a company, talent initiatives need to be carefully planned, executed and reviewed:

> + Give feedback: Include coaching for future success and change rather than focusing on what was done 'right' and what their weaknesses were.

> + When conducting assessment interviews, ask about how a person would tackle a new assignment and how they would

measure their success.

+Establish criteria for selection, including examples of seeking to learn, overcoming obstacles, seeing mistakes as learning and bouncing back from setbacks.

+Present 360-degree feedback and other kinds of assessment not as a static picture but as a snapshot in time, with indicators for change and growth. Back this up with coaching to make the change.

+When introducing learning opportunities, whether they're formal programmes or on-the-job, present skills as things that can be learned rather than innate. Don't talk about filling a gap in their skill-set, but instead about opportunities to master new skills.

+When setting goals, frame them as improvements rather than absolute achievements. The research suggests that if employees believe that they can grow but sense the company does not value that, they will not grow to the same extent. The structure of goals is a clear indication of the company's true beliefs, so goals that describe progress rather than absolutes are consistent with a growth mind-set culture.

+In performance management and rating systems, measure people against their effort or their own past performance rather than each other. A study by Ruth Butler[7] showed that when people are compared to others they adopt more of a fixed mind-set. They felt the point of an exercise was to show how good they were. Those that were compared with themselves, however, against how they did on early questions compared to later questions assumed the point of the exercise was to help people to get better. The study showed that not only did these people actually get better, they were also better at finding the best strategy to solve the problems they were working on. Also, people seeing themselves getting better provides intrinsic reward in the brain. Companies that adopt this type of approach in performance management systems help to reduce the inherent threat of evaluation and also nurture people's ability to fulfil more of their potential - potential that would be suppressed by fixed mind-set evaluation systems. Companies such as Juniper Systems and The Gap are adopting this approach, as are a number of clients we have been working with.

+ Make sure the manager's role is - and is seen to be - one that includes performance coaching, not simply as being the sole judge of performance. Engage employees in monitoring their own performance standards and seeking feedback.

A talent strategy based on growth will look across the whole workforce; it will seek out people who have a history of developing and changing rather than simply qualifications, a high IQ or the 'right' education. It will provide opportunities for job rotation and skill development, and employees will be encouraged to take on stretch assignments, new challenges and new roles.

Overall, the strategy will convey the idea that the organisation values effort and dedication, not just ready-made aptitude.

Case study:
Recruiting for growth mind-set in global retail

We were asked to help a global retail company with a growth mindset to recruit and develop store managers more effectively.

The rate of expansion of this retail company is enormous. At the beginning of 2012, they were opening three stores a week in China alone. The company has a unique culture that has been a major element of - and possibly even the main reason *for* - their success. The store manager role is pivotal and encompasses a much wider, more empowered remit than in most retailers. Store managers in effect manage a business with profit and loss responsibility and are empowered not only to buy for their store, but also manage and develop employees within the culture, values and operating philosophy of the company.

But there was a combination of different factors that prompted a need for change. These included:

> + Rapid growth across the globe
>
> + Exacting standards
>
> + A preference for helping people from within the company to rise to become store managers rather than bringing in experienced retailers
>
> + A business plan that required them to accelerate the num ber of store managers available to run new stores.

All of this put pressure on the recruitment practices and the speed at which people could be developed to take on store manager roles. The directors understood that exporting practices and people from the company's home country did not always work in countries with a different culture and work philosophy, yet the company wanted to keep the best of their very successful culture and highly effective ways of working.

We were asked to create a success profile across the international businesses to define what made the biggest difference when it came to the success of their store managers. We also created a profile for those store managers who had been assigned from the home country to international locations, to train and pass on the culture to newly established stores. These profiles told the company the approach, beliefs and behaviours typical of those who were able to translate success from one country to another, and also what was required of a local company to grow into a truly international one.

This enabled the international businesses across Asia, Europe and America to understand the mind-set and behaviours of the most successful individual store managers and we then created tools that would help them to hire people with the same attributes and to accelerate their career development so they could take up and succeed in the store manager role.

The challenge

Together we faced a number of challenges, some of which were known at the start of the project and some that emerged as the work progressed. The first was the sheer variety of the countries we were working with, and the fact that in each different country, regional managers felt they already understood the ingredients necessary for success and were reluctant to have a profile handed to them from the international head office.

The second challenge was that the client already had a profile, created by the president, for more senior roles. We needed to ensure that this was integrated into our model. The profile that the president designed was only for senior leaders but we recognised that unless there was a clear flow from the store manager profile to the senior leaders' profile, there would be a disconnect for people's career path and limited acceptance.

The third challenge concerned the politics between the head office and the international businesses. Our client was in the international business side, and although the project had been endorsed by the global head of HR, there were many other stakeholders who we did not have direct access to at all stages of the project. Helping the client balance the pace of change that these stakeholders could manage with winning acceptance of the change itself across a large number of people operating in multiple regions was no easy task.

The company culture

The founder and president of the company is a remarkable man. He has great vision and a unique style of leadership. At the time we worked with him and his colleagues on this project, they were not aware of the Carol Dweck research, but nevertheless one of the defining features of the company culture was - and is - a growth mind-set.

However, when we looked at how they hired people, we found an expensive and relatively slow process, the most worrying element of which was the number of people who went all the way through the process only to be rejected at the final interview. This interview would take place with the region's most senior manager, who was always someone who had grown up in the company and held deeply to the culture and beliefs. Throughout the process, HR and store managers asked the standard questions about biographical history and reasons for wanting to work in retail and for that company in particular.

The final interview asked one question all around the world. 'What is your dream?' It's the ultimate growth mind-set question!

This was asked because the president felt strongly that every employee should have an ambition, something that was important to them that working for the company could help them realise. Many candidates were just too young to have thought about this pretty profound question and so were rejected at the final stage. Part of our ambition was to help the company keep the essence of this question - and make the most of the growth mind-set - but to unpick beliefs that underpin it to make it more accessible to young candidates.

We also noticed something very encouraging during the success profile interviews. We kept meeting people who were open about their failures and how the company had given them another chance. Some had failed time after time, sometimes costing the company a great deal of money, and they weren't in low-level or less influential roles - they were some of the most successful people in the company, responsible for running regions, bringing in huge amounts of revenue and expanding fast. The company truly lived a growth mind-set and encouraged people to learn from set-backs in order to be successful.

Creating a profile for success

We made sure that we identified the secrets of success across all the different regions from South Korea, China and Hong Kong to Europe and the USA, interviewing store managers and supervisors (managers who oversee a number of stores) as well as the most senior person in each territory. Senior managers in each region were asked for a bit of background information, what success meant to them personally and what they thought were the challenges their businesses faced. We asked store managers about their sense of purpose and their beliefs, capabilities and work habits, and also about what kind of environment enabled them to do their best work - what policies had helped them to succeed and which had hindered them? It's worth pointing out that in any successful business there are contradictions; this was no exception, as we discovered when collating our findings. Most case studies ignore these awkward obstacles so that the story hangs neatly together. We, however, want to share some of them because they illustrate what happens when people don't have a shared language that matches their organisation's idea of success and also how creating such a language translates directly into business results.

Contradiction: Rules versus a growth mind-set

Having formulated such success profiles many times before, we knew that it's always the beliefs and mind-set that make the difference to an individual's or an organisation's success - not the behaviour. So rather than create a competency framework with a prescription of how people should behave, we wanted to identify the characteristics and mind-set that set the most successful apart alongside examples of how these played out in different cultures.

The problem was that the company had a very detailed instruction manual that detailed every action and task a store manager should complete in order to succeed. The company believed so strongly that this manual was the secret of their success that it was only available in hard copy and everyone who had a copy had to sign for it and wasn't allowed to take it out of the store. Indeed, part of their assessment for promotion to store manager involved being able to recite rules from the manual.

At first we were rather puzzled with how this fitted the culture and beliefs we had heard from the president, which were all about the company's growth mind-set. Store managers we interviewed talked about the manual and confirmed it was invaluable but, they said, only when they were first appointed. Once they had learned the manual they knew what to do and then the best managers began the growth mind-set process of building on the advice it gave and adapting it to their store, their staff and the national culture they worked in.

When we fed this back to our senior stakeholders we got two very different reactions. Some people categorically denied that what we had found was true. Another group, which included the president and the global head of HR, saw that this *was* true and the success profile gave them the picture of how the most successful set a purpose for their role (their dream if you like) and also outlined the beliefs which helped them fulfil that purpose. Many of their beliefs and habits, as you would expect, reflected a growth mind-set, like helping new recruits learn by asking questions designed to help them think what a customer would want rather than just telling them what to do, and also encouraging people to make suggestions and try new things in the store.

The success profile we created, then gave the company a tool which they could use to spread the beliefs that guided the most successful staff in place of issuing a much clumsier, one-size-fits-all set of rigid behavioural guidelines.

Contradiction: The secrets of success

Many regional managers were initially reluctant to be interviewed. They knew their jobs and were pretty sure they knew the secrets of success for their particular region and, outwardly at least, had little interest in reading a success profile.

The regional managers and every employee interviewed received feedback on the success profile which was emerging and were also asked to give input to the final model. This process helped the most successful understand more about how they achieved success and had the added benefit of validating the final profile and convincing the regional managers there was something to learn.

As each regional profile was completed, we drew out similarities and differences across and within each area regarding the culture that helped (or hindered) managers' success. By profiling each region, business heads could discuss and understand their own profile and how it compared with the best of the best across the globe. This was another principle of mirroring a growth mind-set; the process should help people to learn more about their own success and that of others, how it was achieved and how it might be emulated. It had the added advantage of melting resistance to the whole process because everyone could see how their region had contributed to the whole.

The end result was a group profile that illuminated:

> + The factors that made the most difference to the success of store managers.

+ How the best store managers ran their store, developed their team and role-modelled the values of the company.

+ How store manager candidates could accelerate their training and skills development by adopting the same attitudes and sense of purpose as the most successful.

+ The criteria for recruiting people who would fit the culture and thrive in it.

Accelerating the development of store manager candidates

Hitherto, the company had set little store in off-the-job training and staff development, but we were able to use the success profile to build an evaluation and on-the-job development tool to help store manager candidates take on the store manager role. The same tool would help current store managers to take on bigger roles too, such as area manager of a group of stores or general manager of a flagship store - along with the responsibility for teams of hundreds of people.

This tool was integrated with the existing, largely task-based evaluation process. It ensured store manager candidates understood and excelled at the tasks required but at the same time developed the mind-set and attitudes that drove success. Task-based elements weren't, in our view, strictly necessary but since they were familiar, we included them to give any sceptics time to see how the tool worked in practice. This worked better than setting out to contradict deeply held beliefs directly.

Even in a growth mind-set culture there will always be pockets of fixed mind-set; either individuals feel safer holding onto established policies and processes or they hold strong beliefs about a fundamental element of the company's success. And when it comes to cultures that hold a growth mind-set, examples of successful attitudes and behaviours melt resistance more quickly and more easily than logical arguments.

Alongside the behavioural elements, we ensured that definitions of certain beliefs and outcomes were clear and that examples of good and poor practice were given to help people see the difference between behaviour and beliefs. For example, we incorporated one of the success factors we'd found in the design of the tool itself. Rather than managers telling their team members what to do or how to do it, the most successful store manages used an approach and a set of beliefs they called 'teach thinking'. These store managers asked powerful questions to get their team members asking why and how they should carry out a given task. Questions like, 'How will the customer feel when they see such-and-such?', 'What would you like a colleague to do for you that maybe you could do for them?', 'What would you do if you had such-and-such an issue?'.

This teach thinking technique not only passed on the standards required in the store, but it did it in such a way that employees learned the beliefs associated with success by having the insight for themselves. We know from neuroscientific research that with insight comes the motivation to act, and it also changes the structure of the brain permanently so that a person is much more likely to act that way again.

Recruiting for a growth mind-set

To help with the recruitment challenges the company faced we developed a new approach that, rather than focusing on the volume of applicants, concerned itself with identifying candidates who could succeed in the culture and quickly become store managers - candidates who had a growth mind-set which could grow into a dream and a sense of purpose.

The process was derived directly from the success profile and included a number of selection tools that provided useful data and ensured that the candidates had a good idea of what was required for success. We also wanted the process itself to be a valuable experience for the candidates whether or not they ended up joining the company so, for example, we designed a selection exercise that enabled the candidate simultaneously to show how they worked with others, to learn about the company and to make suggestions about how the company could improve their recruiting experience. It was the very definition of a growth mind-set exercise.

Passing on skills

Once the selection and development tools were designed, we ran workshops to train store managers and HR staff to use them, and we also conducted train-the-trainer workshops to enable managers to train their staff. Again, it was important that this training reflected the pertinent factors from the success profile and the growth mind-set culture. Some of the ways we did this were to structure the workshops based on our brain-savvy learning model (see Principle 5). We used the elements of the model in the following ways:

'What's in it for me?'

We were aware that a number of people weren't convinced about the new recruiting methods and to some extent were attending the workshop to gather evidence to use back in their region to persuade people that they should *not* adopt the approach. Again, if we look at this through a neuroscience lens we see the threat elements from CORE. The new method threatened:

> + Their sense of certainty. They didn't know how this would work out

> + Their options. They were expected to follow a methodology that, for the most part, they had not been part of creating and which for many cut across their beliefs about how the company needed to recruit

> + Their reputation. What they currently did was being questioned - and by their senior managers, no less - who had bought into the success profile model

> + Their sense of equity. None of this seemed fair!

These threats had to be addressed and mitigated. We did this by helping participants understand the rewards they would gain from adopting the new recruiting methodology and development tools:

> + We designed exercises to help people work out for themselves what was good about the tools rather than simply telling them.

> + We also designed exercises that helped people to get under the skin of the new recruiting approach and know what it would feel like to candidates.

> + We helped employees come to the conclusion for themselves that significantly reducing the volume of candidates processed whilst improving the fit would save them time and also save the company a lot of money. One lever for convincing them was the enhanced reputation this would gain them with senior managers who would save time and get better staff through adopting the process.

To some extent the reward factors were easier for the store managers to see because they had more to gain from hiring better staff - smaller staff turnover and improved chances of meeting their objective of developing more store manager candidates.

Insight

Some of the elements we built into the workshops included helping participants see where they had adopted a growth mind-set and how this had aided success, and also where holding a fixed mind-set had held them back. We produced a set of flash cards with phrases that typified the contrasting mind-sets and asked participants which ones suited the company culture best. This allowed them to learn about their own mind-set, and this exercise alone left many people more open to learning the skills on offer.

Application and habit

Elements of the training included videos that demonstrated how to use the tools we'd designed. But we also needed to get people to go out and actually apply these tools and create new behavioural habits. So we included opportunities for participants to tailor what they did in a day-to-day capacity for their store or region. We explained the principles behind the design of the training and the use of the tools, and then we suggested how people put these together in different ways to fit their region or store whilst still meeting required standards and aims.

Practice and discussion

We encouraged the company to adopt two key learning elements. The first was to create space between workshops where people could go off and practice their recruitment skills and then come back together to debrief, learn more and share experiences. The second was to set up a community of master recruiters who could help and coach others new to the process.

Mood

Finally, we always make a point of creating a light-hearted atmosphere in the workshop as well as helping the client to recreate this back in the workplace. It wasn't difficult with this particular company as it has a strong culture of positivity anyway, where people celebrate success and congratulate one another on a job well done.

The results

We had a number of goals and measures of success when we started the project, some quantitative and some qualitative. One of the qualitative goals was getting the success profile and tools accepted across the international regions. We had verbal agreement from everyone including the president of the company that the profile reflected the route to success, but this wasn't going to be enough to make it stick. People had to find their own reasons for adopting it.

One of the ways we guided their thinking was by producing sample tools and making them available for stakeholders to experiment with in their own business area. When, even against managers' expectations, the in-store development tool was adopted in the home country then we knew we'd achieved a major success. This sent a clear message to the other regions that the profile and tools were sound and that the senior stakeholders believed in their value.

Effective and efficient recruiting

After a full cycle of using the tools, the results showed that the number of people who were made offers at the final stage went from 46% to 75% and the number who accepted those job offers from 78% to 95%. We also saw more people screened out earlier in the recruitment process. With the volumes being recruited, this represented savings worth around 2 million dollars in the first year alone. Managers were spending their time more profitably, direct recruitment costs were down and the company's reputation also benefitted because candidates were usually customers too.

The client said, "The new recruitment tools have enabled us to streamline our recruiting by eliminating many candidates early in the process and improving the success rate of final candidates presented to senior management. This new approach has also created a better candidate experience resulting in an improved offer acceptance rate."

Accelerating promotions

Our other target area was, as we've said, to accelerate the number of people who reached the standard to become a store manager.

Again, in the first year of using the evaluation and development tools we saw 28.6% of candidates promoted within one year and

57% within 18 months. This compared to zero percent of the previous cohort after one year and numbers in single figures for the 18-month threshold.

In summary

Defining and sharing the success profile across different regions gave people a say in what makes a difference. This helped gain buy-in to the process and ensured important universal values were included as well as regional differences. We were careful to use the client's own language and, because the examples came from within the company, people quickly identified with and adopted the model for hiring and talent identification. We also found, as one might expect, that making the tools as simple as possible meant that there was greater up-take and application in the business.

You can never do enough in terms of demonstrating how the tools will work and giving examples of them prior to tailoring them to the client company. Allowing stakeholders to discover for themselves what the tools and changes in the recruitment process could achieve, as well as the benefits that could accrue, was critical and proved to be much more important than logical arguments, cold stats or cost savings. The overwhelming learning was that we should always be looking for ways to manage the CORE threats and to create imaginative CORE rewards.

At the end of the project the client told us, "Integrating the success profile has meant we have created a continuous model of success from entry to Director level in the company. We can use this to accelerate development, hiring and promotion."

Where else does mind-set matter?

Mind-set impacts most of the talent areas in a company. Areas where there will be a particular impact include:

Performance management policy and practice

If you or your managers hold a fixed mind-set then performance management is more likely to be about controlling poor performance rather than developing people to be the best they can be. A whole host of differences will prevail, such as the willingness to have tough conversations - or indeed any constructive conversations at all about development. A strong reliance on ratings and rankings is also often associated with a fixed mind-set, so always bear in mind the mind-set in the organisation if you're trying to remove ratings and develop a feedback-lead process.

Recruitment and promotion

Have another look at your recruitment specification. Are you looking for someone who's done the role before, has all the experience and can hit the ground running, or are you looking for someone who will grow into the role and still have capacity to develop as the organisation changes and grows? Check that advisors and recruitment agents understand your preference for growth mind-set candidates. The same type of questions should be asked when reviewing promotion policy.

Learning programmes

This is the other area to check along with the mind-set of the coaches you use. We will deal with this in more detail in the Principle 5.

Tools

Changing mind-set

First of all, ask yourself how growth-oriented your own mind-set is. (Remember - mind-sets are more of a tendency than something concrete.) Then think about the characteristics you need in your business, bearing in mind that your particular company may reward a fixed mind-set. If you're aiming to adopt a growth mind-set, Carol Dweck's research has shown you can change through the language you use and actions you take:

+ Praise effort, not accomplishment

+ Coach on tactics, not just results

+ Encourage experimentation

+ Think of set-backs as learning opportunities – and treat them as such

+ Run post-project reviews and focus on learning.

What do you believe about your own abilities?

Do you find yourself stuck doing your job the way you always have? Are you a 'natural fit' for your role? Does your role match your talents and abilities, and do you like being in a role you know you can succeed in? Or are you the kind of person who'd prefer to take a risk over a sure thing? If you recognise the qualities of a growth mind-set as the way you'd like to be, you're already on your way. Here are some simple steps for coaching yourself, which you can also adapt to help managers coach their teams.

Step 1: Learn to hear your fixed-mindset 'voice'

As you approach a challenge you're very likely to hear the voice in your head, casting doubts:

"Are you sure you can do this?"

"You've never tried this before!"

"It's going to be really embarrassing if you fail and people realise you thought you could do it."

"Maybe this just isn't for you."

And if something goes wrong for you, the voice might be saying:

"This would have been easy if you just had the talent for it."

"This happened last time, you're never going to get this."

"It's not too late to back out."

"Now *everyone* knows your limits!"

If you come in for some criticism you might hear yourself saying:

"I couldn't deliver the results without backup."

In relation to the person delivering the criticism, you might tell yourself:

"They really don't know what this job involves."

And even if your boss is giving you some very specific, constructive feedback, you may be hearing:

"I'm disappointed in you. I thought you were capable but it seems I was mistaken."

Step 2: Your interpretation

Everyone is going to be presented with different opportunities, face different challenges and setbacks, and come in for some criticism. It's how you react to them that's the key. Fixed mind-set: It's your talents or abilities that are lacking. Growth mind-set: You need to work in a different way, try something new, make more effort or expand your abilities.

Consciously check yourself when you catch that type of fixed mind-set internal voice. So ignore the voice telling you that you can't do this, and remind yourself that it's natural to be nervous in a new role, but in three months' time you'll be on top of it.

And instead of giving in to that temptation to keep your head below the parapet for this one, tell yourself that if you don't try you automatically fail.

Privately brainstorm a list of times when you've been successful in mastering something new. Write that list down, and keep it to hand. Update it. Visualise seeing yourself successfully completing the project, and get a feeling for how it's going to be on the other side of it. Seek out the right kind of positive, open-minded people to support you. When you hit a set-back, don't assume that you just haven't got what it takes, but give yourself a break: "What's so wrong with trying? Successful athletes have to practise and fail on their way to the top."

Identify what you're passionate about and concentrate your efforts there. And keep a record of the milestones as you progress. If you're getting criticism from someone, instead of pushing it away make a real effort to view the situation from their perspective. Consciously tell yourself, "If I don't take responsibility, I can't get better. I can always learn something."

Step 3: Follow up with the growth action

Build the habit of creating growth mind-set explanations, and learn to act on your new voice. Consciously ask yourself, "What would the growth mind-set action be here?"

It will feel uncomfortable at first. It really helps to write down these ideas and intended actions to make them more tangible.

Changing the talent culture

If you're now sitting with you head in your hands saying, "I can see all our managers have a fixed mind-set. Our talent strategy is never going work," you're falling into a fixed mind-set yourself!
You can turn this around.

Developing a growth mind-set culture

5 ways to develop a growth mind-set in your talent development culture:

> 1. Educate managers and employees about the brain and how abilities aren't inherent - they can be learned.
>
> 2. Always try to learn from mistakes. People with a fixed mind-set tend not to. People with a growth mind-set improve their performance based on understanding their past failures.
>
> 3. Reframe the purpose of activities from being good at something to getting better at it.
>
> 4. Rating and performance evaluation systems should aim to measure progress and effort rather than simply how capable an employee is. Rather than comparing people to each other on a fixed scale, compare an individual's current performance with past performance, and ask whether their ability has developed.

5. Finally, the message from the top that encourages people to improve rather than to be the best is really, really important.

Principle summary

Mind-sets are determined by the beliefs that individuals hold. This mind-set will affect their entire psychology, determining how they view everything from risk and opportunity to learning and failure.

Someone with a fixed mind-set believes that people are born with unchanging talents, skills or intellect. A talent policy based on this belief is about recruiting and retaining the most talented.

A growth mind-set, on the other hand, believes that no matter how smart people are they can always get better. These people strive to improve regardless of how good their current performance is.

The mind-set of the leadership creates a culture which impacts the talent policy practice of managers.

Mind-sets can be changed through training.

Managers who adopt a growth mind-set are more likely to coach, give performance feedback and seek out stretching assignments for employees.

There is evidence that organisations with a growth mind-set are more adaptable.

References

1   Carol Dweck, Mindset: The New Psychology of Success, *Random House*, 2006

2   Carol Dweck and Heidi Grant Halvorson, NeuroLeadership Summit 2014 San Francisco

3   Jason S. Moser, Hans S. Schroder, Carrie Heeter, Tim P. Moran & Yu-Hao Lee, 'Mind Your Errors: Evidence for a Neural Mechanism Linking Growth Mind-Set to Adaptive Post-error Adjustments', *Psychological Sciences*, October 2011

4   PA Heslin, D Vande Walle & GP Latham, 'Keen to help? Managers' implicit person theories and their subsequent employee coaching', *Personnel Psychology*, vol. 59, 2006

5   Mary C Murphy & Carol S Dweck, 'A Culture of Genius: How an Organisation's Lay Theory Shapes People's Cognition, Affect, and Behavior', *Personality & Social Psychology Bulletin*, vol. 36(3), 2010, pp. 283-296

6   Carol Dweck & Heidi Grant Halvorson, Lecture at NeuroLeadership Summit, 2014

7   Ruth Butler Task-involving and ego-involving properties of evaluation: Effects of different feedback conditions on motivational perceptions, interest, and performance. Journal of educational psychology. Volume 79 1987

Further reading and viewing

Carol Dweck, The Power of Believing that You can Improve (TED Talk): https://www.ted.com/talks/carol_dweck_the_power_of_believing_that_you_can_improve?language=en

Carol Dweck, The Power of Yet (TED Talk): https://www.youtube.com/watch?v=J-swZaKN2Ic

Carol Dweck, Mindset: How You Can Fulfil Your Potential, *Robinson* (February 2012)

In Search of Growth Leaders *Wall Street Journal*. Sean d. Carr,

Jeanne m. Liedtka, Robert rosen and Robert e. Wiltbank July 7, 2008. http://www.wsj.com/articles/SB121441083243003809

How Companies Can Profit from a "Growth Mindset", HBR November 2014. https://hbr.org/2014/11/how-companies-can-profit-from-a-growth-mindset

Will Smith, Mindset Wisdom: https://www.youtube.com/watch?v=XkziAM_ZyDM

Principle 4: Emotions Win the Day

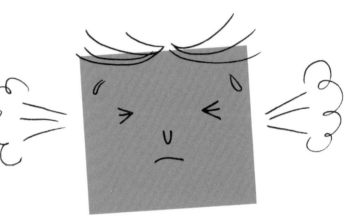

"I'M FINE!"

"I'm angry"

A handful of questions to turn over in your mind before you read on:

Are emotions marginalised in your organisation?

Are leaders trained to understand how emotions affect decision-making?

As a leader, are you aware of the role of bias in decision-making?

What techniques are employed to mitigate bias?

Are leaders taught how to manage emotions in a constructive way?

Do your staff understand the role emotions play in clients' decisions?

The science

Many people think that the workplace should be an emotion-free zone. Similarly, few organisations help employees understand and manage their own emotions, let alone each other's. So it's not surprising that most organisations don't recognise the role emotions play in virtually every aspect of daily office life.

Learning about the brain is one way to help leaders understand more about emotions and especially how to manage emotional triggers better. That's why, more and more, we're hearing about celebrities adopting emotional control techniques, from Andy Murray learning about the brain in order to manage his nerves to Will Young practicing mindfulness techniques.[1]

We'll look at the science behind emotional control, positive emotions and decision-making. All three areas activate different brain regions, and knowing about how the brain works can help leaders make better decisions and avoid bias as well as promote a positive culture that fosters creativity, problem-solving and better client relationships.

The Emotional Brain

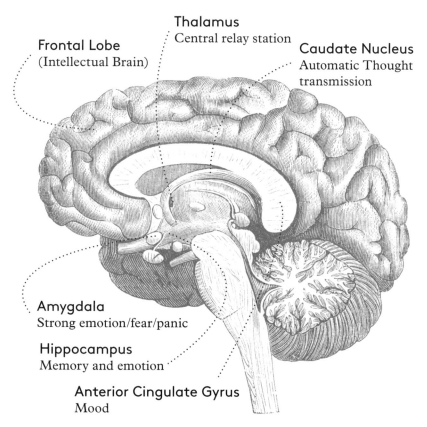

Thalamus
Central relay station

Frontal Lobe
(Intellectual Brain)

Caudate Nucleus
Automatic Thought
transmission

Amygdala
Strong emotion/fear/panic

Hippocampus
Memory and emotion

Anterior Cingulate Gyrus
Mood

How does emotional control work?

We all use terms that reflect our emotional state every day, even when we don't really mean to. We might say, 'I dragged myself to the gym,' or 'I made myself get up,' or 'I lost my cool.'

Our ability to understand and control emotions is one of the things that separates us from other animals, yet as adults we hardly ever teach people about how this works and how to get better at it. Whatever emotional control we manage to pick up as children is often all we have to keep things wired tight throughout the rest of our lives. Yet what many people are doing, whether they're celebrities or the people we see commuting to work every day, is picking up that learning again and applying it to the job they do.

Emotional control can be complex, but it's an important tool that we need to know how to use if we're to accomplish what we set out to do. Take self-control, for example, it allows us to focus and persist when we'd rather take a break; it's what allows us to manage our impulses rather than have our impulses manage us.

As social animals we're primed to relate and engage. But every social interaction has its stresses and different things can push our buttons and perhaps trigger negative behaviour, like when you snap at a junior team member or well up over heartfelt thanks. Emotions are also responsible for our jumping to conclusions or not checking the logic of our decisions. What's happening in the brain is that the prefrontal cortex is being dominated by the limbic system, a set of structures responsible for our emotions and the formation of memories. This domination can, in extreme circumstances, result in what's been termed as 'going limbic', when the strength of response from the amygdala hijacks our executive brain, resulting in memory blanks or uncontrolled expression.

Memories and emotions are intrinsically linked, and remembering an experience which has a strong emotional element can activate a limbic response. This might be positive (your recent promotion), or negative (the CEO spotting a mistake in your spreadsheet). The amount of attention you pay to your emotions, the strength and volume coming at you in a period of time and the balance between positive and negative, will all have an impact on how you do your job and ultimately on your performance. Emotional control or regulation is about understanding your triggers and avoiding them, or dealing with the consequences in an effective way.

Emotional control is linked to success

Walter Mischel's Marshmallow Test, the famous long-term study that began back in the late 1960s, is probably still the best-known example of emotional control research, and demonstrates the close link between self-control at a young age and success later in life.[2]

His Stanford research team used a simple but effective test to measure pre-school children's ability to delay gratification. The children were presented with a marshmallow and it was explained to them that if they could resist eating it for 15 minutes while the researcher was out of the room, they would be rewarded with a second marshmallow. Videos of the tests show the perfect agony of restraint. The most successful children had strategies for distracting themselves from succumbing to temptation. Following up with the participants years later, Mischel found that the children who had been able to resist outperformed their peers on several scores including academic results, income and social relationships.

The kind of self-control needed to resist marshmallows seems very different to the kind involved in performing well at work or on educational tests. However, neuroscientists are demonstrating how widely disparate forms of self-control all rely on a common neural mechanism. Indeed, the kinds of self-control that depends on this system vary much more widely than the marshmallow and SAT cases.

Imagine being in a foreign country where they drive on the opposite side of the road. This takes motor self-control to override your normal driving habits. At the other end of the self-control spectrum, imagine trying to understand the beliefs of a colleague who has a completely different solution to a thorny work issue. Trying to take this person's perspective on the issue also involves great self-control as you try to inhibit your own way of seeing things. Motor self-control and perspective-taking self-control are as different as can be, yet both rely on the same neural mechanism.

Motor self-control

Motor self-control refers to any time your body seems compelled to do one thing but you know you need to do another, like the example above of driving on the opposite side of the road. Scientists use a simple test to study motor self-control within the confines of an MRI scanner using what's called a 'go-no-go' task. Typically, participants see a series of letters appear on the computer screen, one at a time. Participants must click a button for each letter *unless* it is a particular letter, B for example. Usually 80% or more of the trials are so-called 'go' trials - they're supposed to press the button. These 'go' letters might occur about once a second, one after another, and so a participant gets into a rhythm or habit. Nearly all forms of self-control involve overriding some kind of habit response, a response the brain assumes it should follow and thus is expecting to make. And so, every so often, the 'B' appears on the screen and when this happens the participant must not press the button - it's a 'no-go'. For the participant, this feels like withholding a response, stopping the habit that was all ready to go. The one constant across these studies is that the right ventrolateral prefrontal cortex (RVLPFC) is more active during 'no-go' trials, when self-control is needed, than during 'go' trials.[3]

Other regions of the brain light up, too, including left ventrolateral prefrontal cortex, supplementary motor areas and basal ganglia, because brain regions tend not to work in complete isolation. But the RVLPFC is the one brain region that seems to be active regardless of the type of self-control being tested.

Demonstrating that particular brain regions are active during a particular form of self-control is helpful, but it doesn't tell us whether those brain regions are actually doing anything that's vital to *successful* self-control. Examining patients with damage to particular brain structures, however, can give us further insight. That's why Aron and colleagues carried out similar 'go-no-go' tests in a variety of patients with damage in different brain regions.[4] Only those with damage in the RVLPFC demonstrated impaired performance on the task. No other damage in the brain was associated with this.

Cognitive self-control

In a work context, we're more interested in cognitive control. During cognitive self-control, individuals try to modulate their own thoughts, control what does or does not come to mind or try to influence how one thought or belief might affect other cognitive processes that logically should be kept separate such as when, for example, you're trying to focus on what a colleague is saying but there's a distracting noise or an interesting conversation taking place just outside your cubical. Again, there have been various studies conducted to test RVLPFC involvement - though they're a little different to the 'go-no-go' ones.'

In one study, participants were instructed to try not to think of a white bear. This turns out to be very challenging (as you have probably just noticed!), and sure enough, while participants were doing this, the RVLPFC was active.[5]

In another, people were given a series of photographs, and learned to associate one specific picture with another specific picture, grouping them into mental pairs. Later on, they were shown a picture and asked not to think of the one associated with it, and their success at this was linked with RVLPFC activity.[6]

In a third study, Goel and Dolan asked participants to inhibit a certain belief in order to provide the logical answer to a question. The participants were shown syllogism, a kind of logical argument that applies deductive reasoning to arrive at a conclusion based on two or more propositions that are asserted or assumed to be true. They had to decide if the conclusion logically stemmed from the premise. For example, only expensive things are addictive, cigarettes are not expensive. Therefore cigarettes are not addictive. The first premise is false but the conclusion logically is accurate. When participants were able to suppress the belief that the conclusion was false and get the right logical answer the RVLPFC was active.[7]

These types of studies are particularly interesting when we think about the workplace because they help us understand what's going on in the brain when we want to manage bias or overcome psychological associations like 'only people from certain universities perform well' or 'you need to have worked in the home region to get promoted above a certain level.'

Luckily, adults are quite good at passing Mischel's Marshmallow Test. However, they fail on analogous tests quite frequently. In studies surrounding a phenomenon called temporal discounting, individuals choose whether they would prefer to receive £10 right now or £15 in a month. We know from previous studies that people prefer immediate rewards and discount the value of rewards in the future. That is, people prefer the smaller reward now to the larger reward later even when this is not logical. A study examining this found increased activity in the RVLPFC when individuals chose to wait for the larger rewards, presumably inhibiting the impulse to take the immediate reward.[8]

Perspective-taking self-control

Perspective-taking is perhaps most intriguing element of self-control because it's so different to the other forms, and in business in particular it's not usually even thought of as self-control. But just think about when someone has a competing perspective and you're trying to understand it. There's limited data on this, but from the research that has been done, it seems that a patient with damage to the RVLPFC has limited ability for perspective-taking when their own views need to be inhibited to achieve it.

For example, if a patient with this kind of injury had no stake in a game and was entirely indifferent to the result, he could understand the feelings of two competing sports fans when one team scored - the delight of one fan and the dismay of the other. Once he started watching a game where he himself supported one of the teams though, this ability broke down; he was unable to suppress his own emotions and to understand other people's emotions. The patient mistakenly believed that others would feel the same way he did, whether they supported the same team or not. So he could take a perspective when he was ambivalent, but when it came to overcoming his own emotions his RVLPFC was not available.

A separate fMRI study backs up this result. Participants were asked to look at images of needles or cotton swabs being applied to another person's hand. A natural response, of course, would be to show empathy for the pain inflicted by the needle, so on most trials participants' own perspective was aligned with what they saw - needles hurt and cotton swabs do not.

In some instances, however, participants were told that the hand was anaesthetised and no pain was felt, and in these cases the participants needed to inhibit their own immediate response (to feel empathetic pain) to be able to empathise properly - the hand felt nothing, and therefore why should they? In these latter trials, the study found increased activity in the RVLPFC.

Because the RVLPFC is active in all studies to date in forms of self-control, Matt Lieberman has referred to the region as the brain's braking system.[9]

Lieberman goes on to suggest that when we activate one area of self-control we simultaneously activate others. Turning on this system might put the brakes on any habitual responses, whether relating to movement or thinking, not just a specific one we are trying to control. This is intriguing as it's not how self-control feels to us when we practise it. It feels like we inhibit one response at a time.

In his study using 'go-no-go' tests, Lieberman found that when participants inhibited motor activity whilst looking at pictures that would elicit an emotional response such as horrible accidents or emotional scenes, their amygdala activity was similarly - and proportionally - inhibited.[10] Thus, even though participants felt like they were only inhibiting a motor response, they unintentionally inhibited their emotional response as well. This makes perfect sense if RVLPFC is seen as a common mechanism in the brain's braking system. Turning on the braking system for any reason is likely to have wide-ranging effects.

'Use your words'

This braking system can also be turned on unintentionally. Parents and teachers often tell children, "Use your words." It's supposed to calm the child down when they are overly emotionally aroused. The idea is to get them to think about what they're experiencing and put it into words. It is, incidentally, very good advice.

One of Lieberman's studies involved showing emotionally charged pictures to participants, for example people laughing, frowning or crying.[11] Sometimes they were asked to choose a word that described the emotion of the person in the picture (this is called 'affect labelling' in the jargon), sometimes they were asked just to think of a gender-appropriate name, and other times they were asked simply to look at the picture. Lieberman found that the RVLPFC was more active during affect labelling than during gender labelling.

Counterintuitively, Lieberman and his colleagues found that putting feelings into words diminished participants' emotional responses to the pictures even though this involved attending to the emotional aspects of the pictures - a finding backed up in other studies.[12] This led the researchers to conclude that affect labelling is a form of unintentional emotion regulation.

So can adults learn to regulate emotions better through 'using our words'? Well, there's only a little data but the results so far suggest this is so.

A study by Evian Gordon at the University of Sydney has shown that people who have the greatest emotional control, especially those with good emotional resilience, are also more productive at work.[13] Also, Lieberman's team studied whether mindfulness meditative practices can increase the benefits of putting feelings into words.[14] (Mindfulness involves deliberate, non-judgmental awareness of one's own experiences and emotions; it bears a strong resemblance to affect labelling because it requires the brain to inhibit immediate thoughts and shifts in attention). They found that those who report being more mindful showed greater RVLPFC activity and less amygdala activity while affect labelling compared to those who reported being less mindful.

Emotions and decision-making

Work by the internationally recognised neuroscientist Antonio Damasio at the University of South California has shown that there's an emotional element to all our decisions.[15] It's something that economists have to grapple with a lot. (From their point of view, it would be great if people could be relied upon to make cold, calculated decisions. But people don't. So the definition in economists' circles of a good decision is one that aligns with what people *should* do if they made optimal choices.)

One of Damasio's experiments is famous in neuro-economist circles. Participants are given £20 each, and asked to bet on the toss of a coin. They are told they can place £1 bets on 20 tosses of a coin (there's nothing tricky about the coin - it's chosen at random). Each losing bet will cost them just their £1 stake, while each winning bet will earn them £2.50. What would *you* do?

If you were going to bet at all, from a rational, cool-headed perspective you should bet every time, because the amount you can win is higher than the amount you are likely to lose. The laws of probability are in your favour. Most people with intact brains opted not to take the rational approach, particularly once they had won a little. In another study, when participants had damage to the areas in the brain governing emotion they just kept on betting and won much more!

Another of Damasio's studies involved such people with damage to the limbic area of the brain. As a result of their injuries, these patients were unable to experience emotions. They could say how they *would* feel if they saw something bad or something good, but they would speak quite impassively about an upsetting event or family trauma. And they also found it very difficult to make decisions. They could describe logically what the process should be, but struggled to make even simple commitments like deciding the date of their next appointment or which restaurant they would like to go to. This suggests emotions and choice are intrinsically linked. In fact, even those we believe to be purely logical decisions are arguably *always* based on emotion which is why, for example, we talk about decisions that 'feel right'. Damasio's view is that emotions provide convenient tags that help us consider our options, marking factors as good, bad or indifferent.

Just think about what happens when we're confronted by more complex decisions, where each option has pros and cons that can't be easily weighed. Let's say you're thinking about buying a new car. Do you buy a small car with good mileage, or a larger car with more room for the children? Or think about what you've got to weigh up when you want to change jobs. Do you go for the exciting opportunity in a sector you don't know but where the money's good, or do you stay with an organisation in a sector you've mastered but where the remuneration's not so great? There isn't a calculable answer to these types of decisions - even if sometimes we try to act as though there is.

It turns out that the decision-making networks and emotional centres are physically linked in the brain. Networks in the limbic system are devoted to processing emotions, while corresponding regions in the cortex integrate emotional information with what we know about the world. Emotions are expressed through body sensations or a state of mind that provides cues to decisions that we want to make. This is totally independent of our ability to analyse data. Damasio doesn't believe that emotions work in opposition to reasoning, however, but that they provide essential support to the reasoning process.

Neuro-economist Baba Shiv says we have to use a different definition for complex decisions: "A good decision is one in which the decision-maker is happy with the decision and will stay committed to it."[16]

This is where the science of decision-making begins to clash with entrenched business beliefs. Most business people spend time constructing neat, logical rationales for their decisions, whether that's a hiring option or the company strategy. What they tend to miss is the role of emotions. Try asking yourself how many of your plans to get the management committee to agree a budget or new policy take into account their emotional state and not just the perceived risks and benefits? And how often do you take into account your own emotions when you need to make a decision?

In *Thinking Fast and Slow*, Daniel Kahneman proposes that we have two ways of thinking.[17] There's a fast, instinctive and emotional brain that he calls System 1 that specialises in identifying and responding to danger as well as rewards such as food, sex or social connection. Then there's System 2, a slower, more deliberative and more logical brain that analyses data. Kahneman says that because the more cautious and analytical System 2 is lazy and tires easily, we often accept the quick-and-dirty assessments of the intuitive and largely unconscious system. "Although System 2 believes itself to be where the action is, the automatic System 1 is often where decisions are made," he says.

Kahneman's analysis suggests we should be taking more time to check our System 1 intuitive decisions and decision-making habits by slowing down and engaging System 2 - our logical, rational brain. However, given the sheer pace of life and the value we put on getting things done quickly, we often go with the System 1 intuition without taking the time to check with System 2.

The application

The impact of emotions on decision-making

Damasio's findings have enormous implications for decision-making in business. A purely logical case for a change in policy or direction would miss a key component if it failed to take into account the less rational but no less real factors driving the decision-maker.

Think of a situation where you've presented a strong proposal with facts, reason and logic on your side. You thought there was absolutely no way the person with budget approval could say no to your perfectly constructed argument. To do so would be impossible, you think, because there is no other logical solution. And then the decision-maker comes up with a totally illogical alternative. You're completely floored and spend the rest of the day ranting to your colleagues about this irrational individual and feeling thoroughly frustrated.

This is typical of what most people do when they sit down to plan their strategy, or to think about getting buy-in to a policy, or selling any other recommendation they want to get adopted. And it's what we nearly always do when we want to get our boss or a client to agree a proposal. We go in armed with the facts, and attempt to use logic to persuade them.

Although emotions are an intrinsic part of the decision-making process, they don't always guide us towards the most profitable ones. Shiv, who has demonstrated this phenomenon with patients who have brain damage in the emotional regions, calls these results 'frinky', a word his son made up to mean counterintuitive and funky.[18] Take the brain-damaged patients who did better on that coin-tossing experiment described above, for example. Shiv says this is because they did not experience the effects of what's known as Prospect Theory or loss aversion in behavioural economics.[19] The healthy participants passed up opportunities to place a bet, and as fear mounted with each coin toss they were less and less likely to take the gamble. They earned an average of only $22.80. By contrast, brain-damaged patients who felt no loss aversion earned an average of $25.70.

The relevance of this in business is multiple, think of investment decisions and those where a project is going wrong but you have invested time and energy. These are all areas where your emotions will drive you to make decisions which may not get you the best outcome.

The power of hormones

So we know that how you feel affects how you decide. But how you feel is in turn affected by the mix of hormones in your body. Neuroscientist and former Wall Street trader John Coates found that the risk appetite of traders was influenced by the hormones testosterone and cortisol.[20] They took more risks when testosterone was high but became averse to risk when cortisol peaked.

Shiv, too, says the time to make tough choices is in the morning when our hormones are most likely to favour decision-making. Serotonin is at a natural high, calming our brain and making us less fearful about risk, whereas later in the day, as serotonin levels start to decline, we find it more difficult to be decisive. Also it's best to check whether you're feeling hungry or thirsty - test results show that people take on less risk to achieve financial gain after a satisfying meal than before.

And a study at Duke University was the first to show that sleep deprivation is another factor that can change the way the brain assesses economic value.[21] It demonstrated that sleep deprivation increases sensitivity to positive rewards while diminishing sensitivity to negative consequences. "Even if someone makes very sound financial decisions after a normal night of sleep, there is no guarantee that this same person will not expose you to untoward risk if sleep deprived," says co-author Michael Chee. Getting a good night's sleep is going to put you in a better state to make important decisions, so make sure you go to bed early before making that big decision.

Give yourself time

It's also useful to take time to reflect on a decision. The saying 'sleep on it' is backed up by the science. It may seem obvious, but neuroscientist David Creswell has found that people who had to make a decision based on many competing factors made better decisions (judged by experts) when they had time to reflect on it.[22] Even a few minutes helps. So in a meeting, give yourself or your stakeholder time before forcing a decision and make the suggestion, "Shall we take a break for coffee now, and come back to this when we've had a chance to consider it?"

Your decision-making checklist:

+ Check for any unconscious bias such as loss aversion when you're making an important choice

+ When you need someone else to make a decision, build in an emotional as well as a logical argument. Consider what their emotional starting point will be on the issue and how you can shift their emotional thinking

+ When you're making a decision, check your mood and the time of day and try to make important decisions in the morning or when you've eaten and are physically comfortable

+ Finally, give yourself time to reflect on data, especially if it's complex. Ideally, sleep on major decisions.

Decisions and bias

There are several aspects of the way we make decisions that can hinder and help us in business (see also Principle 7). Here we'll look at how people make decisions on organisational issues like recruitment, investment, the make-up of teams as well as numerous other day-to-day and strategic matters.

Though we may be able to explain why our brains have gradually evolved to make decisions in the way that they have, they haven't evolved as quickly as society has. We naturally develop biases and habits that help us make good decisions but these same biases and habits can also lead us to make poor ones. That's because the way the brain works means we miss important information or limit the things we take into consideration. So we have to be able to spot when bias is influencing us in any given context.

This, of course, is the reason so many UK companies are providing training in decision bias and unconscious bias more generally - and it's a trend that's already well established the States. It has been reported that 20% of large US companies provide unconscious bias training, a ten-fold increase in the last five years.

But is any of this making a difference? Can we be trained to overcome unconscious bias? Or is it all a waste of money? Maybe it is. Because these biases are so numerous (and some say there are as many as 150 lurking down at an unconscious level) training may raise our awareness of them but it won't significantly improve our ability to reduce them or overcome them.[25] We - all of us - are generally pretty bad at being aware of our own thoughts and we're inclined to underestimate how our thoughts and behaviour impact on others. One thing the training *can* do, though, is persuade people of the value of having a diverse and inclusive culture and of finding ways to improve decision-making.

Addressing bias

One way of addressing bias in decision-making is to take more of an organisational development approach, to shift the focus from the individual and look at the whole system. An organisation's processes and the groups within it can be used to create structures which identify and mitigate bias and use group decision-making to counteract individual bias.

Heidi Grant Halvorson and David Rock have proposed that one means of facilitating this type of approach is first to categorise bias into different types in such a way that all the biases within a type can be mitigated in similar ways.[26] Their bias categories, which they call SEEDS, are as follows:

Similarity biases

The two most prevalent forms of similarity bias are in-group and out-group preferences. We hold a relatively positive perception of people who are similar to ourselves (the in-group) and a relatively negative perception of those who are different (the out-group). Even when we're not aware of these two biases, they are reflected in our behaviour. For example, we're more likely to hire in-group members - and once we hire them, we're likely to empathise with them and favour them, their ideas and their performance.

The best way to manage this bias is to find areas of similarity with those who appear different so that we can bring more people into the in-group. This means paying closer attention to the goals, values, experiences and preferences that we share with the out-group. This causes the brain to re-categorise these individuals and thus creates less bias.

Expedience biases

Expedience biases can be described as mental shortcuts that help us make quick and efficient decisions. As described above, Daniel Kahneman pointed to the brain's two ways of making decisions, fast and slow. Fast decisions just *feel* right. That's what makes us follow them. When you need to make decisions based on more objective, less accessible information, your brain's slower, more analytical system has to get involved to review the fast brain's impulses and correct its mistakes. But the slow brain requires more cognitive effort and concentration, so we don't use it as much as we should.

For example, one expedience bias is availability bias; the tendency to make a decision based on the information that comes to mind most quickly instead of taking different perspectives into account. This bias inhibits us from considering all potentially relevant information or even looking for it, severely limiting our objectivity.

Experience biases

The human brain has evolved to regard its own perceptions as correct and complete. In other words, we tend to assume that what we see is all there is to see, and all of it is accurate. But this doesn't take into account the many background processes in the brain that combine to construct our experience of reality, like our expectations, past experiences, personality and emotional state.

To offset these types of bias, we have to step off the easier decision-making path very deliberately. We need to create incentives to challenge ourselves and one another, perhaps by identifying our own mistakes and encouraging a culture where it's acceptable to ask others to challenge our ideas. For instance, we might institute a process of having different people review major decisions or ask people with different perspectives to contribute. We might also mitigate expedience biases by breaking a problem into its component parts.

Distance biases

Proximity is a strong, unconscious driver of decision-making. Brain scan studies have shown that one network in the brain registers all types of proximity, including conceptual proximity (such as whether or not you own an object) as well as proximity in space and time. The closer an object, an individual or an outcome is in space, time, or perceived ownership, the greater the value assigned to it.

For example, given a choice between receiving £100 today versus £150 in three months' time, the majority of us will choose the former thanks to that aforementioned phenomenon, temporal discounting. A distance bias encourages short-term thinking instead of long-term investment and can also lead us to assign entirely disproportionate values to certain products or projects that we have, in one way or another, been close to.

To mitigate this kind of bias we need to take distance out of the equation. To do this, evaluate the outcome or object as if it were closer to you in space, time, or ownership. For example if you are putting off doing something - buying a car, booking a holiday or working on a project, imagine you own the new car now or that you have already had the holiday or succeeded at the project you are putting off progressing.

Safety biases

As we've seen, our tendency to pay more attention to negatives like threat than we do to positives like reward is the result of how we evolved to survive. A hunter-gatherer whose brain responds quickly to the threat of a snake would be more likely to survive than one whose brain responds first to the charm of its colourful markings. This is why, when it comes to considering a transaction or investment, we're more focused on avoiding loss then the potential gain. That's what we mean by a safety bias.

Another safety bias is the framing effect, first identified by Amos Tversky and Daniel Kahneman in 1981.[27] When an opportunity is framed as a gain, people tend to be relatively conscious of the risk involved. But if the risk is framed as a way to avoid a loss, then people are more likely to ignore that risk or to justify it. This is true even though the objective information is the same in both cases.

To mitigate safety bias, try adding psychological distance to the decision. Imagine that you're giving advice to someone in your shoes rather than making the decision for yourself; when we're making decisions for others we're less biased because the threat network is not as strongly activated. Or imagine that the decision has already been made, and you're seeing it from a later point in time. Recasting events this way from a more objective, distanced perspective makes those events less emotionally-charged and less personal, and therefore we're able to get a clearer, more objective view.

Organisational development approach

First of all, help people to understand what bias is and how it works, share the science about why our brain responds in this way and emphasise that bias is a natural thing despite the pejorative associations that come with the term in everyday conversation. This is an area where training people is valuable.

Then, using the type of classification above, help people identify bias habits and to familiarise themselves with the terms best used to discuss them accurately, like 'distance bias' and 'similarity bias'. Finally, set up processes so people can help each other and themselves to mitigate bias. This will include sharing information about what a team can do when faced with potential bias in the categories above.

Using the brain to combat its own biases

That region of the brain, which includes what Lieberman calls the braking system is active when people are able to spot bias.[28]

When people are able to apply this mental brake, review their decisions and take a more objective view or when there's a chance to check their assumptions and intuition with others, then the influence of unconscious bias can be mitigated. However, it takes discipline to apply the brake and to decide to trust colleagues' judgement - to listen to their opinion and to be open enough to change tack. These types of factors work best when they're part of the culture - part of 'the way we do things around here' - where the prevailing behaviour is to apply the mental brake.

The other means of mitigating bias is mindfulness. The more mindful a person is, the more they're aware of and open to their subjective experience, the more they use their RVLPFC, improving their ability to label emotions, neutralise the threat response and reduce bias.[29]

The happiness advantage

Many if not most people in the business world share a common if unspoken assumption: If you work hard, you will be more successful, and if you are more successful then you will be happy.

By researching top performers at Harvard, at the world's largest banks and at Fortune 500 companies, psychologist Shawn Achor discovered a different pattern, however.[23] His decade of research shows that training your brain to be positive at work leads to success rather than success leading to happiness. Achor says that 75% of job success is predicted not by intelligence but by optimism, social support and the ability to manage energy and stress in a positive way.

Neuro-economist Paul Zak turned his attention to a similar subject, developing a formula he calls the Ofactor theory of organisational design which states that *Trust x Purpose = Joy or Happiness*.[24] His research was undertaken with companies that have taken his Ofactor organisational trust survey and also taken part in on-site experiments in which they measure a variety of physical factors, including people's production of oxytocin, that hormone discussed in relation to trust in Principle 2. Zak calls oxytocin 'The Trust Molecule', as he believes it drives cooperation, bonding and empathy.

His research reached two important conclusions on which his formula is based. First, trust and developing a strong sense of a company's purpose are linked. Second, organisations that achieve both these things clearly have happier, more engaged employees. Zak's team also tested whether happiness led to more effective working practices. They asked people to do cognitively taxing tasks that had to be completed accurately and quickly for payment to be made. Comparing those in the top quartile of happiness with those in the bottom quartile, the top group was 5% more productive. People with high happiness scores were also able to reduce stress at work 200% better than those with lower scores.

The researchers also divided participants into groups of four and asked them to find a solution to an unusual problem that they had not seen before and to do it against the clock. They found that happy people felt closer to those with whom they worked. In turn, those who were in the highest quartile of closeness to colleagues were 22% better at finding innovative solutions and enjoyed it 10%

more than those in the bottom quartile. They also discovered that the higher productivity of happy employees is about 50% due to existing personality traits (they were happy before they joined the company) but the other 50% is a response by employees to the organisation's culture.

Emotions and client relationships

There are myriad areas we could cover when it comes to clients and their brains, but let's narrow it down in the interests of simplicity to two: How clients' brains want to connect with you and how they actually decide who to work with.

Our brains hates salesmen

Think about a situation when someone has tried to sell you something. You know the scenario. The hearty smile, the over-familiar language and posture. They're probably standing too close or asking to use your first name before you've even shaken hands.

What's your reaction? Probably to get out of the situation, right? This is the brain's threat response in action. It's signalling that this person may not be trustworthy. Of course, as individuals we're more subtle than that - more nuanced - but remember that this reaction is unconscious and emotional, not logical, rational or sophisticated. The rational brain hardly gets activated, at least in the first few minutes. Survival required a brain that could react to threat without thinking and it still does so when confronted by a social threat just as it does when it encounters a physical one.

It's the same when you're starting your pitch to a prospective client. The challenge is to ensure that the primitive part of the audience's brain hasn't written you off as a foe, so that their rational brain can then process the data and evaluate the merits of what you're saying. This is one reason why there is so much talk about the importance of making a good first impression, of connecting personally before pitching.

The client's decision-making process

One decision the client's brain is making - and it may be the only one to begin with - is whether they want to be in a relationship with you. (For most people this is an unwelcome sentence. It's awkward. Uncomfortable. It doesn't make you feel good. What you are experiencing is a threat response. More on that in a minute.)

When a client is making this decision there are two systems in the brain that are active, the limbic system which includes the amygdala, and the prefrontal cortex. Your goal is to make sure there is a balance between the two and that when the client comes to make a decision they're using both of these systems. These are the decisions that stick! What does that mean and how is it accomplished? Getting the two systems to connect

The amygdala is responsible for signalling the fight-or-flight response, as we discovered back in Principle 1. To re-cap briefly:

This response is triggered by a release of chemicals. In order to survive day-to-day dangers, early mammalian brains had to develop a system that gave them an early warning of danger.[30] Today, the amygdala is still at it, and within seconds of meeting a person it'll send us a stream of messages along the lines of 'like', 'dislike' or 'not sure yet, proceed with caution'. Usually, these more basic messages operate below conscious awareness and simply show themselves as a vague impression of trust or distrust of the person we're meeting. That's you at a client meeting!

So when you start communicating with a potential client, you need to send positive or neutral signals to their amygdala - their security guard if you like - so the unconscious sense is 'this person is safe', and even better, 'This person is safe and I like them'. These messages allow you to influence the part of their brain where the rational decisions are made, the prefrontal cortex.

As we discussed in Principle 2, humans developed a large brain, and specifically a large prefrontal cortex, that gives us the ability to connect with and understand each other, helping us to live and work together. It's why we're wired to experience a sense of reward from social interaction.

In pursuit of these connections and interactions we've developed those extraordinary powers that mean we can understand what another person is thinking, what their goals and motivations are likely to be and even to predict another's behaviour to some extent.

The region of the brain in charge of these processes is called the medial prefrontal cortex.[31] It's right in the middle of your head, just behind your eyes. It's active when you think about your own behaviour, when you think about your favourite sweater or an important memory, or when you're reflecting on your own personality and skills. And it's this bit of the brain that's absolutely crucial to connecting with your client.

One way to think about this practically is to bear in mind that your potential client can't be thinking and assessing about your technical expertise and thinking about whether they would be happy working with you at the same time. They'll switch from one train of thought to another and back again. So, when you meet them, remember that they won't be exclusively focused on the PowerPoint you're presenting because they'll also be wondering how they feel about the prospect of working with you, how their stakeholders will feel about you and your team and how they can describe the benefits of working with you. If you only focus on strategy, logistics and expertise and miss the personal engagement, you're not activating all the relevant parts of the brain.

A potential stumbling block here is that most companies value and talk about the economic and strategic aspects of business more than the social aspects. This in turn pushes you to focus on your expertise over bonding with the client. Just add up roughly how many more training hours you've spent on expertise rather than client understanding? What is the number? Five times more? Ten? Obviously some of this will depend on the stage of your career (you need a base of expertise, after all) but you must also be able to engage with and understand the client or that expertise is worthless.

There's one final thing to remember when trying to appeal to both your client's thought processes. When messages from the two parts of the decision-making system are contradictory, we need to use our frontal cortex to resolve the conflict. Anxiety disrupts this process by prompting the amygdala to flood our brain and body with the stress hormone cortisol, putting the prefrontal cortex out of commission. So if you're in charge of the venue, providing a comfortable, relaxed environment for your client meetings is more important than you might think.

We're born biased

"Most of our judgments and actions are appropriate most of the time," says Daniel Kahneman in *Thinking Fast and Slow*. As we know, our fast, intuitive brain often jumps to conclusions or takes shortcuts that the slower, more rational brain doesn't question and hence creates bias.

This bias, of course, plays its part in decision-making. David Rock suggests that loss aversion, minimising uncertainty and emotional reactions to proposals are common.[32] "These three groups of biases steer people toward minimising danger even when there isn't any;

to make choices based on a feeling of certainty, even when there isn't any; and to like an idea or not, even when there isn't any actual data."

In essence, this means that clients - just like the rest of us - may *think* they're making entirely rational decisions when they aren't. Biases such as loss aversion spring from past experiences or memories that are often unconscious. When they distort a client's decision-making, they need to be examined on a conscious level to rid them of their power. Raising these potential issues as part of your presentation or discussion brings them to consciousness without embarrassing the client. This could mean, for example, helping the client see that pouring more money into a moribund project will be damaging, or that their attachment to a solution they created in the past won't work going forward.

Honest signals

Some neuroscientists talk about 'relaxing the emotional brain.' It's a slightly simplistic phrase, but basically it means reducing or even eliminating any possible threat response in a client's brain and making sure you're seen as a friend rather than a foe.

That's why establishing rapport is so essential, by making clear that you're like them or, if you're not, at least your not different to them in a threatening sense. This creates a sense of reward when being around you and provokes positive emotions in the limbic system to which the rational brain will look for evidence to corroborate its conclusion that you're good news.

Psychology has for many years emphasised the importance not just the words we use but also the body language and tone of voice that accompanies what we say. We're always on the lookout for what's authentic, what's important and what doesn't ring true. These skills seem purely intuitive but research by Sandy Pentland at MIT sought to verify and quantify them.[33] Pentland found that we act on and are influenced by what he calls the 'honest signals' people give out, like the tone of voice being consistent with the words, or the degree of tension or relaxation in the body being consistent with how we talk to the client. He measured these signals using those sociometric badges to which we refer in Principle 2.

Pentland says honest signals have a real impact on the success of individuals and teams, accounting for as much as 50% of the performance of a group. He also researched people giving pitches and could predict, based on body language, tone and energy, who would win the business with 87% accuracy. The most successful pitchers score high marks in the following:

Influence: The extent to which people speak in a similar pattern.

Mimicry: The reflexive copying of body language and gestures.

Activity: Increased activity levels normally indicate interest and excitement.

Consistency: Consistent emphasis and timing is interpreted as a mark of mental focus, while a lack of it may signal an openness to influence from others.

People can be trained to modify or control these honest signals, imbue their communication with more energy and to get their body language backing up their verbal language.

Practical strategies

Probe for clients' real needs and goals. Don't just cater to what they *say* they want. When you understand and share your clients' goals, you'll also understand their challenges more clearly and be more motivated to help them - and this'll show itself in your 'honest signals'. Then they'll be inclined to trust you and tell you what you need to know.

Build rapport. This is the immediate priority. If you can begin this before you even meet, through a phone call or even a quick email, this will establish your interest in the potential client.

Address contradictions. If there are contradictions and confusions in what the client says they want, you'll be tempted to provide a rational answer immediately. This may not help, considering the research by David Cresswell, where people made much better decisions about complex issues when they had just a few minutes to reflect.[34] Engineer downtime - maybe suggest a coffee - and avoid going into a purely rational, emotionless pitch. If you over emphasise the rational reasons for working with you, you may get the 'yes' you're looking for but without the necessary commitment.

Manage your state of mind. It's hard to concentrate on the client and your own signals at the same time. Your brain just can't manage that many things at once. The best way to ensure you project honest signals is to manage your state before you walk into the room. Get curious about the client, not just about their business but about them personally too. If you're feeling nervous, boost your confidence with some power poses. Amy Cuddy gives a good demonstration of this and the science behind the method.[35]

Make the environment match the relationship. Foster a climate of safety and empathy by cultivating a warm, safe, empathetic relationship. You also want to provide a situation where the client is physically relaxed and comfortable. Think about where the meeting will take place. Does it welcome the client, or is it chilly and intimidating? You want the venue to seem inviting, uncluttered and comfortable, a place where they don't feel rushed.

Reframe the issue. Think about how you can help the client reappraise their issue or take a step back from it to be able to see more possibilities. Using powerful questions that help the client see a new perspective is one way to achieve this. Another technique is to help the client have a picture of a future where they've solved the issue successfully. Asking questions about what this will look and feel like will put the client into that future state and help them both discover new approaches and feel good.

Use stories. Telling stories both to ourselves and to prospective clients is a powerful way to talk to both brain systems at once. Listening to how your clients talk about their issue and the way they make sense of the experience is an important part of deepening your connection with them. Your pitch, then, should help them reframe their story in a way that is less liable to trigger a purely negative emotional reaction.

Case study: Connecting emotionally with clients and colleagues

The challenge

An accountancy firm had observed that the analytical nature of their work led their people unconsciously to look for problems in everything, to take a problem-orientated approach in conversations and relationships, and generally to focus on the negative. Of course auditors - like lawyers and some other professional services - should look for problems. That's what they are paid by clients to find. But it becomes an issue when people can't compartmentalise these abilities and begin to extend them to areas of their life where different skills would work better.

A pessimistic, fault-finding mind-set doesn't help build relationships either with clients or with colleagues at work or at home. Shaun Anchor calls this 'The Negative Tetris Effect', a phenomenon where noticing problems and scanning for issues locks people into a negative spiral in all areas of their life.[36] This happens because we're bombarded with competing stimuli for our attention, we develop habits that act like a filter, a bit like a spam filter on your computer. Your brain filters for what's familiar to you and you notice more of that. Scientists estimate that we remember or consciously deal with only one out of every hundred pieces of information we receive. The rest is dumped in this mental spam folder, hence if your job requires you to be critical or dig for issues then you develop the habit of doing this even where it's not necessary or helpful, like in your home life or when you are building a new relationship with a client.

The programme

The accountancy firm introduced a programme to help partners understand the impact of their own emotions on client interactions, team energy and business success. The company wanted to improve the corporate culture, initially in the tax business and then across the organisation as a whole. Their hope was that this change would improve its client relationships and relationships in the firm.

The firm worked with the consultancy who developed the methodology for the NeuroPower[37] framework, a neuroscience-based model that identifies six ways that impact how people perceive information and respond in relationships. Their work explores what have been termed 'The Six Needs of the Social Brain' - those elements that drive individual, team and organisational performance.

The six needs are:

Relatedness - the need to be a valued member of a group (see Principle 2).

Expression - our need to notice and express emotion.

Leading the pack - the need to gain higher social status or to enhance our place in the relationship hierarchy.

Interpersonal connection - the need to connect socially with others.

Seeing the facts - the need to have data or personal experience of something.

Hope for the future - how we imagine and understand new possibilities.

The Six Needs approach provides a new lens through which to view the complexity and intricacies of human behaviour, revealing the core elements of human motivation. It offers people a comprehensive approach to understanding themselves and others in the work environment. These needs affect the way people lead, communicate, build teams and relate to others.

The basis of the model is that our habits and preferences mean we focus on one or two of these needs more than the others. So some clients may have developed a habit of needing to connect closely with others more than knowing the facts for example. Or another client may be much more concerned with facts and the future than with bonding and being empathetic. We also expect others to have the same preferences and priorities as we have ourselves. It's this assumption that can impact communications and understanding. The NeuroPower model also says that there is an order of needs and preferences in any high-performing relationship, and if the early preferences are not met then later ones won't be either.

In the first part of the programme, partners looked at their own emotional profiles (these are called 'core beliefs' in the model used) and those of their colleagues and clients. They learned to analyse their profile, identify behaviour triggers and to adjust their behaviour to improve relationships with others.

The model helped the partners look at how the brain's limbic system drives people's reactions, mental models and behaviour. This includes how they resist change, their triggers for conflict, what motivates them, their preferred communication styles and how they make decisions. This part of the programme also allowed the partners to explore how emotions impact on the effectiveness of individuals and their relationships with clients. They learned how to use conflict positively - make use of conflict rather than fight it such as utilising different views on how to tackle a project - to drive agility, creativity, innovation, constructive problem-solving and unbiased thinking.

The understanding their emotional profile and the impact of their core beliefs on interactions provided great personal insight. In addition, experiential simulations enabled partners to practice new behaviours and tools in a safe environment on challenges that were similar to real work challenges. They got better at reading other people's emotions, engaging more personally with clients and their teams, and asking how people felt rather than simply asking what they wanted. All this involved overcoming their own self-created narrative about why a client didn't want a particular solution and moving towards asking for new business or additional work and building long-term meaningful relationships.

The programme also covered the labelling of emotions as a means of managing difficult conversations and conflicts as well as identifying faulty thinking - testing assumptions that could be holding back a relationship or masking an issue with what the client really wanted as opposed to what the partner assumed they needed. The training and practice helped partners recognise and manage their emotional reactions and to pause for a moment to engage their rational brain rather than let the threat response manage the conversation. For example, partners were encouraged to ask for client feedback, overcoming a fear of what they might hear. They were also challenged to understand that they were often operating from assumptions rather than a fundamental understanding of their clients' needs.

Tipping the negative bias

Appreciative enquiry techniques, which include identifying what has worked well in the past and the circumstances where things have gone particularly well, were also used alongside questioning techniques to guide the culture towards more positive curiosity, warmth and optimism.

The use of positive psychology that focused on the strengths of each partner helped to raise collective energy towards the organisation's ambitions, improve levels of engagement and fostered collaboration by leveraging strengths rather than criticising people's weaknesses. For example, positive psychology guru Martin Seligman[38] and appreciative inquiry expert David Cooperrider[39] were engaged to lead the firm's partner conference and to work with partners to engage clients in positive conversations, and Tal Ben Shahar, another positive psychology expert, taught positive principles including re-framing questions.[40]

The firm is now using their neuroscientific understanding of habit to encourage partners to form new behavioural patterns by practising new behaviours in client relationships and communications for 30 days. Their work has led to an appreciable increase in the pipeline of new work.

The client said, "NeuroPower provides an extraordinary leap forward. It has enabled us to fast-forward strategically, and has helped us stay ahead of the curve. The value it has created in our business comes through at all different levels, from formulating strategies to engaging personal relationships. The value has definitely exceeded the investment."

Where else does understanding emotions matter?

Emotions and emotional control are relevant to virtually all aspects of business, but some of the areas that deserve particular attention:

Decision-making and especially potential decision biases.

Diversity and inclusion initiatives, which can benefit from a greater understanding of how the brain works and the potential impact of emotions.

Wellbeing, stress reduction and resilience. These will improve the more people understand about positive emotions.

Business development and sales. Emotions play an important role in decision-making and the quality of relationships.

Finally, as in our case study below, understanding your own and others' emotions can be useful in improving both internal and external relationships.

Tools

Emotion versus reason

The best approach to making good decisions is a middle path in which we use both head and heart. Over time, observe the patterns of how you think under different circumstances. This means bringing more of your thought process into your conscious awareness:

+ Notice the content of your thoughts.

+ What kind of language do you use to talk to yourself - is it kind, harsh?

+ Does the language vary and, if so, when?

+ What's your decision-making style? Do you tend to over-analyse, generalise or cut to the chase of a problem? How does your style change in different circumstances or for different types of decisions?

Decisions and stress

Fear and excessive stress are both big obstacles to making smart decisions. One way to manage stress and its impact on decision-making is to reappraise your experience. Try using these ideas:

Tackle tough decisions when you're mentally rested.

When you're anxious about your mental performance, tell yourself, "That's just my brain." This'll help you to step back and be more objective.

Make changes to your thinking patterns. Consider using mindfulness, whether it's in the form of formal meditation or just simply paying more attention to what you're feeling and thinking.

Decision fatigue

We all reach a certain point of the day when the quality of our decision-making starts to go downhill due to the brain's resources being depleted. To manage decision fatigue, bear these guidelines in mind:

+ Avoid back-to-back meetings that require focus and decision-making. Take short breaks and a few minutes here and there for refreshments.

+ Make your most important decisions earlier in the day or after a break, when your mind is more alert and you have more energy.

+ Avoid trying to think about too many things at once. Focus your attention on one thing at a time, perhaps by simply writing lists. Once something's written down, you've already started to clear some head-space for it.

+ Don't be afraid to sleep on it. Decision fatigue can lead to making the easiest possible decision - no decision at all. A break, whether it's overnight or just an hour, will improve the quality of the decision.

Emotional contagion

We all practice self-regulation every day in our home and working lives, with varying degrees of success. For example, scientists have discovered - rather shockingly - that our stress permeates out through our skin and infects, as it were, the people sitting close to us. It's a distressing thought-picture, particularly for any parent, but it highlights our responsibilities: Don't infect the team!

Try this simple tool when you notice your stress levels rising or feel yourself getting a bit 'limbic': Go for a walk around the office or outside and notice the feeling of your feet in your shoes. Concentrate on the feeling. If you notice your attention going elsewhere, that's okay. Bring your attention gently back to the feeling of your feet in your shoes. This simple exercise is called mindful walking and can be done in five minutes.

Labelling emotions

Matt Lieberman has found that using simple language to name emotions *lowers* the arousal of the limbic system, producing a quieter brain state that allows the prefrontal cortex to function more effectively. The implications of findings such as these for business are profound. It means that if people suppress their emotions in order to be - or seem to be - 'professional', they actually make it harder for themselves to function professionally.

Use these steps when you anticipate experiencing a difficult emotion or when you're feeling it:

+ Give the emotion a name. Something simple that you recognise. It does not have to be a name everyone would use; you can create your own. For example what one person might call anger another might call it irritation. If you find it difficult to name the precise emotion just make a name up.

+ Say the name to yourself, write it down, and draw a picture. Anything that gets it out.

+ Step back and take a minute or two to notice how you feel.

This might all sound very straightforward - and it is - but neuroscientific research shows it works!

Priming your mind

It's possible to manage negative triggers by using 'priming', which is when we fill our heads so full of a particular idea that it seems to crop up wherever we look. For example, when you decide to buy a particular make of car you prime your mind and as a result you seem to see them everywhere.

It's easy to prime our brains in a negative way. Think of an archetypal bad morning. You've slept badly and then you slept through the alarm, you spilled your coffee on the way into the office and then found you've left behind some important papers you were working on at home.

"This," you say to yourself, "is not going to be a good day." And then - not surprisingly - it isn't. Your brain has been primed to be on the lookout for everything that goes wrong.

You could, of course, prime your brain differently to notice the positives in your day. So set yourself the goal of noticing a certain number of positive events each day or the positive in every challenging situation.

The social control model

Stanford psychologist James Gross has developed a model for emotional regulation, assessing the pros and cons of the different techniques.

Avoidance takes several forms, from not getting into emotional situations by avoiding the person who annoys you to distracting yourself by reading a book or focusing on something else. The successful children in Mischel's Marshmallow Test employed various avoidance techniques.

Suppression is embodied in the attitude of the British stiff upper lip, can be bad for your health, raising your blood pressure and heart rate. It also uses up more brain energy and fails to deal with the cause of the emotion. In fact, there's some evidence that it increases the intensity of it.

Reappraisal involves looking at the situation in a different light and interpreting events in a more positive way. It can be a successful strategy, dealing with the root cause of the emotion and reducing amygdala activity.

Mindfulness, as discussed, has been shown to reduce our reaction to emotional triggers and also has several health and concentration benefits. Taking the time to become more mindful through a meditation practice can have long-term results.

Gross makes the point that all of these techniques require practice and, like a muscle, the more we use them the more our abilities develop. This it true whether it's a supportive technique like mindfulness (along with all its associated benefits), but remember that it's also true of negative techniques such as suppression (and all the associated side-effects).

So when a colleague asks for space to think about an issue that's causing them stress, go out of your way to respect the request, and ensure you're training yourself and your leaders in the supportive techniques because you can rest assured we're all quite adept at the poor ones!

Principle summary

Emotions are fundamental to how the brain works. Our two mental systems - the rational and the emotional - don't work in opposition to each other, but rather in harmony.

Understanding how the rational and emotional brain work together can lead to better decisions, improved wellbeing and less bias.

Positive emotions may be fleeting but cumulatively they improve our wellbeing, social connections and also our health.

Understanding the triggers for our emotions improves control and potentially results in better decisions.

References

1   'Andy Murray wins Wimbledon with emphatic victory over Novak
    Djokovic', the *Guardian*, 2013:
    http://www.theguardian.com/sport/2013/jul/07/andy-murray-
    wimbledon-2013-novak-djokovic

2   Walter Mischel, Ebbe Ebbesen & Antonette Raskoff Zeiss,
    'Cognitive and attentional mechanisms in delay of gratification',
    Journal of Personality and Social Psychology, vol. 21(2), 1972

3   Matthew D Lieberman. The brain's breaking system (and how to
    'use your words' to tap into it) *Neuroleadership Journal* Vol 2. 2009

4   AR Aron, PC Fletcher, ET Bullmore, BJ Sahakian & TW
    Robbins, 'Stopsignal inhibition disrupted by damage to right
    inferior frontal gyrus in humans', *Nature Neuroscience*, vol.6, 2003.

5   JP Mitchell, TF Heatherton, WM Kelley, CL Wyland, DM
    Wegner & C Neil Macrae, 'Separating sustained from transient
    aspects of cognitive control during thought suppression',
    Psychological Science, vol. 18(4), 2007

6   BE Depue, T Curran & MT Banich, 'Prefrontal regions
    orchestrate suppression of emotional memories via a two-phase
    process', *Science*, vol. 317, 2007

7   V Goel, & RJ Dolan, 'Reciprocal neural response within lateral
    and ventral medial prefrontal cortex during hot and cold
    reasoning', *Neuroimage*, vol. 20, 2003.

8   SM McClure, DI Laibson, G Loewenstein & JD Cohen, 'Separate
    neural systems value immediate and delayed monetary rewards',
    Science, vol. 306(5695), 2004.

9   ET Berkman, L Burklund & MD Lieberman, 'Inhibitory spillover:
    Intentional motor inhibition produces incidental limbic inhibition
    via right inferior frontal cortex' *Neuroimage*, vol. 47, 2009.

10 E Berkman & MD Lieberman, 'Using neuroscience to
    broaden emotion regulation: theoretical and methodological
    considerations', *Social and Personality Psychology Compass*, vol. 3,
    2009.

11 MD Lieberman, T Inagaki, G Tabibnia & MJ Crockett, 'Affect

labelling is a form of incidental emotion regulation: Subjective experience during affect labelling, reappraisal, and distraction'. *Emotion*. 2011 Jun;11(3):468-80.

12   MD Lieberman, 'The brain's braking system (and how to 'use your words' to tap into it)', *NeuroLeadership Journal*, vol. 2, 2009

13   CA Boettiger, JM Mitchell, VC Tavares, M Robertson, G Joslyn, M D'Esposito & HL Fields, 'Immediate reward bias in humans: Fronto-parietal networks and a role for the Catechol-O-Methyltransferase 158Val/Val Genotype', *Journal of Neuroscience*, vol. 27, 2007

14   D Creswell, B Way, NI Eisenberger & MD Lieberman, 'Neural correlates of dispositional mindfulness during affect labelling', *Psychosomatic Medicine*, vol. 69, 2007.

15   Antonio Damasio, Descartes' Error: Emotion, Reason, and the Human Brain, *Putnam Adult*, 1994.

16   Marina Krakovsky, How Do We Decide? Inside the 'Frinky' Science of the Mind, Stanford Business, 2010

17   Daniel Kahneman, Thinking Fast and Slow, Farrar, Straus & Giroux, 2011

18   Marina Krakovsky, How Do We Decide? Inside the 'Frinky' Science of the Mind, Stanford Business, 2010

19   D Kahneman, D Lovallo & O Sibony, 'The Big Idea: Before you make the big decision...', *Harvard Business Review*, vol. 98(6), 2011.

20   John Coates, The Hour Between Dog and Wolf: Risk Taking, Gut Feelings and the Biology of Boom and Bust, *Harper Collins*, 2012.

21   Vinod Venkatraman, Scott Huettel, Lisa Chuah, John Payne & Michael Chee, 'Sleep Deprivation Biases the Neural Mechanisms Underlying Economic Preferences', *The Journal of Neuroscience*, vol. 31(10), 2011.

22   David Creswell, James Bursley & Ajay Satpute, 'Neural reactivation links unconscious thought to improved decision making', Social, Cognitive, and Affective Neuroscience, 2013.

23   Shawn Achor, The Happiness Advantage, *Virgin Books*, 2011.

24   The Ofactor survey: http://www.ofactor.pro/

25   Heidi Grant Halvorson &David Rock, 'Beyond Bias', *Strategy + Business*, 2015: http://www.strategy-business.com/article/00345?gko=d11ee

26   Heidi Grant Halvorson &David Rock, 'Beyond Bias', *Strategy + Business*, 2015: http://www.strategy-business.com/article/00345?gko=d11ee

27   Daniel Kahneman & Amos Tversky, 'Choices, Values and Frames', *American Psychologist* vol. 39(4), 1984.

28   MD Lieberman, 'The brain's braking system (and how to 'use your words' to tap into it)', *NeuroLeadership Journal*, vol. 2, 2009.

29   U Kirk, 'Neural substrates of corporate decision-making', *NeuroLeadership Journal*, vol. 4, 2012.

30   Elizabeth A Phelps & Joseph E LeDoux, 'Contributions of the Amygdala to Emotion Processing: From Animal Models to Human Behavior', *Neuron*, vol. 48(2), 2005, pp. 175–187

31   David M Amodio & Chris D Frith, 'Meeting of minds: the medial frontal cortex and social cognition', *Nature Reviews Neuroscience*, vol.7, 2006, pp. 268-277.

32   David Rock, Your Brain at Work: Strategies for Overcoming Distraction, Regaining Focus, and Working Smarter All Day Long, *HarperBusiness*, 2009.

33   Alex (Sandy) Pentland, 'To signal is human', *American Scientist*: http://web.media.mit.edu/~sandy/2010-05Pentland.pdf

34   JD Creswell, J Bursley & AB Satpute, (in press). 'Neural reactivation links unconscious thought to improved decision making', Social, Cognitive, and Affective Neuroscience.

35   Amy Cuddy, Caroline Wilmuth and Dana Carney (2012). The Benefit of Power Posing Before a High-Stakes Social Evaluation. *Harvard Business School Working Paper* 13(027).

36   Shawn Achor, The Happiness Advantage, *Virgin Books*, 2011.

37   Peter Burow. NeuroPower: Leading with NeuroIntelligence. *Copernicus Publishing*; Third Edition edition. 2013.

38   Martin Seligman, Authentic Happiness: Using the New Positive

Psychology to Realise Your Potential for Lasting Fulfilment, *Nicholas Brealey Publishing*, 2003

39   David Cooperrider & Suresh Srivastva (2000). 'Appreciative Inquiry in Organizational Life', *Research in Organizational Change and Development*, vol. 1, 2000

40   Tal Ben-Shahar, Happier: Learn the Secrets to Daily Joy and Lasting Fulfillment, *McGraw-Hill Education*, 2007

Further reading and viewing

Daniel Kahneman, Thinking Fast and Slow, *Farrar, Straus and Giroux*, 2011

John Coates, The Hour Between Dog and Wolf: Risk Taking, Gut Feelings and the Biology of Boom and Bust, *HarperCollins*, 2012

Dan Ariely, Are we in control of our own decisions? (TED Talk): http://www.ted.com/talks/dan_ariely_asks_are_we_in_control_of_our_own_decisions?language=en

Dan Ariely, Predictably-Irrational, *Harper Perennial*, 2010

Amy Cuddy (2012). Your body language shapes who you are. TEDGlobal.

NeuroPower: https://www.youtube.com/user/NeuroPower1

Martin Steligman, The new era of positive psychology, (TED Talk): http://www.ted.com/talks/martin_seligman_on_the_state_of_psychology?language=en

David L Cooperrider, Ph.D., Case Western Reserve University: https://www.youtube.com/watch?v=P3MLkDl2MHc

Tal Ben-Shahar, Happiness 101: https://www.youtube.com/watch?v=5-RVECUWOGQ

Principle 5: Create Brain-Savvy Learning

A few questions to mull over before you get going:

Do people need to learn new skills and ways of working for your strategy to succeed?

Benefits for programme participants of learning the new skills or ways of working and thinking?

Will attending the programme reward participants' CORE elements?

Do people understand the goals of the programme and has time been spent ensuring they're personalised?

Are you creating an atmosphere where people want to learn, where they can have fun whilst they're doing so?

Are the programme elements effectively spaced out and paced so people have time to assimilate the material?

Are key ideas being generated through insight rather than instruction?

How are people reflecting on the learning?

The science

It's extraordinary how helpful neuroscience can be when it comes to designing a company's learning strategy, and even more extraordinary how few organisations are making the most of it in the design and structure of leadership and learning. Learning and development practitioners say they're being more commercial and business-focused, but we still hear that programmes aren't producing the behavioural changes that they're supposed to deliver. We estimate that only about 1% of new behaviour sticks on skills-based learning programmes like leadership development.

Some of the points that make up brain-savvy learning design may already be part of your programme. But understanding the science behind learning and behavioural change - even though you might not mention the science explicitly - will mean you can audit your learning strategy effectively and make sure you're getting the best return on your investment. Participants don't have to know why and how you've designed the learning strategy the way you have, we call this 'behind the curtain', but following an approach that works with the brain will increase the odds of behavioural change sticking.

This chapter is structured slightly differently to the others. It is structured around our brain-savvy learning model. We have given you the science and the practical application for each part of the model.

Learning and the link to business strategy

We often find that when we talk to people in learning and leadership development, they say that their programmes and learning strategy links to the business strategy, but when we go on to talk to the participants we find that link is sometimes a bit tenuous. Sometimes the link has been lost completely.

Communicating this link between the learning and the bigger picture helps participants understand at both an emotional and rational level what the company is doing and why. It makes clear the purpose of the learning and change, and it helps to reduce the sense of threat and provide the motivation for learning.

So what tools are at your disposal when it comes to ideas, language and models that link to the business context as well as each other, and that fit easily into the overall objective? You're looking to build up a picture of the new behaviour and the mind-set you're trying to instil, leading the brain down a natural learning path that minimises the effort needed to understand and also makes recall easier. Whilst this might seem obvious, we've all been in the situation where a stakeholder suggests adding a new concept or a new set of skills 'as we have the group together' and suddenly you're trying to shoehorn a totally unrelated piece into the design.

As anyone involved in any kind of programme design knows, you should aim to make content as interesting as possible by using a variety of media and colour, and also make sure you're using a common language across modules and programmes. Ideally, you'll design a few easily replicated models and ideas that work across all the company's learning events. It's not uncommon for us to find three or four different models - feedback models for example - used across a company in different programmes; whilst this may provide choice, it can also create confusion and inhibit habit change.

Finally, try to make sure that information is expressed in terms of the various agendas, goals and aims in your organisation, and that you repeat but deepen ideas over different levels of seniority and mastery.

Learning strategy model

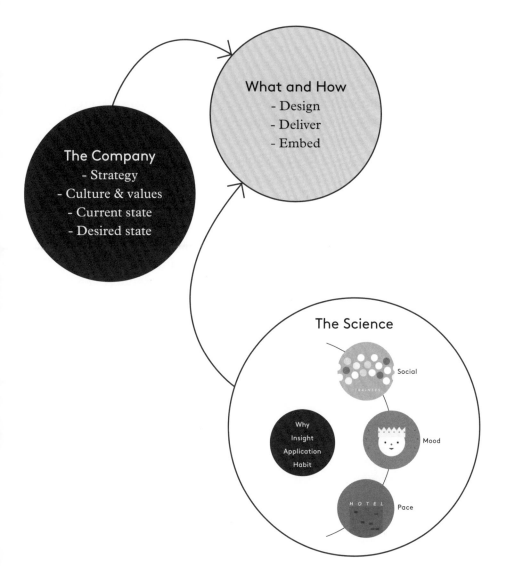

How the brain learns

Put simply, the brain learns in two ways:

Creating new networks
Neurons pass electrical impulses between one another, and neurons that fire together repeatedly create stronger, more established links. The more new connections you create to an idea or insight, the better; the more the new information is presented in different ways and the more it is used, the more likely it is to stick.[1] When we learn this way ideas are put together in a linear way; one idea linking to the next or parts of a skill building up to the ability to do something new.

Whole-body learning
Mirror neurons are thought to allow us to imitate the actions of others. It's the way children learn and it's believed that this is how our ancestors learned to use tools. This learning happens pre-consciously, which speaks to the importance of on-the-job learning from good role models.[2] This type of learning isn't linear, building from one point to another, we learn the skill all at once, but the new skills still need to be reinforced to make them stick and to make the new neural pathways as strong as possible.

Whether the brain is creating new networks via a linear piece by piece process or you're engaging in some whole-body learning, it'll be easier if you ensure consistency, reinforcement, linkages, application and use role models to demonstrate examples of the learning in action.

How to make your learning strategy suit the way the brain works

As we've said, for learning and leadership development to be truly strategic it should be explicitly linked to the business strategy and culture of the company. This model should remind people to make this link when it comes to needs analysis, design and positioning of events. Linking learning to the realities of the job is typically less of an issue, although the need to ensure learning is focused on the future rather than what was useful in the past can still be a struggle.

We use a particular model of learning to guide behind-the-curtain programme design. Below, we've taken each element of the model and given you the brain science that supports it along with the practical implications.

Model for learning and behaviour change

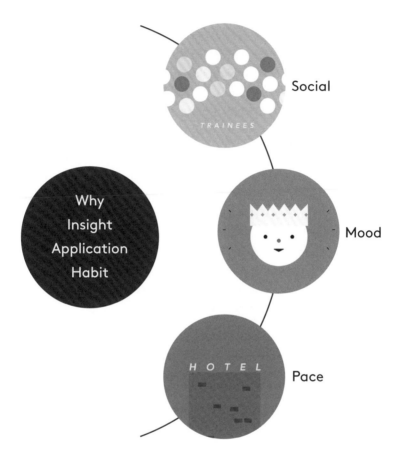

"What's in it for me?"

This is one of the first questions running through the brain of anyone you're targeting for new learning, whether it's informal, on-the-job learning or a formal programme or workshop.[3]

This question of motivation kicks in before anyone is even invited to learn something new. Essentially, when you ask someone to learn something new, you're asking them to realign their group identity. Humans are essentially social beings and one of the first things we do is categorise people into in-group (people similar to us) and out-group (people who are different).[4]

Learning interventions and especially high-profile programmes where there's competition to get a place will automatically create new in-groups in the form of programme participants and alumni. If people think that by taking part in the programme they're separating themselves from a valued in-group then they'll be reluctant to participate. But they'll feel good about the prospect of attending a programme with high-potential colleagues or being offered a place on a course where numbers are limited, so bear in mind that these can be powerful motivators.

One of the aims of the programme may be to mix up people from different functions across the organisation. Evidence shows that the boundaries of people's in-groups *can* change if you present evidence that challenges their preconceptions.[5] Front office people can learn something from service functions, and sales people can learn from accountants, for example. In order to overcome resistance to in-group change you need to create an awareness of the benefits of introducing participants to a valuable new network.

Also bear in mind that change is usually inherently threatening to people's CORE elements(see Principle 1).[6] There are ways to create feelings of reward that mitigate the threat, however, like learning in a community or the reputational boost that comes from being more skilled. So ensure that your pre-programme communications mitigate threat and maximise reward so that learners will be receptive to new skills, ideas and change.

It's important that participants understand that being invited onto a particular course isn't implied criticism of how they're currently working. So present the learning as an opportunity to get better, to master something new or to learn something which will benefit them personally and enhance their success. In other words, learning needs to be framed in terms of a growth mind-set and the associated benefits (see Principle 3).

A second way of answering that 'What's in it for me?' question that helps with the application of new learning is to connect the content with the learners' role and beliefs about their own success. For example, suppose there's content about a new way of carrying out performance reviews. If a learner asks him or herself, "How will knowing this content relate to my role and my success?" it creates links between the new content and an existing neural network. Researchers Kim and Johnson used fMRI to explore activation in a brain region called the medial prefrontal cortex (MPFC), which is active when we're thinking about ourselves or reflecting.[7] The researchers asked participants to rate how much they liked images they were shown. Later, the images were randomly assigned as belonging to the participant or to another person. People were more likely to remember the images assigned as 'theirs' and there was activity in the MPFC associated with the memory.

It's also worth letting people know 'what's in it for them' on a personal level. A clear vision of the future helps people maintain new behaviours and strive harder to achieve the change.[8]

Practical implications

Within and across programmes, make the links to why it's important to learn new skills, change behaviour or think differently as explicit as possible. The goals of the programme or event should clearly link to the business strategy, as we've said, but they should also be personalised to the individual learner either through mechanisms like a discussion with the boss, through using 360 feedback, self-assessment tools or pre-event reflection questions that help potential participants think about the relevance of the programme to their success. This helps to answer the question 'Why should I attend this programme, learn this new behaviour or adopt this new way of thinking?' It also reduces uncertainty and enhances the reputation of those who adopt the proposed change.

Learning is easier when people intuitively understand the themes and when, where possible, the new knowledge or behaviours are demonstrated through role models. So see if you can build in education and training for role models and ensure they speak the same language, use the same models and purposefully demonstrate behaviours to their colleagues. And when we talk about role models, they don't have to be there in person, or even be actual people - they can be case studies, videos, examples, stories or people identified by the learners in or outside the company.

Grabbing people's attention

The science of how we learn is compelling but sometimes it can be pretty counterintuitive. The first thing you need to secure is people's attention. Unless you have this, they won't learn anything! In today's businesses, where there are competing demands on people's attention, getting it isn't easy.

And this is one of the counterintuitive bits. Part of the reason it can be hard to grab is that attention isn't one discrete brain process.[9] We focus in many ways, for different reasons, using different parts of the brain. Sometimes these parts of the brain work together, sometimes they compete.

Take the simplest example - the startle reflex. That's the one that makes us jump when we get a shock or hear a loud noise. When this is triggered, a chain of neurons from our ears to our spine activates the fear response in a fraction of a second, boosting our heart rate, tensing our shoulders and making us cast around to see if whatever shocked us represents a threat. This reflex requires almost no brain power and has been observed in all animals. Needless to say, you're unlikely to want to use this in learning!

Top-down and bottom-up attention

Our attention is attracted in a different, more complex way when we hear our name called across a room. This stimulus-directed attention is controlled by pathways through the temporoparietal and inferior frontal cortex regions, mostly in the right hemisphere. These areas process raw sensory input but they don't concern themselves with how we should respond immediately to it. Neuroscientists call this a 'bottom-up' response.

When we consciously pay attention to something, when we're listening to someone who's telling us something we want to know, remember or understand, for example, a separate 'top-down' pathway activates. The signals are conveyed through a dorsal pathway in the brain's cortex, the part that does more complex processing. This lets us focus on what we're hearing and tunes out sights and sounds that are not immediately important to that task.

When it's doing this, our brain works like a set of noise-suppressing headphones, with the bottom-up pathways acting as a switch, ready to interrupt if something more urgent needs to capture our attention.

Attention spans

Various studies have demonstrated that our brains can only give something our full attention for less than about 20 minutes.[10] After that time, it's less and less likely that we'll retain information we're presented with. What happens in the brain when we lose and then regain attention is governed by the two separate systems. There's the dorsal attention network, located high in the brain, which is active when we chose to focus on things like goals or intentions. So listening to the boss explain their vision for the new leadership behaviours and working out what it means for us is likely to be activating this system.

The second system is the ventral attention network. This directs attention to things coming in from our senses and is effectively a safety system, keeping us alert to potential danger. The problem comes when the alerts are not central to our continued survival but relate to less critical matters - like a new email landing in the inbox and your phone going *ping*.[11]

The two systems work together - the dorsal system gets a bit of a rest when the ventral system directs our attention elsewhere. This rest also gives the dorsal system a chance to refocus and notice what might have changed while it had been distracted. Of course, all of this can happen in less than a second, sometimes without us even being aware we've switched focus.

It's likely that in a learning environment there is also another system which is active - the brain's braking system (see Principle 4).[12] This inhibits our impulses, and whilst it's useful in stopping us from flitting from one thing to the next, it's tires us out. That's another reason why taking frequent 'brain breaks' is important.

These features of attention have an impact on how our memory works. As we might expect, constantly flitting from one focus to another (as when we're multitasking) has been shown to reduce our ability to retrieve information later on.[13]

Exploitation vs exploration

Paying attention to what needs to be achieved in the present (exploitation) activates different parts of the brain to those we use when concentrating on future imperatives (exploration).[14] Not surprisingly, exploitation (implementing strategy initiatives, for example) requires concentration on the job at hand, whereas exploration (thinking up the next strategy or a new product) demands a more open awareness of future possibilities.

Exploitation is accompanied by activity in the brain's circuitry for anticipation and reward, which suggests it feels good to be on familiar ground. But when we switch to exploration, we have to make a deliberate cognitive effort to disengage from that familiar routine. The brain will experience discomfort, sometimes even pain, which means we're disinclined to do this.

This is more difficult if we're short on sleep, when we're stressed or mentally overloaded. To sustain the outward focus that leads to innovation and new ways of working, we need some uninterrupted time to reflect and refresh our focus.

Practical implications

The research into processing multiple inputs has implications for the form of the materials best suited to a learning programme.

The brain cannot process different input to the same brain system at the same time - it needs to switch between them. So having a complex slide showing written information whilst the trainer talks about it means that the listener has to switch their attention from the slide to the speaker and back again because both are being processed by the language systems in the brain. But talking and simultaneously showing a visual picture which illustrates the words does not produce the same issues. This is because visual processing takes less cognitive effort and because the language and visual systems can operate simultaneously.[15]

Delivering content

You should aim to divide learning into small, easily assimilated chunks to accommodate the brain's 20-minute attention span:

> + Include multi-media messaging that engages multiple senses and increases neurological connections.

> + Maximise brain-based rewards by ensuring positive CORE and personal rewards for learners

+ See if you can get the participants to connect with one another and agree the ways of interacting through clear, simple ground rules.

+ Vary the activities so the brain has a chance to refocus and reset. Ideally these new activities use different parts of the brain's processing ability. For example, if people have been sitting listening for a while then they'll welcome a chance to move and talk or reflect and write.

Insight

Insight in this context refers to that moment of clarity when a solution comes to you or a connection is made between new material and existing knowledge and you know instinctively that it's correct. This happens when the brain puts together unconnected neurons, usually when it's quiet or reflecting on something other than the issue at hand.

When people have insight they also have a burst of energy and a dopamine reward in the brain, and the process also permanently changes the brain at a physiological level by creating new neural links.

We're not talking about general creativity here - that's a process, a way of thinking and perceiving. Insight is also different to intuition, which is a nudge or a hint about the direction you need to take, rather than the whole solution.

How do insights work?

Mark Beeman of Northwestern University is probably the best-known and most respected neuroscientist working on insight.[16] He summarises the elements that make up insight in three ways:

> + There's unconscious processing - when solutions come to people when they're *not* thinking about the problem in the same way as they did before, like when someone asks a powerful question or they genuinely put themselves in someone else's shoes.

> + There's the relaxed mind - when someone's calm and in a good mood.

> + And then there's the sudden answer - this is when the solution comes, it's a surprise but they're confident about it; they just *know* it works.

So here's a bit more detail on those elements, with the scientific evidence pointing to how insight happens and how you can create the optimum conditions for it.

Unconscious processing

Beeman's research suggests that insight tends to involve connec tions between small numbers of neurons. An insight is often a long-forgotten memory or a combination of memories aligned in new ways. These memories don't have lots of neurons linking them to-gether, which is why we need a quiet mind to notice the new con-nections and the insight they provide. A busy mind with little down time tends to overlook the insight.

Inward-looking

Beeman has also found insight happens when we are looking 'be-yond the box'. Our attention can be externally focused (reading this chapter) or internally focused (an image has been generated in your mind's eye by a word on the page). We tend to flick between these two states all the time. When people have insights they are often 'mind-wandering', according to psychologist Jonathon Schooler, rather than focused on the problem.[17] Mark Beeman has recorded alpha wave activity in the visual and auditory cortex just before the moment of insight, which indicates that people shut out external stimuli to save brain resources for noticing the insight.

A relaxed, positive mind

Beeman can predict which method someone will use to solve a prob-lem (logic or insight) by the type of activity in their brain immedi-ately before the problem is presented to them. He says our mental state determines our approach, and also our personal preference.

In a similar study, Joydeep Bhattacharya of Goldsmiths and Bhavin Sheth of the University of Houston identified that the brain knows how it will solve a problem eight seconds before the conscious an-swer appears.[18] Sheth suggests this could be the brain capturing transformational thought in action (the 'Aha!' moment) before we're consciously aware of it.

The sudden answer

So here's another slightly counterintuitive point: If you want insight then stop trying to solve the problem.

A distinctive feature of problem-solving is that people get stuck. They go round and round the data and the issues and can't see the solution. This happens because we tend to get fixated on a small set of solutions. The more we work on this same wrong solution, the more we prime the brain for that solution and the harder it is to think of new ideas. Insights tend to happen when people give up, at least temporarily.

Psychologist Stellan Ohlsson's Inhibition Theory indicates that we need to inhibit the *wrong* solutions for the right one to come to our attention.[19] Also, conscious effort tends to involve a lot of neural activity, which can reduce the likelihood of noticing the quiet signals of insight.

Beeman also found that these sudden answers tend to be correct: 92-94% of insight answers were correct compared with about 80% of answers produced by logical analysis.

Practical implications

To design for insight creation rather than instruction. This means:

> + Introducing new ideas in a relevant context for the learner. For example, linking learning to strategy or personal goals, as discussed above.

> + Understanding the current mind-set of the learner and positioning content accordingly. In practice, learners will all have different starting points so designing content to be flexible and ensuring that learning outcomes can happen at different times is important. This requires facilitators who understand the overall goals and who can think on their feet, monitoring where individuals are and then using the things that happen in the room to make links. They should also know when to push a point home and when to leave it for reflection.

> + Using powerful questions to generate insight, and offering new and different perspectives such as stories, personal anecdotes and external examples.

> + Giving learners time to reflect is essential and designing in active reflection tools, especially when the stakeholders for the programme believe people need to be busy. We use techniques like coaching on the go, which provides all the benefits of coaching whilst they're walking. The movement seems to reduce inhibitions and free up thinking space.

+ Designing programmes with an overnight stay, say from lunchtime to lunchtime. This provides participants with the natural downtime of sleep (see Principle 8) which is known to enhance the making of new connections.

Insights can be fleeting, so it's important to capture them when they do happen and to fix them in the mind. So try reinforcing them by discussing them, setting goals about their application, applying them to a current situation or to oneself - or using the insight experientially whereby you incorporate it into a new habit plan or a briefing for the team.

Applying learning to the job

Even the best programmes in the world are no use if the learnings themselves aren't applied, so it's vital that participants understand the value of the learnings and how to apply them. It's also important to facilitate genuine insight as this can transform an idea from being merely interesting into something that begins the process of changing behaviour. Finally, applying new knowledge helps reinforce the connection between a new idea and a new way of working.

At a neurological level, applying information or insight increases the connections in the brain.[20] Pieces of information are not stored in the hippocampus as discrete memories as they would be on a computer hard drive, for instance, but are instead made up of webs of data stretching across the brain that are linked together. The more associations there are connecting the original information to a memory, the stronger the links are and the easier it is to recall that information later on.

When we make a conscious effort to store new knowledge through reasoning or insight, our memory retention improves. Even if the initial conclusion we reach is wrong and we have to re-examine our thinking before reaching the correct one, it produces better recall than just studying the right answer for the same period of time. Also, immediate feedback on any errors significantly increases accuracy of future retrieval.[21]

Historically, we've tended to believe that repetition is the way to ensure memory moves from the working memory system in the brain to the long-term memory. We now know this isn't sufficient. Both psychological and neuroscientific research show that the key to learning and building long-term memory is to create ownership of learning content.[22] This ownership occurs when participants are motivated to understand, when they can put the information into a context which is relevant to them and when they can apply knowledge in their own way.

This means that learners should be encouraged to do something with the insight or information they're gained. The more grounded and profound the application of knowledge - the more thought they have to put into it and the more ways there are of applying it - the more likely it is to be retained. For example, asking learners to elaborate on ideas engages the hippocampus, which is at the heart of memory creation.

Even though genuine personal insight is the best way to ensure memory retention and recall, research by author Eric Jenson suggests that it also helps to present learners with data and then ask them to organise or reorganise it themselves or add their personal experience, perhaps by creating a leadership model for their specific organisation or a tool for working with a particular team.[23] These personalised tasks are more effective than providing a pre-defined, one-size-fits-all model.

Metacognition

Metacognition means thinking about thinking. It's a skill that, when well developed, is an important part of effective learning.[24] There are many ways to get people thinking metacognitively, such as helping them to understand what they already know and what they don't know, and asking them to think about how new information is relevant to them and their success. For example, getting people to reflect on their learning at the end of each day has been shown to enhance application and retention.

Knowing what you know

Self-evaluation is the most well known method of increasing learners' awareness of what they know and don't know. Giving short tests of knowledge and understanding and quizzes have been proven to enhance learning.[25] Research has also shown that memory is enhanced by retesting a short time later (see the section on Spacing, below).[26] These tests, whether they're given as part of the programme or the participants take it upon themselves to formulate them, reinforce the links between information and application because every time a person retrieves knowledge, the link between a cue and that knowledge is reinforced. This approach works particularly well when incorporated into online or e-learning programmes, for example giving people a short quiz at the end of each part of the programme and also as a light-hearted exercise during face-to-face events.

Debriefs

Debriefs can take many forms such as quizzes, reviews and visualisations. All of these trigger retrieval of the recently learned information and improve long-term retention. Asking the learner to visualise situations in which they could apply their new learning or to make decisions within the context of the new data also helps reinforce what has been learned. Again, these activities increase associations between information and application.

It isn't easy to monitor how much new information is being absorbed by learners in real time, but you can engage them in activities that provide external validation of the process. This might simply mean getting people talking to each other about ideas rather than sitting back and listening to presentations. Or it might involve encouraging participants to invent their own ways of applying new knowledge and analysing their work in order to get an idea of how well information is being integrated. In our experience, not only does this aid application but it's also more energising and fun for participants. You can read about some of the ways we've done this in the case study.

Reflection

Reflection offers ways for learners to apply content and to make their own connections between new ideas and their existing knowledge.[27] This will be more valuable than simply telling them about the connections between the content and their work. Tools and exercises that require people to think about how they can apply new ideas work well, bearing in mind the brain's attention constraints, as they offer opportunities to vary activities and also give the brain a chance to relax without having to resort to traditional refreshment breaks. For example, you might give learners questions and tasks that ask them to apply learnings to themselves or their team. Find out or ask them to find out what they know and what they may still need to understand, and then set up the conditions for insight by creating the space and time for quiet, internal reflection. One way to do this is to encourage learners to reflect on their thought process surrounding a solution. Ask the question, "How many different ways are you considering applying this knowledge?"

Peer learning, group work and storytelling are all common in learning environments. One thing they all have in common is that they involve learners thinking about themselves in the context of the broader social environment. Connecting new information with the self is one way to create a network of associations that enhance activity in brain areas involved in memory, which has been shown to help with recall as well as application.[28]

Habit

Embedding new knowledge, skills and ways of thinking is really part of the application process, but in our learning model we single it out for particular attention because we find it is an area that's often neglected. You can read about the science of forming new thought patterns and behavioural habits in Principle 6.

Embedding the practical application of new skills and insight relies on incorporating habit creation at every stage of the learning. When learning takes place on the job, helping learners to create new habits speeds up skill-development and consistency of application. When habits begin to be built in a formal programme, it increases the return on the investment. The tools we use to do this are also laid out in the relevant section in Principle 6.

Mood

Work by Jessica Payne at the University of Notre Dame shows the brain learns best when it's in a good mood, when it's mildly stressed, and when it has had a good sleep.[29]

There's plenty of anecdotal evidence that being in a good mood helps problem-solving, and it's well-supported by the science. Participants who were happy when they arrived for an experiment or who were put into a positive mood in the lab solved 10% more problems overall, and solved 20% more of them by insight, a result that supports Beeman's research showing that a positive mood helps people have more insights.[30]

Barbara Fredrickson's research on positive emotions has shown that a positive mood induces a broader focus of attention, allowing more creative and flexible responses that are good for tackling complex issues and learning.[31] Negative emotions tend to increase physiological arousal, narrow focus and restrict behaviour.

Mild stress

Too much stress reduces memory for neutral facts, such as the background details, but enhances negative memory and, in the long-term, reduces hippocampus functioning. So the emphasis here is on the word 'mild'. There is also the possibility that learning in an environment that is highly stressful may increase the retention of information but with an accompanying avoidance state; people remember things but don't want to recall them because that would entail revisiting the negative memory.

Research into the Flow state (see Principles 1 and 8) has shown that the ideal conditions for work and learning are a balance between the level of challenge in a situation and the participant's perceived ability to carry it out. If it's too low, people coast. If it's too high, they panic. In any learning programme, stress needs to be reduced, but only to the point of Flow. So, no jumping off cliffs - either physical or mental. Instead, design exercises that stretch participants just beyond their comfort zone[32]. It's important to anticipate the capabilities of the participants so that the intensity can be dialed up or down depending on the individuals in the group.

Pace

When training budgets are under pressure and you find yourself having to do more with less, the obvious response is to cram more content into less time, work longer hours on the programme and keep the pace brisk. However, there are key pieces of research that should inform your decision-making on the intensity of your learning programmes and events.

It's well known that synapses in the brain (the connections between neurons and other cells that allow for the transmission of information) grow when they're learning. Previously, educators and scientists believed that learning was cumulative; in neuroscientific terms the synapses links started small and got progressively bigger and stronger.[33] But it now seems that synapses that have recently been strengthened are peculiarly vulnerable, and more stimulation can actually wipe out the effects of learning. More recent research has shown that, in the short-term, synapses get even stronger than previously thought but then quickly go through a transitional phase when they weaken.

We've all had course participants joke about 'brain overload' at the end of a long day or following an intensive online programme. It's real. More training during this phase is actually counterproductive. There's no point trying to cram more information into the timetable - you're wasting your resources.

It's also been shown that when people have to process complex information giving them time to reflect, if only for a few minutes, makes their decisions much better.[34]

Spacing learning

The importance of spacing - having some space between learning and review sessions - can be a little counterintuitive but is nevertheless one of the most important research findings. People tend to believe that cramming the learning into one intense session, as we probably all did before exams, is the best way to learn. This belief is so ingrained that even when people perform better after spacing, they tend to be unaware of it. In one study researchers found that 90% of participants had better performance after spacing than cramming but even so, 72% of the participants reported that they still thought that cramming was more effective.[35]

Here are some useful guidelines for spacing in different learning contexts:

+ Spacing within a single learning event can be achieved through a reflection break. During experiments, this has led to significantly better recall of written passages than passages read all at once. These effects were also shown to be long lasting and persisted for at least a week. The optimal spacing seems to be a function of how long the information is needed for. A review of spacing research found that for a test undertaken seven days after the final study session, the best retention came from a spacing gap of one day; for a test 35 days later, the optimal spacing gap was 11 days; for a test 70 days later, the optimal spacing gap was 21 days.[36] The authors suggested 10–20% of the test delay would be optimal.

+ But in a work environment, learning is seldom done with a single test date or formal check on learned materials in mind. Learning needs to be continually retrievable, both in the short term and the long term. Research indicates that revisiting the information three times is ideal.[37] This research used an understanding of new concepts, similar to the type of material people might need to learn in a work context. Revisiting the information just once and after a few days brought memory up to about 40% on a test a month and half later. However, revisiting the information three times and with a handful of days between each session brought memory on that test up to about 55% - 60%. Adding additional learning sessions helped, but not enough to warrant the additional effort. This is the type of spacing that can be achieved in virtual programmes or in a series of webinars or modules.

+ When building spacing into a programme, the science suggests that an ideal gap is one that includes sleep. A 12-hour spacing gap during the day (with no sleep) is helpful, but not as good as 12 hours overnight, and sleep is especially relevant for more challenging material.[38] Sleep has been found to improve retention, insight and making connections between new and old knowledge, and of course it requires no extra cost, effort, or additional total time devoted to learning sessions. Sleeping helps transform pieces of information into long-term memories before they decay and also helps us to disregard irrelevant information.

Practical implications

In our own programmes we manage spacing by using a variety of techniques that provide repetition as a means of learning without it feeling like the same material is being re-issued over and over in the same context, for example by beginning each module with a review of the learnings from the previous one and reviewing the application of ideas. Repetition can also happen through facilitation techniques like priming. Priming allows the brain to build the new concept into a larger context, increasing efficiency in learning.[39] Methods we use to do this include sharing how ideas were applied and getting learners to provide their own related material or sharing new material.

One thing to remember about spacing is that despite the research on its benefit, people tend to believe it is less important than other learning strategies. Although it outperformed methods like mind maps by roughly 15%, participants in the study thought that they had learned more in the mind mapping exercise.[40]

Social

Humans are social animals - we're wired to thrive in communities (see Principle 2). Using the reward response triggered by social connection by creating communities of learners is one way to enhance learning and its application. An additional benefit is that the brain networks activated in social interaction will then be more likely to be linked to the new content. These networks include the medial prefrontal cortex (MPFC), a region important for processing identity, self-evaluation, and self-relevance.[41]

In his research, Matt Lieberman set out to see what happens in the brain when an idea is assimilated in such a way that it will be passed on or shared with others. Lieberman and his colleagues thought they would find brain areas associated with memory and deep encoding activated - areas that are used to try to hold on to critical information. In fact, those parts of the brain did not stand out in the study[42].

What they found instead was strong activity in the brain's medial prefrontal cortex, a network of brain regions central to thinking about other people's goals, feelings, and interests. It seems we employ our social abilities when we take in new information, testing whether the information would be of value to others who are important to us and not simply assessing its direct personal value.

Lieberman described this phenomenon as 'being an information DJ'. He suggests that this process of filtering information according to its importance to others activates the reward systems in the brain, increasing the person's sense of reputation in the group. The medial prefrontal cortex is active when new memories are formed and new material is learned in a social context. This indicates that socially useful information (or information that will be useful to people who are important to them, like a manager's team) should enhance opportunities for making new neurological connections which are potentially stronger than those formed by simply committing data to memory.

This brain region, the medial prefrontal cortex, would not usually be involved in forming new memories relating to technical skills, processes or technical data. Connecting these kinds of ideas to a social context such as a team or task force provides an opportunity to generate richer, stronger connections to new ideas than might otherwise be possible.[43] For example, learning safety procedures can be pretty tedious, but the learner might consider a situation in which a colleague, knowingly or not, cuts a corner in terms of safety and how the learner will then support that colleague towards better safety. In thinking this through, the learner will be activating the social circuits in the brain and generating his or her own connections between the new content and that social connection.

Get the learners teaching

We can make the most of all this research by turning learners into teachers and facilitators. Consider the phrase 'If you want to learn something, teach it'. There are many practical ways of doing this, from having learners pass on their insights from pre-work questions (see above), or dividing them up into small groups and asking them to take turns teaching certain elements of a learning programme. Even simply preparing to teach something without actually doing so is more effective that trying to learn something in isolation.

The social nature of the human brain means that adding a social angle to learning magnifies the effects of each of the other aspects we have discussed above. For example, in the case study on social connection which follows, you will read how we ask participants to present back their insights and learning to the rest of their business group. That social interaction in which the teaching or sharing occurs is one that is perfectly suited for focusing attention on the essential material. No one wants to appear to have had very few insights or ideas about how to apply the workshop content, and so doing this with colleagues who were also on the workshop means there's a social benefit of hearing others' insights and revisiting the material. It also provides the types of benefits we describe in the pacing section earlier in this chapter. The spacing is built in because simply by teaching or sharing at a different time, spacing has occurred.

A move toward leveraging the power of social learning can be as simple as a subtle shift in the way the facilitator closes a session. Where we may have ended by asking people to state what they learned, we can instead ask them whom they will share a learning with or how they will use the learning with another person.

Busting some
learning myths

Myth no. 1: The 70/20/10 strategy

Is this the number you are striving for in your learning strategy? Because according to a survey in 2014 by Lumesse, the talent software firm, less than 5% of companies achieve the 70/20/10 learning mix although many more are aiming for it.[44] In case you haven't come across this or have never really understood it, the theory says managers and leaders become successful and effective by learning roughly based on this mix of experience:

> 70% from tough jobs
> 20% from people (mostly the boss)
> 10% from courses and reading

The original idea was about how high-performing managers learned their stuff. That study, first identified in research by McCall, Lombardo and Eichinger, has since been verified by other studies[44]. The trio published their research in 1996. Later the idea was modified by learning professionals to align learning practice with strategy. The most noted of these was Charles Jennings, who worked at Reuters.[45] In his opinion, 70/20/10 is more of a reference model than a recipe, and that's a good way of putting it rather than as a model to slavishly strive to implement.

The model, in the context of learning strategy, indicates that effective learning and development comes through experiential and social learning in the workplace (the 70% and 20%) rather than through formal workshops or e-learning programmes (the 10%). Structured and directed learning, so the theory goes, can be useful but it rarely, if ever, provides the complete answer.

It's true that we usually build skills and capabilities through experience and practice supported by encouragement and personal motivation. This is what the concept of 70/20/10 is getting at. Whilst this can be helpful in moving away from a reliance on classroom-based learning, many companies have struggled to give the 70/20 parts of the process the necessary backing, and not a few learning professionals find it hard to know exactly how to help do this. This is exacerbated in some HR functions that have a shared service model which assigns regular learning programmes to a minimal level of service and removes too much of the expertise which is needed to support social learning and to help managers with creating on-the-job learning.

There are other problems with this theory that aren't widely acknowledged. First, with the pace of change occurring in organisations across many professions, the skills and the mind-set for future success is changing. There isn't always the expertise available in a workplace where 90% of the learning is meant to be happening (70% on job and 20% from others, mainly the manager). In fact, it's more than likely that in such a fluid business environment the way things were historically done is not how they need to be done in the future. So, for learners, the experience on offer from senior managers or colleagues may not be relevant, the skills may be out of date and good role models few and far between.

Take, for example, a profession such as the law, which sets great store by junior lawyers learning at the feet (as it were) of the master. Historically this has worked well. But as the demands of clients change to a more commercial focus - they don't just want their legal issues solved, they want them solved in a way that meets their particular business strategy and goals - learning from senior, more experienced legal experts is less and less useful to junior lawyers. They also need role models who ask probing questions, understand the client's business context and probably the competitive landscape, too. That's not to say these role models don't exist but they are not as numerous as they need to be, nor are they necessarily able to unbundle how they do the 'commercial' part of the role.

Some recent research by leadership and learning consultancy DDI supports a view that the 70/20/10 model is in need of revision. They conducted a survey of 13,000 leaders and asked them what experiences had contributed to their expertise, where they had learned the most and how they allocate their learning time. The results, published in the Global Leadership Forecast 2014/2015 found that rather than 70/20/10, the leaders actually spent 55% (on the job) 25% (learning from others in the work place) and 20% (formal learning) - a doubling of formal learning and a drop in informal experiential learning compared to the prevailing wisdom.[46]

Lumesse, the aforementioned talent software firm, say that 50/26/24 is the average learning mix in most companies right now and, given this new research by DDI and the pace of change, it suggests that this looks to be the right mix.

But rather than obsessing on the ratio, the focus should be on how formal learning is actually used, consistently and over a sustained period, back on the job. Assessing and measuring this is where the real gains can be made.

Myth no. 2: You can't learn skills via webinar

One way to capitalise on the science of how the brain learns is to use a variety of different ways to help learners make the most of the learning experience. For example, we know that the brain retains information best when it arrives in small chunks, over a period of time and with opportunities for reflection and practice in between. We also know that the brain likes to learn with others. That makes virtual learning programmes and webinars and related technology perfectly suited to effective learning. Webinars can mean that learners get maximum benefit from the time they put in.

One way to structure a virtual or webinar-based learning event is to include three elements to each phase: knowledge, processing and application.

Knowledge is either introduced in the workplace or the information is presented in a relevant context, perhaps in the form of a video, some reading, an interview with a client or colleague, a self-assessment or a reflective process prompted by questions as mentioned above.

The processing stage begins when the group comes together to discuss the information, to think about the reasoning behind it and its potential application.

The third element - application, takes place in the workplace and is where the learning is applied and put into practice.

Another consideration when designing such a programme is outlining what's expected of participants and instilling a suitable mindset. You could, for example, prepare them to be responsible for their learning by asking them to select a sponsor from within their own organisation and including a Personal Learning Agreement, a simple contract between the learner and their manager or sponsor that helps them keep track of their progress and defines the support they require.

You might also include on a learning platform an online library of tools, frameworks, videos and techniques tailored to the learners, enabling them to form a social learning community in which they can share their learning, successes and tips for applying the learning.

Myth no.3: Learning style

We are urged, and we always have been, to apply the Learning Styles Theory to programme design, and prospective clients often insist we show how the design will meet participants' different learning styles. This Learning Style Theory isn't one theory, there are actually a variety of slightly different ones, but the most well known is probably Kolb's Experiential Learning Theory.[47]

Kolb's theory is typically represented by a four-stage learning cycle and four styles of learning. The cycle holds up fairly well to modern research but the learning styles do not. The cycle is:

Concrete Experience - a new situation, experience or reinterpretation of existing experience is encountered.

Reflective Observation of the new experience.

Abstract Conceptualization - reflection gives rise to a new idea, or a modification of an existing abstract concept. This is akin to insight.

Active Experimentation - the learner applies the new idea to the world around them that is their job.

Kolb's theory also says different people naturally prefer a very particular learning style and that various factors influence a person's preferred style such as social environment, educational experiences or the basic cognitive structure of an individual's mind.

There are many different theories that suggest different learning styles. Many of the theories contradict each other, but that's not really the issue. The issue is this: Are any of them correct and do they help people learn?

People like the idea of different learning styles because the theories make intuitive sense. Surely, people think, we all have a preference for learning in different ways. Some of us like learning practically, some experientially and others theoretically.

For example, it's often said that people have a preference for the way in which information is presented - verbally, through experience, in writing or via other forms of visual presentation such as a model. Again, there are variants of this theory but a widespread one is that many learners are visual learners. Visual learners, think in pictures and like to learn via visual aids that represent ideas using methods other than words, such as graphs, charts, diagrams and symbols. Auditory learners' preference is for lectures, discussions, tapes and so on. Kinaesthetic learners prefer to learn via experience; they like moving, touching, and doing, and tend to like experiments and role play and so on.

The use of these ideas in programme design suggests participants have access to materials and information in all the modes so they can pick their preferred one. Participants can, it is claimed, use the model to identify their preferred learning style and thus optimise their learning by focusing on the mode that benefits them the most.

But the brain doesn't work that way.

It's true that we do store memories in three distinct ways and it's possible that some people may be better at visualising things or remembering certain things via sound. But that doesn't mean delivering learning in one mode for some people and a different mode for others is necessary. Scientists have tested the theory by showing pictures or saying words to research participants and then seeing which they remember best. There was no discernible difference in learning. When we ask people to learn or remember, we're really asking people to learn about the *meaning* of something. It's not enough simply to recall a word – we have to know its meaning if the learning is to be useful.

We do know that it's easier to learn certain things visually, like the shape of a product, and other things by hearing it, like a tune's melody - that's true of most people but is more to do with the nature of the thing to be learnt rather than the preference of the learner.

So why has this Learning Styles Theory persisted for so long?

Partly it's because it seems to make sense intuitively. Something close to the theory is right but the specific basic assumptions of the theories are wrong. It's also partly because, once we know the theory, we unconsciously filter data to match it.

A more productive way to think about programme design is to concentrate on implementing the right type of learning exercise according to the type of information and delivering it at the right time. And this means categorising the information rather than the learners and their learning style.

Another reason for the enduring popularity of the Learning Styles Theory is that changing the medium (from visual to auditory to kinaesthetic and so on) appears to work because it stops our brain getting bored, not because we naturally prefer one specific style of learning.

Case study: Creating a brain-savvy learning strategy

The challenge

One of our clients, who were in the process of making significant changes to their operating model, came to us because they saw an opportunity to overhaul their approach to learning and development. Specifically, the human resources director had an intuition that their learning methods and the strategy being used for learning and leadership development in the company was failing to maximise the investments the company were making.

He wanted to take the opportunity to review the learning strategy and the individual programmes, the consultants they used and the delivery of learning across the organisation. He was particularly interested in what neuroscience had to say about how people learn and change behaviour, and also how the company's learning strategy could reflect this.

Education - the 'what' and 'why' of brain-savvy learning

Our starting point was to work with the Learning and Leadership team to help them understand what the neuroscientific community was saying about how people learn and change behaviour. We shared with them the model we had created on brain-savvy learning and how this could fit into an overall learning strategy.

Some of the team were highly sceptical about the methodology. Their attitudes ranged from 'this is no different to well designed learning' and 'our internal clients won't accept programmes which are different to their expectations' to 'this is a threat to my expertise'. Our first job was to help the team understand the neuroscience behind brain-savvy learning for themselves, and we wanted to use this first introduction to the topic as an experiential example of the model we had developed.

The education sessions therefore gave participants an opportunity to experience for themselves learning delivered in a brain-savvy way. For example, rather than simply answering their 'what's in it for me?' questions, we helped the team to understand their motivation and which of the outcomes would be of the greatest personal benefit. And rather than lecturing them about the hard science, we provided experiential exercises and held back the science until the debrief session to explain why, from a neurological point of view, they worked the way they do. This approach went a long way to creating insight and a profound, almost instinctive understanding of brain-savvy learning.

The learning audit

This model enables a company to both audit their overall learning strategy and to look at individual programmes. It can also guide the drafting of briefing documents for suppliers and be used to develop a checklist for reviewing responses and design storyboards. Working alongside the team, we created tools to help our client carry out all of these.

The starting point was to understand the current practice and examine the link to the business strategy and what participants thought of the learning they had undertaken and how much they had applied it.

We interviewed a cross section of stakeholders and programme participants in order to understand how they perceived learning, its links to strategy and the different methods that were being used, from formal programmes to on-the-job learning. This meant that, for the first time, data was available on how stakeholders and learners felt about areas like their responsibility to develop their own skills (most people had not considered this), how individual programmes supported the company strategy (few could articulate this), which programmes were beneficial to them personally and also the amount of learning participants actually applied after attending programmes (a reasonable amount of the technical stuff, it turned out, but less on the behavioural side of things).

The review also provided data on the attitudes to different learning methodologies such as e-learning, social learning platforms (which had been used to support some recent programmes) and webinars, as well as role model-led and on-the-job learning. We were able to collect data on the amount of coaching received and to some extent the quality of that coaching, and also about attitudes to success using fixed mind-set versus growth mind-set questions.

Trends

From carrying out this review and others like it, we found a variety of common trends:

> + Stakeholders rarely have a good understanding of how a learning programme fits with the business strategy, even when this is something like a leadership programme explic-

itly designed to support the strategy. Much more explanation is generally required and the links need to be made more explicit, especially at the early stages and when people are first being invited to attend.

+ Much more explanation is typically needed in terms of people understanding the need for the programme and also what's in it for them. Setting goals with managers before the programme or at the beginning is rarely enough; managers may not fully understand the programme themselves and are generally poor at carrying out the goal-setting discussion.

We have found the most effective methods include:

- A campaign of communication about a major programme made up of short, punchy learning descriptions that focus on outcomes rather than inputs.

- Learners being given much more responsibility for the identification of their own learning needs but in a context that requires them to make a business-centred case for attending learning or for the company providing funding.

- Conversation guides for managers for the goal-setting discussion and also help from HR business partners or learning consultants with the process of identifying who should attend.

- Where a programme is in support of the business strategy and groups of learners across sections of the company are to attend, it's also important to supply some clear branding, a name, logo and colours, and a cascade of the programme. Starting the roll-out with the most senior people and progressing to the more junior. Another tactic that works well is attendance in work groups.

+ Learning and leadership departments don't always dedicate sufficient time and resources to embedding learning. The focus is too much on the event-based programmes, and the split between centres of expertise that design and roll out new programmes and shared services that manage on-going programmes usually exacerbates things. Learning needs to be seen as a process rather than an isolated event, and resources need to be made available to support the programme before, during and after the formal learning.

+ There is, even now, limited use being made of technology such as webinars and social learning platforms as an integral part of the learning methodology. This is especially true for programmes involving more senior people. What's more, the small number of virtual programmes that *are* being provided are typically under-supported. Webinars are more often used as short, one-off sessions rather than as a methodology to support on-going learning or to deliver programmes across geographies. They are usually stand-alone initiatives with little follow-up or embedding. However, when this technology is properly exploited, the benefits to learning are unarguable, as are the cost savings in travel and down time.

+ The 70/20/10 framework has been misunderstood in many companies and is causing learning functions to overlook the need to provide role models and on-the-job coaches who understand the future needs of learners rather than what's worked well in the past. This is a particularly important issue in sectors that are undergoing rapid change.

+ Anecdotally, individuals say they apply only around 1% of the learning they experience from programmes designed to create behavioural change. It's higher for technical learning, but nevertheless it looks like many companies are wasting 99% of their behavioural learning budget and this includes most leadership programmes. This is mainly due to the lack of embedding after a learning event, the lack of experiential learning and the uncertainty in the minds of participants about the link between the behaviours and future success.

+ In our work with companies (and maybe we have been unlucky!) the most conservative attitude to changing the way learning and leadership programmes are designed and rolled out tends to come from the learning function itself. Whilst this is the brain's threat response in action, it's also a worry for the ongoing influence of the function.

Articulating the learning strategy

Back to our case study. The outcome of the review was a clear, simple articulation of the company's learning strategy and how it supported the business strategy. This was a very straightforward document that could be used as a guide for the Learning and Leadership team also came in handy when telling managers how learning supported the business strategy. It included a small number of core principles that would guide the positioning, development and measurement of learning both during programmes and back in the office.

Efforts were made by the client to integrate the strategy and principles into all HR processes including talent, performance and promotion. This is on-going work.

Auditing individual programmes

In addition to an overall review that spanned the breadth of the company's learning strategy, we also took a closer look at individual programmes to ensure that our general findings and recommendations held true on both levels.

We found that the programme design lacked experiential learning even when the vendor claimed to provide this (this has been typical of our findings in other companies too). Many programmes also relied heavily on role plays which are not only unpopular with participants but also, we believe, result in people undertaking practice in a disassociated state which makes it hard to apply the learning back at work.

In this particular case, we found that they used negative role models, applied too much stress to participants and had limited flexibility in the intensity of the event for different learning groups, all of which is typically the responsibility of the facilitators.

We also found there was little or no time set aside for reflection. One point of particular concern was that the learning professionals in the company had limited experience of events that matched the brain-savvy model (except what we had given them) and therefore it was hard for them to assess what was being offered. We overcame this to some extent by jointly developing checklists, asking vendors to demonstrate how they facilitated events and being clear about requirements in briefing documents for vendors.

The outcomes

The client wanted - and we helped design and develop - a leadership programme that demonstrated the brain-savvy learning model.

This had two benefits. First, it enabled the Learning and Leadership team to test the model and to measure the results in terms of actual business and behavioural change. Second, it gave the Learning and Leadership function an opportunity to work on the programme from conception all the way through to embedding. We provided coaching and acted as a 'critical friend' as the programme took shape, helping the team understand some of the nuances of brain-savvy learning in the context of their own company as well as appropriate learning goals and stakeholder expectations.

We used our brain-savvy design principles because we know they ensure participants are more likely to apply learning and new behaviour:

+ Designing a programme and individual elements based on how the brain learns. As part of this, we made sure that participants understood what the benefits would be to them personally if they attended the programme and adopted the new behaviours

+ Generating insight rather than telling people how to behave. The brain is more likely to act on personal insight

+ Reinforcing insight by using tools that help apply learning and continue to apply it back in the workplace

+ Pacing learning to avoid overloading people and providing active reflection such as coaching on the go

+ Packaging content into digestible chunks and using multiple learning methods and media

+ Providing short learning modules and using review techniques to reinforce learning and ensure efficient, effective spacing

+ Applying a scientific understanding of habit formation to create new behaviours and help them take root.

This approach facilitates greater personal change and buy-in from people so it affects the bottom line too: It is, quite simply, a better return on the company's investment.

Embedding behavioural change

Learners were presented with a comprehensive set of activities to embed the learning. These included:

> \+ A site where participants could continue to access materials after the face-to-face programme elements were complete. This also created a community of learners who were willing and able to help each other
>
> \+ Group coaching sessions with participants 3, 6 and 9 months after the workshops
>
> \+ Shorter workshops to deepen skills in key areas throughout the year
>
> \+ New materials supporting the themes of the programme. These were sent out periodically to remind people of their commitments and the insight they had gained
>
> \+ The setting up of a buddy system. The buddy provided ongoing support and coaching.

Workshop participants also committed to how they were going to apply some of their learning from the workshop in the form of a leadership charter for working with their teams.

Tools

Checklist for brain-savvy learning strategy

The learning team in our case study have gone on to use the brain-savvy model to design other learning events. But the biggest struggle, they say, is finding vendors who truly understand the approach and can deliver it in practice.

Here's a checklist of pertinent questions you might ask potential vendors, and the kinds of answers you should keep an eye out for from the more brain-savvy suppliers.

Questions you should expect to ask suppliers	What to expect suppliers to cover in their proposal
What do you need to know about our organisation?	They should ensure they deeply understand your strategy, culture, values and the current state of the skills and mind-set of potential participants as well as how you want them to be when the learning is complete and embedded.
What is your understanding of our need? What process would you undergo to understand this more clearly?	The best suppliers will be keen to understand what, historically and in the current culture, aids learning and what blocks it. They should have a robust process for determining these and be able to help you mitigate the blocks and maximise the enablers in the culture and company processes. Along the way they should be able to reflect back the key stakeholders' hot buttons and needs, the potential participants' mind-set and what will make the programme successful. They should also cover how this learning event or programme fits into the wider learning context for your company.
How, in terms of content and methodology, would you use your understanding of our company in your design? What is your advice to us to ensure success?	The best suppliers take an organisational development approach, looking at the learning culture in its entirety and in the context of the business. Key design principles should mirror the beliefs in your learning strategy, for example a growth mind-set, taking responsibility for own learning and so on. There should be clearly defined behavioural / mind-set outcomes. The content links strategy and other criteria such as increasing energy or increasing connection across the company. The design is done in such a way as to reinforce the messages being delivered. For instance, if taking responsibility for learning and career development is a critical message then you don't want the participants to be spoon-fed all through the learning event. Instead, you require activities that make them seek out learning for themselves. The best suppliers will also give advice on positioning, communications and stakeholder management in the context of the programme.
What are your core design principles?	These should include a design that mirrors the organisational culture (or the cultural changes you are seeking to make), key messages that are clear and re-enforced in each part of the programme and a style that reflects those messages as in the example above. You will want to see clear links between the desired outcomes and the content, and also how learning builds deep understanding by reinforcing messages and using consistent models. The flow of the programme also must be clear and logical and should build from one element to the next.

How do you get people engaged?	The supplier needs to be able to help you show participants 'what's in it for them' and to make clear links to the business strategy and the benefits for the individual in communications to potential participants, their managers and other interested parties. Some ways to do this might include the use of humour, novel ways of presenting the programme such as a catchy title or slogan or other innovative branding. Identifying positive role models can be another tool for helping participants understand the benefits of attending the learning and applying the new skills.
What is the methodology you use to design your sessions? What is the methodology your facilitators use to deliver the event?	We suggest you look for the brain-savvy elements described above like creation of insight, application to real business and personal situations, and a means of embedding the new behaviour. What you don't want are one off workshops, lectures and experts telling people what to do. In the main, theory and models need to be made practical and participants given time to work through how they would apply them in their role. You also want participant to have a felt experience of the new mind-set or skills rather than just a cognitive experience. Probe how this will be achieved and ideally get the vendor to demonstrate to you examples they will be using. Obviously the facilitation should follow the design method and facilitators be capable of adapting their pace and style to match the participants' needs.
How do you ensure new behaviour is embedded? How do facilitators monitor learning goals? How does your design approach meet the brain-savvy principles?	Look for sessions within the design where people plan and create new goals or habits, that foster a desire to make behavioural change and where there are follow-on activities that reinforce the new behaviour and help participants stay on track. These sessions might be in the form of a follow-up with the line manager, coaching or post-event reviews. Look also for suggestions of how people will be rewarded for successfully applying the new behaviour. You're also looking to see evidence of time for reflection, the correct pace for the level and experience of the participants, elements of learning with others and a design that takes account of the positive insights that can come from mild stress and plenty of sleep.
How does your delivery approach meet these principles?	The facilitators should be role modelling the key messages and the content. For example, if a key message is about accountability then the facilitators should be demonstrating their own accountability in the way they run the programme. You would also expect them to get to know the company and use real case studies and realistic exercises, and have a deep knowledge of the content that goes beyond the storyboard. You're also looking for signs that they'll connect with the participants and demonstrate the benefits of social connection as well as monitoring how much people have understood and have had the relevant insights. Typically this happens to different people at different times so the facilitators need to be on their toes. They should also be able to manage the level of engagement of participants and their energy levels. It's very important then, that a facilitator enables people to learn at their own pace. So you want facilitators to demonstrate they can dial up or down the intensity according to the group of participants on any given cohort of the programme.
How do you measure results?	Measurement will often be a function of what you as the person leading the project wants to see. But typically you'll be looking for: Satisfaction with the event (immediate). Application of the learning back in the workplace (medium term). Consistent change in behaviour (medium-to-long term). New ways of working and new habits (long term). Business change linked to strategy (medium-to-long term).

These questions and watch-outs can also be used to write a request for a proposal or to review a proposal. Feel free to adapt these questions slightly and use them to audit your learning strategy and programmes.

Nail the 'Why'

Making sure your people know why changes are happening or why they need to learn something sounds obvious. But getting this message across loud and clear at an individual level rather than an organisational one isn't easy, and sometimes even the reason itself can be hard to define. Understanding the reason behind a decision gives a sense of certainty and helps people understand their options and make choices. This clarity also helps people focus on clearly defined goals, what they will change and what it will look like when they succeed. We also know that outlining definite steps to achieve goals gives a motivational boost, and being clear about what you want to achieve and how you will do it helps to make better decisions about time spent and where to concentrate your energy. Linking goals to a higher purpose in their role and their own success helps leaders and learners stay focused, especially when things get busy.

To this end, try following these steps:

> + Have each person draw up and share a description of their future when the learning is complete and new behaviour embedded. What will they be doing differently?

> + Have each person create a 'skyhook' - an image that's a metaphor for the higher purpose of what they want to achieve in their role

> + Ask them to identify what will be different once they've realised this. Get as much detail down as possible. Some people need a couple of iterations doing this to make adjustments to their description

> + Get them to identify what it will take to make these changes. Have small groups help the individual complete their plan through supporting their ideas and challenging them if they get stuck.

You may want to use this tool to create a collective future across the learner group by combining the individual images, skyhooks and plans.

Focus attention through stories

Stories talk to both our rational brain and our emotional brain and can be a good way of helping people have insight and also engage with changes. A story enables people to envisage the values and ideas being talked about. Telling a story is also a way of creating a deep connection with others. The characteristics of a story that will positively impact are based on the acronym SUCCES[50] (that's right - with the last 'S' omitted!). Each letter refers to a characteristic that can help make an idea memorable:

> **S**imple - find the core of the idea.
> **U**nexpected - grab people's attention by surprising them.
> **C**oncrete - the idea should be well defined so it can be grasped and remembered later.
> **C**redible - make it believable.
> **E**motional – an emotional buy-in will help people grasp the importance of the idea.
> **S**tories – Get people to create a narrative.

Changing behaviour

The application of new learning involves convincing people to change their work habits. Neuroscientist Kevin Ochsner estimates that humans act according to habit 70%-90% of the time, and are guided by deliberate mindful actions only 10%-30% of the time[51]. It's also worth knowing that it's easier to create a new behaviour than to change an old one.

So when designing a programme, make sure you include ways for participants to work out precisely which behaviours and habits will help them succeed. They are more likely to be successful when they:

> **Make the goal public**. We like to be seen to keep our commitments
>
> **Work with someone else** on the new habit, like getting feedback from a buddy or asking a colleague for support
>
> **Plan for what might derail them**. Anticipating stumbling blocks makes them easier to overcome
>
> **Build in rewards** for each step towards success.

The easy path to application

As people become more adept at a skill, the brain no longer needs to work as hard at it – it becomes automatic. Mastering a new skill actually results in decreased activity in brain regions involved in conscious control and attention and increased activity in the default network that is involved in self-reflective activities, including future planning or day-dreaming. Thus skill mastery is associated with increased activity in areas not engaged in skill performance, and this shift can be detected in the large-scale networks of the brain. Giving people time and encouragement for working at new skills helps embed the changes required.

To make new ways of working really stick, it's important, therefore, to keep the new skills or knowledge at the forefront of people's attention. People learn best when:

+ They have a clear idea of how the new skills or mind-set will help them be successful

+ The new skill is applied and practiced in multiple situations

+ They can apply the skill to current work

+ They have a plan to create new habits using the skills. Do this through drawing up clear personal goals, repeated practice, and applauding success.

Principle summary

Learning works better when:

> People understand what's in it for them to learn and adopt the new behaviours

> The material grabs their attention

> They experience insight and can apply it to their own role

> They understand and have time and encouragement to build new habits

And for learning events to be most effective:

> Provide a positive environment; get people into a good mood.

> Get learners helping each other to learn and adopt new ways of working

> Pace learning so that people can reflect, review and revisit it.

References

1   David A Sousa, How the Brain Learns, *Corwin*, 2011

2   Marco Iacoboni et al., 'Grasping the Intentions of Others with One's Own Mirror Neuron System', *PLoS Biology* 2005: http://biology.plosjournals.org/perlserv/?request=getdocument&doi=10.1371/journal.pbio.0030079

3   Debra K Meyer & Julianne C Turner, 'Re-conceptualizing Emotion and Motivation to Learn in Classroom Contexts', *Educational Psychology Review*, vol.18, 2006. And Eric Jensen, Teaching with the Brain in Mind, Association for Supervision & Curriculum Development, 2005

4   David Amodio, 'The social neuroscience of intergroup relations', *European Review of Social Psychology*, vol. 19, 2008

5   Kyle Ratner & David Amodio, 'Seeing "us vs. them": Minimal group effects on the neural encoding of faces', *Journal of Experimental Social Psychology*, vol. 49(2), 2013

6   Evian Gordon, Integrative neuroscience: Bringing together biological, psychological and clinical models of the human brain, *Singapore Harwood Academic Publications*, 2000

7   K Kim, MK Johnson, 'Extended self: medial prefrontal activity during transient association of self and objects', *Social Cognitive Affective Neuroscience*. vol. 7, 2012

8   Peters, J. & Buchel, C. (2010), Episodic Future Thinking Reduces Reward Delay Discounting through an Enhancement of Prefrontal-Mediotemporal Interactions', Neuron, 66(1) 138-148

9   Seth Horowitz, The Universal Sense: How Hearing Shapes the Mind, *Bloomsbury*, 2012

10 René Marois & Jason Ivanoff, 'Capacity limits of information processing in the brain', *Trends in Cognitive Sciences*, vol. 9(6), 2005

11 Katherine Sledge Moore, Clare Porter & Daniel Weissman, Made you look! Consciously perceived, irrelevant instructional cues can hijack the attentional network, *Neuroimage*, 2005.

12   Matthew D Lieberman, 'The brain's braking system (and how to 'use your words' to tap into it)', *NeuroLeadership Journal*, vol. 2, 2009

13   René Marois & Jason Ivanoff, 'Capacity limits of information processing in the brain', *Trends in Cognitive Sciences*, vol. 9(6), 2005

14   Daniella Laureiro-Martínez, Stefano Brusoni & Maurizio Zollo, 'The neuroscientific foundations of the exploration–exploitation dilemma', *Journal of Neuroscience*, Psychology, and Economics, vol. 3(2), 2010

15   AJ Wilkins, N Sihra & A Myers, 'Increasing reading speed by using colours: issues concerning reliability and specificity, and their theoretical and practical implications', *Perception*, Vol 34. 2005

16   Karuna Subramaniam, John Kounios, Todd Parrish & Mark Jung-Beeman, 'A Brain Mechanism for Facilitation of Insight by Positive Affect', *Journal of Cognitive Neuroscience*, vol. 21(3), 2009

17   Bhavin Sheth, Simone Sandkühler & Joydeep Bhattacharya, 'Posterior beta and anterior gamma predict cognitive insight', *Journal of Cognitive Neuroscience*, vol. 21(7), 2008

18   Mooneyham, B. W., & Schooler, J. W.. (2013). The Costs and Benefits of Mind-Wandering: A Review. Canadian Journal of Experimental Psychology, 67(1), 11-18.

19   Stellan Ohlsson, Deep Learning: How the Mind Overrides Experience, *Cambridge University Press*, 2011

20   Lila Davachi & Ian G Dobbins, 'Declarative Memory. Current Directions', *Psychological Science*, vol. 17(2), 2008, pp. 112–118

21   JT Guthrie, 'Feedback and sentence learning', *Journal of Verbal Learning and Verbal Behavior*, vol. 10, 1971

22   L Davachi & AD Wagner, 'Hippocampal contributions to episodic encoding: insights from relational and item-based learning', *Journal of Neurophysiology*, vol. 88, 2002

23   Eric Jensen, Teaching with the Brain in Mind, Association for Supervision & Curriculum Development, 2005.

24   NH Schwartz, BM Scott & DHolzberger, 'Metacognition:

A Closed-Loop Model of Biased Competition–Evidence from Neuroscience, Cognition, and Instructional Research', *International Handbook of Metacognition and Learning Technologies*, Springer, New York 2013

25   Henry L Roediger & Andrew C Butler, 'The critical role of retrieval practice in long-term retention', *Trends in Cognitive Sciences*, vol. 15(1), 2011

26   Katherine A Rawson & John Dunlosky, 'Relearning attenuates the benefits and costs of spacing', *Journal of Experimental Psychology*, vol. 142(4), 2013

27   Brett Benedetti, Yoshio Takashima, Jing Wen, Joanna Urban-Ciecko & Alison Barth, 'Differential Wiring of Layer 2/3 Neurons Drives Sparse and Reliable Firing During Neocortical Development', *Cerebral Cortex*, vol. 23(11), 2012

28   Kyle Ratner & David Amodio, 'Seeing "us vs. them": Minimal group effects on the neural encoding of faces', *Journal of Experimental Social Psychology*, vol. 49(2), 2013

29   Jessica Payne, 'Learning, memory and sleep in humans', *Sleep Medicine Clinics*, vol. 6(1), 2011

30   Karuna Subramaniam, John Kounios, Todd Parrish & Mark Jung-Beeman, 'A Brain Mechanism for Facilitation of Insight by Positive Affect', *Journal of Cognitive Neuroscience*, vol. 21(3), 2009

31   Barbara Frederickson, 'Positive emotions broaden and build', *Advances on Experimental Social Psychology*, vol. 47, 2013

32   Mihaly Csikszentmihalyi (2008). Flow: The Psychology of Optimal Experience. *Harper Perennial.*

33   Brett Benedetti, Yoshio Takashima, Jing Wen, Joanna Urban-Ciecko & Alison Barth, 'Differential Wiring of Layer 2/3 Neurons Drives Sparse and Reliable Firing During Neocortical Development', *Cerebral Cortex*, vol. 23(11), 2012

34   J David Creswell, James Bursley & Ajay Satpute, 'Neural reactivation links unconscious thought to improved decision making', *Social, Cognitive & Affective Neuroscience*, vol.10, 2013

35   Nate Kornell, 'Optimising Learning Using Flashcards: Spacing Is More Effective Than Cramming', *Applied Cognitive Psychology*, vol. 23, 2009

36   Nicholas J Cepeda, Edward Vul, Doug Rohrer, John T Wixted
      & Harold Pashler, 'Spacing Effects in Learning A Temporal
      Ridgeline of Optimal Retention', *Psychological Science*: http://
      laplab.ucsd.edu/articles/Cepeda%20et%20al%202008_psychsci.
      pdf

37   Katherine A Rawson & John Dunlosky, 'Relearning attenuates the
      benefits and costs of spacing', *Journal of Experimental Psychology*,
      vol. 142(4), 2013

38   Jessica D Payne, A Chambers & EA Kensinger, 'Sleep Promotes
      Lasting Changes in Selective Memory for Emotional Scenes',
      Frontiers in Integrative Neuroscience, vol. 6(108)

39   Miranda van Turennout, Lisa Bielamowicz & Alex Martin,
      'Modulation of Neural Activity during Object Naming: Effects of
      Time and Practice', *Cerebral Cortex*, vol. 13, 2003

40   Jeffrey D Karpicke & Janell R Blunt, 'Retrieval Practice Produces
      More Learning than Elaborative Studying with Concept
      Mapping', *Science*, vol. 331, 2011

41   Todd F Heatherton, 'Neuroscience of Self and Self-Regulation',
      Annual Review of Psychology, vol. 62, 2011

42   Emily B Falk, Sylvia A Morelli, B Locke Welborn, Karl
      Dambacher & Matthew D Lieberman, 'Creating Buzz: The
      Neural Correlates of Effective Message Propagation', *Psychological
      Science*, vol. 24(1234), 2013

43   Matthew D Lieberman, 'Education and the social brain', *Trends in
      Neuroscience and Education*, vol. 1 (2012),

44   Lumesse, 2014: http://blog.lumesse.com/2014/08/less-than-5-of-
      companies-use-702010-as-their-learning-mix.html

45   Michael M Lombardo & Robert W Eichinger, The Career
      Architect Development Planner, *Minneapolis*, 1996

46   Charles Jennings, '70:20:10 Framework Explained', FastPencil
      Inc. 2013

47   *Global Leadership Forecast 2014 / 2015*: http://www.ddiworld.com/
      glf

48   D Kolb, Learning Style Inventory: Self Scoring Inventory and
      Interpretation Booklet, McBer & Co, Boston MA,1985

49 Walter Burke Barbe & Michael N Milone Jr, 'What We Know About Modality Strengths', *Educational Leadership*, vol. 89, 1981.

50 From Dan and Chip Heath Made to Stick. 2008 Arrow.

51 Kevin Ochsner (2010). The Formation of Habit. Presentation at the NeuroLeadership Summit, Boston.

Further reading and viewing

Brain-savvy training: http://www.headheartbrain.com/brain-savvy-training/

A moment of insight: http://www.headheartbrain.com/a-moment-of-insight-2/

Jessica Payne, 'Sleep on It!': https://www.youtube.com/watch?v=ZG50ucRyfDY

How insight happens (BBC Horizon): http://www.dailymotion.com/video/xy9csr_bbc-horizon-the-creative-brain-how-insight-works_tech

Daniel Willingham on learning styles: http://www.danielwillingham.com/videos.html

Principle 6: Change = New Behavioural Habits

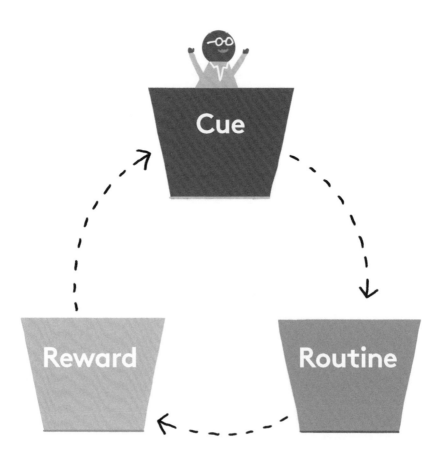

A few more questions to turn over in your head before getting started:

Which habits do you find help at work and which ones hinder your performance?

How easy have you found it to change these habits? Do you have a particular process or technique that you swear by?

How do you encourage people to change work habits during development programmes?

How do you make sure new ways of working are properly embedded?

How do you change habits and attitudes - or how do you think you might change them - across the organisation so that new behaviours really stick?

In your experience of change programmes, what's the most common method of ensuring that new ways of working are embedded?

How do work teams support people to change their work habits?

How do managers help team members adopt new work habits?

The science

Aristotle reportedly said, *"We are what we repeatedly do. Excellence then, is not an act, but a habit."*

But what *is* a habit, exactly? And when does a certain behaviour shift from being a repeated action to an automatic way of behaving? And how can we identify the helpful and not-so-helpful habits we have?

When we first decide to do something new - like not checking our emails every five minutes, regularly going to the gym or applying a new skill we've learnt in a workshop - we're taking action. It's intentional, rational and goal-directed.

Habits, in contrast, are characterised by automatic behaviour: we don't have to think about what we're doing every time we do it. As Aristotle suggests, our intuitive assumption is that actions become habits when we repeat them. But the real challenge for most of us is remembering to act in a new way when we're meant to. And anyway, if we want to form a habit, is just repeating an action enough?

Habits are more than repeated actions

One metaphor used to describe a habit is that of a neural pathway that has been reinforced through repeated use. You might think of it as a footpath that's been used so often it's now a deep furrow in the ground. The depth of this well-walked rut makes it difficult to get off the pathway - to break the habit. This footpath metaphor makes intuitive sense; the more you do something the more likely it is to become a habit. But that's not the whole story.

When we're talking about the technicalities of brain function, actions and habits are very different things. They use different parts of the brain that respond and work in different ways. Understanding how and why they're different can help you change your habits and help you to help others to change theirs too. It can even be useful when it comes to changing the habits of groups of people - or even a whole organisation.

Habits are helpful

Habits, as anyone who's got one they want to change will testify, are inflexible and don't adapt to changing situations. Intentions and goals might change, but habits will stay the same unless you do something positive to intervene.

Habits can have a bad reputation. People tend to think of the 'bad habits' - ones they'd rather not have, like biting their nails or eating biscuits in meetings or checking emails when they're meant to be writing a report. But habits can be very useful when we need to trigger behaviour quickly, automatically and with little effort. They can, in fact, keep you alive, and they definitely make life easier, not least because doing things automatically saves energy, leaving you free to do new things like learning complex skills. Neuroscientist Kevin Ochsner says as much as 70% of what you do is habit - and that includes most aspects of your job![1]

Think about a habit of yours. It can be a good one that you believe helps you or it can be a bad one that you'd like to kick. Maybe it's that habit of being distracted by others chatter when you're working on an important report, or maybe it's when you hear the alert tone on your computer or phone and you automatically open the window for emails. You don't consciously think, "Do I want to check that email right now?" or, "Is it best to finish this report?"

Now, if you're not in a hurry then that's fine. But what happens if you really ought to be concentrating on the report? Or you hear the alert and you *still* check the email!

We all do this kind of thing. We go into automatic mode. Let's say you tend to get down to work the minute you enter the office. One day, after a training course, you decide you want to be more connected to the team and spend more face-to-face time with them. You start off well by walking around the office each morning and catching up with each team member, asking questions and listening to their responses. But one day you're late and instead of walking around you have to rush off to a meeting. After a few days you realise you're back to your old routine, walking in and immediately firing up your computer. You've forgotten your intention to connect more with the team, despite what you set out to do.

This is a feature of habitual behaviour. Actions are more goal-directed: you would need to take conscious steps to avoid the email alert (like turning it off) or to remember to talk with the team each day. Good intentions don't seem to be enough.

That's because habits aren't just a natural extension of actions that have become 'a bit more so'. These two systems, action and habit, can and do compete. And when there's a conflict, habit usually wins.[2] We need both actions and habits in our life and work, and neuroscience has begun to uncover the separate brain mechanisms that control these two processes.

Forming habits

Most of what we know is thanks to research done on rats. Take one very simple experiment, whereby rats that pressed a lever in return for a reward a 100 times could be said to be performing an action. As they continued to press the lever even when they didn't get a reward, they could be said to have formed a habit. It's not clear at precisely what point an action becomes a habit, however. You can, no doubt, identify habits of your own that seem to have been formed very quickly, and others that have been much harder to instil.

This change from goal-directed action to habit happens in different brain systems, and more recent research suggests the process requires more than mere repetition.

The action system is dynamic and responsive to changing circumstances. For example, you can change how you contribute at the management meeting when the agenda takes an unexpected turn. Or you can choose to turn off the email alert on days when you have something important to finish.

However, this takes a bit of effort and part of the brain's design is to be energy efficient, which means it's inclined to push energy-hungry activities like conscious action towards more energy-efficient parts of the brain, where habits reside. The habit system is slower to gear up, but once it's running it can be hard to redirect.

So when your prefrontal cortex, which is largely responsible for intentional actions and goal-directed behaviour, gets tired then the habit system kicks in. Researchers from the University of Sydney have conducted experiments that show two neural 'loops' in the brain that code for actions and habits.[3] They've demonstrated how these loops either compete or coordinate to determine behaviour, depending on whether the intention and the habit agree or not. In fact damage to one system can result in behaviour being totally controlled by the other. According to the same researchers, the brain can compensate by making all behaviour habitual or all behaviour intentional.

Habit versus intention

First of all, it's important to distinguish between your *intention* to adopt a new habit and your *plan* to do so. The road to hell, so the proverb goes, is paved with good intentions. Just cast your mind back to the first of January this year - or any year. Most of us have very clear intentions but rather vague plans to adopt those New Year resolutions. The same can happen at the end of a workshop or development course and change programmes are all about persuading people to adopt new ways of working, which means adopting new behavioural habits.

The neuroscience behind forming new habits tells us it's more effective to focus on what you do want rather than what you don't. According to Hebb's Law (named after Donald Hebb)[4] 'neurons that fire together wire together' and this means that focusing on the old habit - even because you want to break it, may actually strengthen it. Focusing on creating a new habit forms new neural networks in the brain and gives you the best chance of embedding the behavior.

When planning a new habit, it's worth thinking about why you want to do it and not just how you will achieve it; there's good evidence that the how and the why are processed by different parts of the brain[5]. Using fMRI *(functional magnetic resonance imaging)*, UCLA researchers have found that when people perform any given action there's activity in pre-motor areas associated with the execution of actions in higher-order visual areas. That's a technical way - *a very* technical way - of saying that visualising your actions is important.

There's more. "Identifying why actions are performed is done by areas of the brain associated with representing and reasoning about mental states," say the researchers. This means you would do well to visualise yourself achieving your new behavioural habit as well as how you will *feel* when you have achieved it.

It's not unusual to see companies or leaders telling people to change how they behave, but it's surprisingly rare that they provide the necessary help and guidance to make these changes. Similarly, when people are learning a new behaviour or skill, they're not always given a clear reason *why* they're doing it and they're very rarely encouraged to *feel* how important to the change it is. Without any of this, not only are these types of efforts likely to fail, but the fallout can be a negative memory associated with learning and change that will impact both in the future.

The application

The habit model

The need to change people's behaviour happens in many areas of business, from introducing a new policy and asking leaders to lead in a new way to asking employees to deal with customers in a more sensitive manner.

We've seen that habits are automatic behaviours that allow us to do a lot more than if we had to think about everything we do. Given how useful they can be and how essential habit-forming is to making new learning and changes stick, we need to examine how can we form new, useful habits and kick those that have ceased to be useful.

Most of the research suggests a three-stage process for creating or changing habits[6]. It involves developing a plan that contains a cue, a routine and a reward.

Many studies have shown that a cue and a routine on their own aren't enough for a new habit to last. Only when the brain starts expecting the reward will it become automatic. Ideally your cue, in addition to triggering your routine, should also trigger a desire for the reward.

Here's an example. Let's say you want to connect more with your team so you decide you're going to spend 10 minutes each morning walking around the office doing just that instead of sitting down and sifting through your emails.

Your cue might be saying good morning as you walk into the office. It can be helpful to use a cue that's already something you do. These are called behavioural chains. So in this example you already say good morning to the team as you walk to your office but, instead of this being the cue to sit at your computer, make it the cue to engage in a longer conversation.

The reward attached to connecting more with your team might be having a better understanding of what's going on in the office and a greater sense of control. Anticipating that sense of control could be what maintains the new routine. Let's look at this in more detail:

Cue

Identify a trigger, something that will remind you to take the action you plan, your new routine. The cue may be a time, a person or a preceding action like saying good morning - as in the example. Cues work when they're linked to something you know you'll do anyway. They work even better when they also trigger the anticipation of the reward. So in our example the first conversation you have triggers the sense of control that you like and feel rewarded by. This encourages you to continue to talk to other team members.

Routine

Define the steps you'll take. These are the specific actions that you're trying to turn into a habit. This might be walking around and talking for at least two minutes and talking to at least three members of your team. The more detailed you are when defining these steps the more likely you are to carry out the routine – and it's a good idea start with small goals and then build on them over time.

Reward

A reward is essential to turning a new behaviour into a habit. The best rewards are neurological and it's even better if there's a sense of real anticipation. That way you get the benefits of the actual reward as well as the good feeling that comes with knowing that the reward's on its way.

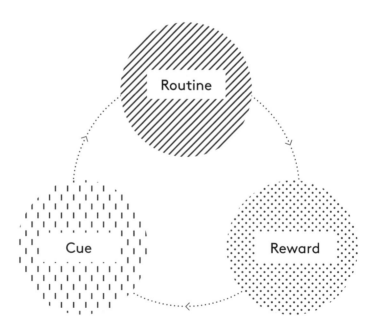

Staying on track: glucose or mind-set?

The conventional wisdom in many businesses is that if people understand rationally why they need to do something then they'll get on board with it. As we've discussed in previous Principles, this just isn't the case.

Think about that statistic we cited earlier in the chapter, that only 30% of what we do is under our conscious control rather than being habit and automatic. So that's 70% of your job you are doing without thinking about it consciously, its happening in automatic mode. Because habits operate outside of our conscious awareness, logical thought alone will not be enough to initiate change. This is why telling people what needs to be done and then leaving it to them to do it, doesn't work much of the time. And if we need to change something outside of conscious awareness is willpower the best approach? Again conventional wisdom in business is often based on assuming that the best people will have the willpower to change.

This is where the cue, routine and reward help, but you also need a plan of what to do if things don't work out quite as you're hoping because sticking to the new routine, based on willpower, can be thrown off track when we are tired, stressed or distracted. So the morning you get a call from the boss on your way to work asking for something urgently is the morning you forget to talk to the team and instead go straight to your computer after saying, "Good morning." This kind of thing can and does happen.

Sheer willpower versus mind-set

Studies led by Roy Baumeister in the US suggest we can shift the balance between the intention system and the habit system through willpower[7].The evidence points toward glucose levels being linked to the amount of willpower you have to resist habitual behaviour: the lower your glucose level, the more likely you are to act from habit. It's a controversial idea, and not one that everybody agrees on, however.

Carol Dweck, a leading researcher on success whose work we refer to in relation to mind-set in Principle 3, is one such person. She believes that it isn't glucose levels that determine our willpower but our mind-set[8]. In other words, if you believe that glucose will help your willpower, then it probably will! Her research also suggests that you need a growth mind-set to get better at forming the habits you want to adopt (see Principle 3). And if you're feeling low or de-motivated, check that you're not taking on a fixed mind-set about your habit (that's the voice in your head telling you you're not talented enough to behave in the new way) when you should be noticing areas where you *can* get better or where you've made progress.

If Dweck is correct, then willpower is not about what you *do* but rather how you think about a situation - which potentially gives you more control. If you're confident in your ability to resist temptation or pick up a new routine then you probably will.

In fact, several studies including Baumeister's have produced results that support this idea, demonstrating that a good mood boosts willpower, so your mind-set and your plan are crucial. And if you're wondering how to change a whole organisation, these conclusions also suggest that creating a positive climate around the change is more productive than using threats.

In a recent paper, Elliot Berkman at the University of Oregon examines the evidence on willpower and says that, rather than a depletion of resources like glucose governing our willpower, it's actually a change in our motivation that makes the difference, as people unconsciously or consciously calculate opportunity costs over time.[9] Berkman is proposing that your motivation and the amount of effort you are therefore willing to exert change as you go through the process of forming the new habit. These changes in motivation mean you may give up before you complete the habit formation because the reward seems less desirable.

Does motivation account for lapses?

Who hasn't started going the gym regularly and then gone on holiday, subsequently falling out of the routine? Or introduced a new way of working across an organisation only to have it trail off after a month or two when you - or the organisation - are under particular stress?

If you want to avoid lapses then there's one more crucial ingredient: belief. "For a habit to stay changed, people must believe that change is possible," says Charles Duhigg. "And most often, that belief only emerges with the help of a group."[10]

For example, social learning communities can help learners support each other to adopt new behaviours. Groups create accountability and belief and keep motivation high, all of which are crucial in helping you stick with new habits.

So if - to go back to our previous example - you want to improve your connection with the team, try asking yourself who could give you encouragement and feedback. If you want to make a habit of going to the gym, is there someone who could be your exercise partner every morning? Or could you hire a personal trainer you'll feel compelled to report your progress to?

The more you can stay motivated or have someone help you through positive reinforcement, the easier it'll be.

Give yourself a break

Nascent habits, no matter how well supported, are easily broken, so it's as well to be prepared for when you relapse. Dan Ariely, a behavioural economist at Duke, calls this The 'What-the-Hell' Effect.[11]

Imagine the scenario. You've been incredibly disciplined about getting to the gym each day, but today you miss a session. Or you've been making time to walk the office each morning but yesterday you were late and didn't do it, and today you forgot. It's tempting to think, "What the Hell," and give up on the whole thing. So now you're ready to trash the whole new habit plan - it's obviously not working - and not only do you skip your gym session but you eat chocolate biscuits all day too. Just because.

The solution is to put down the biscuits and examine your plan. Find exactly where things started to go wrong. Look for small things that changed your cue or your routine. Remember, a habit is a formula your brain automatically follows. Think, "When I see a *cue*, I will follow the *routine* in order to get the *reward*."

So the message is this: Have a good plan. Make sure there are anticipated rewards that are cued regularly. And *don't* beat yourself up.

Don't bite off more than you can chew

David Rock says you can only really work on one or two habit changes at once.[12] We'd suggest that you avoid trying to develop two habits in the same area too. That means don't try dieting and giving up smoking at the same time. It's likely to be too difficult, and you're setting yourself up to fail. Generally speaking, it's best to focus on one new habit and get that running smoothly before attempting the next.

It can be, however, a good idea to choose a habit that can make another overlapping habit easier to take up. For example, if your plan is to make a greater contribution in management meetings and you also want to improve your facilitation skills, you *can* practice both at the same time by facilitating the flow and objectives of the meeting while making an effective contribution.

Balance optimism with realism

We all need to temper our optimism with a pinch of realism. It's true that the biggest predictor of success in achieving a new habit is self-belief - that confidence that we can achieve what we set out to achieve. Having said that, it's important to be realistic about which things will be particularly difficult and to have a plan to overcome those difficulties. This means not underestimating the challenges. Most changes require time, planning, effort, and persistence.

Take the study conducted at New York University, for example, that showed that those who thought it would be hard to lose weight proved to be more successful and lost nearly 11kg more compared with both the control group and those who thought it would be easy.[13] The participants who thought the target was easily achievable actually *gained* weight.

So before you crack on with a new habit, picture what success is going to look like and how it's going to feel. Make sure you've got the right mind-set. Make sure you've set up your cues, routines and rewards clearly, and don't forget to balance that vital self-belief with some cold, hard realism.

Whilst the science can't tell you how long it will take to embed your new habit, you need to celebrate your successes along the way and not beat yourself up if you have the odd slip. And when your cues change, like when you change jobs or when you are on holiday, make sure you're especially vigilant. That's when the old ways of working can creep back. See yourself creating and embedding those new ways of doing things. And be proud of your new self!

Case study: Creating leadership habits

We were asked to design and develop a cross department leadership programme for leaders who work for the UK government. The programme was to take people from middle management to senior leadership positions.

Whilst all the participants were talented and had already achieved successful careers, most were at a crossroads. Could they go from being 'mere' managers and experts to being leaders of large, diverse teams where vision, strategy, engagement and alignment mattered most?

The government departments were going through unprecedented changes at the same time, so their leadership needed to be at home in an environment that was very fast paced, where the volume of work was exceptionally high and where people were experiencing challenging work conditions due to downsizing and a fundamental redefinition of success.

The challenge

There were many potential difficulties surrounding the success of the programme, not least getting buy-in across a diverse set of stakeholders and the concerns of the participants themselves. Some of the latter felt they were being pushed too hard but that turning down the opportunity to be on the programme would damage their career. They were also worried about how much time they would need to set aside to work on their own development since they also had very demanding jobs to attend to. A number of participants were moved to new roles at a more senior level before the programme had even finished.

However, we'll put these specific challenges to one side for the purpose of this case study and focus instead on the challenges related to applying new behavioural habits and how the programme design helped overcome them. The overall challenge of the programme, after all, was to engage the individuals in their own development and, most importantly, help them learn to learn so their leadership journey continued beyond the formal one-year programme.

Embedding learning model

Content

+ Snippets of excellence (video models)
+ Mixed media - online, text, blog
+ Experiential. Build a felt sense of the skill and mindset
+ Plan for behavioural habit change

Self

+ Identify the benefits of acquiring the new behavioural habits
HABIT =
CUE, ROUTINE, REWARD
+ Attach the new habit to an existing one. Ensure brain based reward
+ Keep going until behaviour is automatic. Encourage completion of Learning Journal

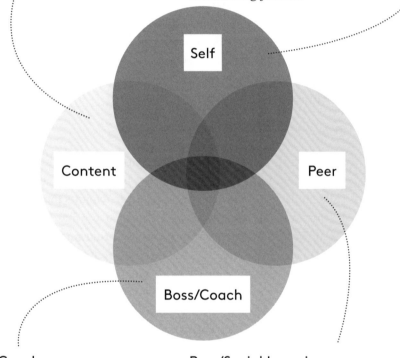

Boss/Coach

+ Link learning to feedback & current performance to create insight on WIIFM
+ Give work based experience opportunities
+ Hold employee accountable for learning
+ Update new habit plan into career plan
+ Celebrate successes
+ Encourage completion of Learning Journal

Peer/Social Learning Community:

+ Creating an "in-group" who provide challenge and support
+ Peer coach
+ Online communities
+ Action learning set/projects
+ Learning buddy - informal or formal

Programme design

The whole structure of the programme encouraged the identification of the new habits that would lead to success and also provided opportunities to start embedding the new behavioural habits during the programme. Much of this was done 'behind the curtain'; we did not explicitly tell participants why certain activities were included and how they helped develop new habits, but the design followed our embedding model.

The programme used multiple channels to develop insight, new behaviours, new knowledge and opportunities to practice in a risk-free environment. (We'll cover each of the elements and how they helped to embed the new habits identified by participants.) This was an individual-centred process because we wanted each person to be able to work on the habits that would make the most difference to them specifically.

Since the programme had four modules as well as coaching, we were able to support and monitor participants' progress. Participants were given the opportunity to update the habit plan at each module if appropriate. One of the things we know about developing a new habit is that people quickly become accustomed to having it and 'forget' how they used to behave. Whilst this is good in many respects it can rob people of their sense of achievement. Therefore celebrating success was one element we were careful to build into coaching and module content.

Our starting point was to share the mind-set research from Carol Dweck and to carry out an exercise where participants assessed their own mind-set, fixed or growth, about their leadership journey. Our thinking was that unless people held a growth mind-set they would limit their progress both on the programme and in their leadership journey more generally (see Principle 3).

We were also explicit about the importance of habits in the first module. We shared the neuroscience behind how habits are formed and changed, and we introduced the cue, routine and reward model. Participants then discussed with one another the new habits that would be most useful for them to develop.

They came up with no shortage of new habits they identified that they needed. The challenge was to pick a habit which would make the biggest difference but which was relatively easy to adopt in order to encourage them from the outset. This was different for each participant, of course, because they were all at different stages in their leadership journey.

In terms of using the habit model, people found little difficulty in identifying the cue and the new routine. The difficulty lay in identifying the reward, and especially in identifying a reward that they could anticipate the pleasure of rather than simply trying to convince themselves that they found the new routine a pleasure in itself. We used the CORE model (see Principle 1) to help people identify the rewards that would work for each of them. So, for example, the reward might be about creating greater certainty or more options in their leadership style, or perhaps a greater sense of reputation or equity. Linking the two models had the added advantage of making CORE a practical tool.

Embedding new habits

We approached this in a variety of ways:

1. **Line managers**: Each participant had consulted with their line manager, which reinforced the habit chosen and also provided an opportunity to get feedback and help with applying the new behaviour in his or her day-to-day job. Some managers took this very seriously, noticing the new behaviour, giving feedback on the difference it had made and praising the effort involved. Not all participants had a manager who was particularly interested or supportive, however. In these cases we encouraged people to get support from peers and colleagues.

2. **Social learning platform**: We supplied a social learning platform where participants could review additional materials, revisit the materials and models used in the face-to-face modules, report back on successes and struggles, and share experiences with colleagues.

Participants were also able to form groups and share additional content they had found. The platform helped to keep the groups connected and active between modules and established a support and challenge group: they'd hold each other accountable for applying their habit plans when they went back to their respective jobs. The social learning platform worked better for some people than others, though. Younger participants were more open to using the platform and also more open about how they were getting on with their habit plans.

However, we did see increased use as the programme progressed, even from the initially reluctant; one of our 'behind the curtain' design elements was itself to create the habit of using the platform by channelling useful and informative materials to it. For example, it was the only place to get access to pre-work for the workshop and supplementary materials like videos. The facilitators were also active on the platform, posting questions, making suggestions and encouraging participants.

3. **Long-term project**: Participants proposed a project they wished to work on during the year and then in the final module presented their findings to senior leaders who were sponsoring the programme. The projects were an opportunity for participants to practice new behaviours. For example, one participant, who we'll call Amy, had identified a new habit she wanted to embed.

She was a highly intelligent and creative person who usually knew instinctively the solution to an issue and understood the organisation well enough to be able to identify what would be accepted and what wouldn't. This had been the root of her success to date. She understood that whilst this made getting the job done fairly easy for her it tended to alienate others who ended up having either to go along with her ideas or actively resist them.

Amy recognised that this style was not helping her engage her team and would almost certainly hold her back in the long run. Her new habit, therefore, was to lead by asking insightful questions so that the group came to a creative answer together.

In her coaching, Amy had identified that what stopped her doing this was a belief she was usually right and asking questions to get others to have the insight would take longer than just telling people the answer. So the first challenge was to deal with this belief that she usually had the best answer to a problem, or at least to find an opportunity to practice in a safe environment where the stakes were not too high and she could test whether her belief held true. The group she was working with on the project on the programme was ideal for practicing this new approach.

She adopted her new behaviour for the very first project meeting. It went well and this encouraged her to try the same approach with her team back in the office. By the end of the programme this had become an embedded habit. She no longer had to plan her questions or hold herself back from giving a solution when she needed the collective intelligence of the group or when she wanted buy-in. As her confidence grew, she added other elements to her habit plan that extended her range of leadership behaviours.

4. **Action learning sets**: The group formed action learning sets that were another means of getting participants to work on and embed the new habits they had identified. These became a core support network for the group and one that continued after the formal programme finished.

5. **Coaching, mentors and sponsors**: Each participant had a number of hours coaching over the course of the programme. The coaches used were also the facilitators of the face-to-face modules, so they were able to support and reinforce learning and behavioural change as well as help participants get over the occasional lapse into a fixed mind-set or old behaviours. Coaching was also useful in noticing change, both in coaching sessions and modules, and reinforcing and celebrating success.

Each participant also had a very senior sponsor from a different government department. The sponsor was a valuable resource as a role model and was able to unbundle the behavioural habits they had developed and which had contributed to their success. Participants shadowed their sponsor on a 'normal' day and on a 'tough' day and then debriefed their mind-set and beliefs around the issues they had been dealing with during the day.

The client said, "Head, Heart + Brain have delivered a best-in-class programme for our leaders of the future. It is rare to work with an organisation who put such a personal effort into creating a bespoke leadership programme. They managed to combine the latest thinking, profound personal development work for participants and genuine insights from the world of neuroscience. The impact to the individuals involved and our profession's capability journey is evident for all to see."

Where else does creating habits matter?

Habits apply anywhere you're trying to make a change. These changes could be personal, professional, and they might even apply to the whole organisation wherever and whenever employees are expected to do something new or different. Therefore it's important that habit-forming ideas are built into:

Learning and development programmes

Policy and process changes

Re-organisations

Culture changes

Don't forget that changes aren't any use if they don't stick, so ensure that any habit-change approach like coaching or development programmes continue long enough for the new habit to be properly embedded.

Tools

Using the habit model

The cue

Habits are triggered by cues - those triggers or signals that prompt us to act in a certain way. Working on the cue will help make a habit. For example, if you want to create more thinking time then you may decide to spend 10 minutes each morning reflecting on what is coming up in your day before you turn on your computer. Your cue might be something as simple as sitting down at your desk: that's when you start your reflection time.

Identifying a good cue can be crucial. They tend to fall into one of the following categories:

+ a specific location

+ a set time

+ a particular emotional state

+ certain other people

+ a preceding action

Don't forget that you can use those 'behaviour chains' that make use of your current routines instead of trying to fight them. (Hanging up your coat is your current behaviour followed by sitting at your desk - so you might link this to the new behaviour of reflection.)

Experiment with different cues until you find the one (or a chain of them) that works best for you.

The routine

Define the steps you're going to take. Specifically, these are the actions that you're trying to mould into a habit. It helps to write down your routine so you know the exact steps. For example, if the routine is to reflect each morning then you might block out these times in your diary so that other meetings or obligations don't encroach on the time.

The concept of *If-then* planning has been shown to help establish new routines, too. This means, for example, that instead of just having the intention to reflect more, your *if-then* intention might be, "*If* I block out my diary each morning for 10 minutes *then* I will be able to reflect on my day."

If-then planning can also help you anticipate things that might knock you off course. "*If* I am interrupted in my reflection time *then* I will take a walk at lunchtime to reflect."

If it's a physical routine you're trying to establish, Shawn Anchor, the happiness researcher mentioned in Principle 4, advises having everything in your path so it takes less than 20 seconds to access what you need: Gym shoes by the door; training gear on the chair beside the bed; out the door in 30 seconds flat, give-or-take.

The reward

As we've said, rewards are an essential part - perhaps *the* essential part - of turning the new behaviour into a habit.

Rewards have some key characteristics. For example, if you're trying to get into the habit of going to the gym, your reward might be the endorphin rush you'll feel once you get into it, or that post-workout smoothie. So *think* about that smoothie. Allow yourself to anticipate the reward. The anticipation is actually more important to the brain than the reward itself. Rather than trying to make yourself enjoy the routine itself, your aim is to get your brain to crave the reward, whether that's the post-workout feel-good or the delicious smoothie.

Tiny Habits

One method of embedding new habits that can be particularly useful is based on the work of BJ Fogg at Stanford University[14]. Fogg calls the approach 'Tiny Habits'. The method isn't all that different to the previous tool but is based on making the new habit very, very small:

Decide what you want to change.

Write a clear statement of the new behaviour you want. Think of the smallest thing you can do. The trick is to make the new behaviour tiny. *Really* tiny. Tiny as in after-I-clean-my-teeth-I-will-floss-one-tooth tiny.

Identify and write down the cue and routine. Maybe that's 'Once I open my email (cue) I will clear two new emails in my inbox'. The cue is really important. It needs to be deeply rooted and something you always do.

Set yourself up to make it easy. If you're going to start flossing your teeth then have the floss in plain sight on the bathroom shelf. If you're going to get practicing your piano chords then pick a cue that's near the piano so you don't get distracted on the way from one room to another. If you want to get talking to your team each day, pick a time and preceding activity that you know you will do every day, like taking your coat off.

Get the reward sorted. Give yourself a mental high five or pat on the back when you've carried out the new behaviour. This produces a shot of dopamine in the brain and makes you feel good, encouraging you to do the activity again to get the mental reward.

If it doesn't work, don't give up. Think of the first couple of weeks as a trial period during which you can try a few different approaches until you hit the right formula.

Why this works

It seems to be that the smallness of the new behaviour prevents you from making up excuses about why you can't do it, and once you start doing it you're so pleased with yourself that you extend the behaviour. For example, talking to one team member leads to talking to two of them, and soon enough you find you're talking to the whole lot of them. Or if you find yourself just flossing that one tooth like you promised rather than your whole mouth, then there's no sense of failure there: you achieved what you set out to achieve.

Fogg runs a free week-long coaching programme via email to help you get the cue and routine just right. You can join the programme at www.tinyhabits.com.

Creating habits for the organisation

The habit model can also be a useful way to implement sustained change at an organisation level.

The cue: When introducing a change such as implementing a new process or policy, a well-communicated business cycle can act as the cue. Linking the cycle to existing business events that are properly embedded (such as the business planning cycle or end-of-year results) can make it easier.

The routine: Again, the business cycle can provide a routine that people begin to follow. And routines can be reinforced through training to improve elements of the new policy or process.

The CORE model can guide this reinforcement (see Principle 1).

For example, provide certainty about the steps to be taken, options within the policy, enhanced reputation to early adopters, and equity in availability of resources and a sense of fairness in how the whole policy is implemented.

The reward: This entails building in rewards at an organisational level. They can be of more than one type and tailored to different groups, be they work units, teams or groups of specialists. Again the CORE model can be a useful way of thinking about these rewards, such as reputational rewards like a Coach of the Year award, or shared team rewards that feel equitable.

Social rewards are particularly rewarding, and you can harness the power of social connections to build them (see Principle 2). You could create cross-functional teams that work together to implement the new approach, reward managers for the quality of their adoption or set up healthy competition between groups, using measures such as the health of the talent pipeline or the speed of career progression across business units, depending on the change you're trying to make.

Awareness habits

Knowing the circumstances that boost or hinder your self-awareness and levels of focus on what is going on around you is critical to noticing your habits. This avoids you forgetting the change you want to make and hence to embed the new habit you want.

Awareness barometer

Create an awareness barometer

> 1. Keep a check on how much you *really* notice. Start with small things like your partner's clothing, the taste of your coffee (most of us drink it without really tasting it) or how you clean your teeth.
>
> 2. Then start monitoring yourself in meetings and throughout your working day. Create a scale, say 1-10 and mark how aware you think you have been after each meeting. Then build up to doing this during the meeting. Complete your rating whilst you can remember the details but are also able to step back from them. With the benefit of stepping back from your own involvement in the content of the meeting you should be able to notice points you may not have done in

the past, like a colleague looking uncomfortable or having an edge in their voice.

3. Just the act of starting the barometer will help you to be more aware.

Monitor the results of your increase in awareness and track how helpful it is in terms of increased self-awareness and noticing signals about your colleagues and team's feelings.

Principle summary

Habits and intentional behaviour are different things and are run by different parts of the brain.

It's easier to develop a new habit rather than change an old one because of the way the brain functions.

Creating new habits is easiest when there's:

> A cue - something that reminds you to act in the new way.

> A clearly defined routine - these are the specific steps you want to take.

> A reward - anticipating the reward is more powerful than just receiving it.

Make sure you believe you can make the change and make plans in advance for avoiding or managing any setbacks.

References

1   Kevin Ochsner, The Formation of Habit, NeuroLeadership Summit, Boston, 2010

2   Matthew Lieberman, 'The X- and C-systems: The neural basis of automatic and controlled social cognition', *Fundamentals of Social Neuroscience*, 2007

3   Bernard Balleine & John O'Doherty, 'Human and Rodent Homologies in Action Control: Corticostriatal Determinants of Goal-Directed and Habitual Action', *Neuropsychopharmacology* vol. 35, 2010

4   Donald Hebb (1949). *The Organization of Behavior*. Wiley & Sons.

5   Robert Spunt, Emily Falk & Matthew Lieberman, 'Dissociable Neural Systems Support Retrieval of How and Why Action Knowledge', *Psychological Science* vol. 20(10), 2010

6   Kevin Ochsner, The Formation of Habit, NeuroLeadership Summit, Boston, 2010

7   Roy Baumeister & John Tierney, Willpower: Rediscovering the greatest human strength. *Penguin*, 2011

8   Veronika Job, Gregory Walton, Katharina Bernecker & Carol Dweck, 'Beliefs about willpower determine the impact of glucose on self-control', *Proceedings of the National Academy of Sciences* vol. 7, 2013

9   Michael Inzlicht & Elliot Berkman, 'Six Questions for the Resource Model of Control (and Some Answers)', *Social and Personality Psychology Compass*

10   Charles Duhigg (2012). The Power of Habit. *Random House.*

11   Dan Ariely, The (Honest) Truth About Dishonesty: How We Lie to Everyone – Especially Ourselves, *Harper*, 2012

12   David Rock, NeuroLeadership Summit, San Francisco, 2011

13   Amy Wysoker, 'A study of beliefs relating to weight loss and weight gain', *Newsletter of the Long Island University School of Health Professionals and Nursing*, 2002

14   B.J. Fogg. http://tinyhabits.com/

Further reading and viewing

Know Yourself Better – and Succeed at your Goals (animated video): http://www.headheartbrain.com/know-thy-self/

Gremlins - What Gets in the Way of New Behavioural Habits (animated video): http://www.headheartbrain.com/gremlins/

Kelly McGonigal, The Willpower Instinct: www.youtube.com/watch?v=V5BXuZL1HAg

The What the Hell Effect, Dan Ariely (video): https://www.youtube.com/watch?v=GKVLoUmtHqI

Principle 7:
Create Brain-Savvy
Working Habits

Before you get stuck in to this Principle, take a moment to consider these questions:

Are you exhausted at the end of each day?

Are you so busy you never seem have time to think?

Do you really enjoy your job or do you think that enjoying your job's a luxury few people have?

Does your brain feel like it's full most of the time?

Are people around you often stressed?

Does your team often make mistakes or jump to conclusions?

The science

Habit 1: No thinking time

Most work cultures value attention, concentration and focus. Taking breaks or time out for reflection are not generally seen as productive but we're seeing a number of scientific studies that suggest there are enormous benefits to taking a little downtime.

These breaks, which most people see as 'not working', may actually be when the brain is doing some of its most productive work. The research shows that, when we are relaxing or daydreaming, going for a walk or taking a reflective break, the brain does not really slow down or stop working. Many important mental processes actually *need* this change of pace. Downtime helps the brain stay attentive, encourages productivity and creativity, and is essential to achieving high levels of performance and memory formation. It also helps us learn from the past and plan for the future, and has been linked to better self-awareness and understanding of others as well as higher-quality ethical decisions.

The areas of the brain doing all of this make up what's called the default system. In a thought-provoking review, Mary Helen Immordino-Yang, who is an associate professor at the University of Southern California's Rossier School of Education, says that when we're resting, our brains are not idle or unproductive.[1] They are, she says, in fact carrying out essential mental processes that affirm our identities, develop our understanding of others' behaviour and instil an internal code of ethics. They're also making sense of what we've recently learned, sorting through our thinking, resolving contradictions and reflecting on our actions and motives.

This seems a bit less weird when you step back and take some downtime yourself. You know that whilst your mind is wandering you're probably replaying conversations and rewriting mistakes as a way of learning. Perhaps you're mentally rehearsing the presentation you're working on or having that difficult conversation with the boss in your head, or lingering over the satisfying praise you got for helping a senior manager. Maybe you're sorting through all those mental to-do lists and ruminating about how you can run your life better. You may find yourself recalling scenes from childhood and then jumping into how you want to be in the future. And you might give yourself to a kind of personal performance review, questioning how you have treated others, what you could do better and where you made a difference. This reflection or introspection is one way you form a sense of self - the story you continually tell yourself about who you are.

People who take time to reflect are surer about their own point of view, tend to be more confident, understand others' motives and goals more accurately and are better at making complex decisions and solving complex problems.

Mark Beeman, Professor at Northwestern University, has made similar discoveries regarding the brain's background workings that tap unconscious mental resources greater than those used during more analytical or conscious thinking.[2] Being in this unfocused default mode allows us, he says, to make new connections in the brain and to see an old problem anew. And that's when insight comes to us.

This is why you get your best ideas in the shower, walking along the road, working out at the gym or at some other time when your mind's not focused on a particular problem. As we saw in Principle 4, David Cresswell, who works at the Health and Human Performance lab at Carnegie Mellon University, has found that when people have complex data to consider, giving them some down time - even if only a few minutes - makes their use of the information more effective and their decisions much better.[3]

So perhaps the next trend in business will be using your unconscious mind more. So there's another reason to put your feet up for a few minutes.

Habit 2: Multi-tasking

We can only multi-task if the things we're doing are using different parts of the brain or if one of them is already deeply embedded in our automatic habit system. So you might be able to find your way to a conference room when you know the way well whilst simultaneously talking on the phone about something important. But the chances are that if you haven't been to the room before then you'll either get lost or lose the thread of the conversation. Or both.

Multi-tasking is something modern businesses assume we can do. When we think we're multi-tasking, however, we're actually quickly switching back-and-forth between different tasks rather than doing them at the same time. The research shows that the error rate goes up when this happens and it takes us twice as long to get things done.[4]

If you're in any doubt, try this quick test. Use your watch to measure how long it takes you to count quickly from 1 to 10. Then see how long it takes you to say the alphabet from A to J. Now time yourself to put the two tasks together, alternately saying a letter and a number (A1, B2, C3 and so on). It will, you'll find, take more than twice as long to perform the combined task as you took for each single task, because the brain slows down when it has to keep switching between numbers and letters. For most people the first two tasks take a couple of seconds each. The mixed task typically takes 15 to 20 seconds.

As well as slowing you down, this kind of exercise can also tire out your working memory. Depending on how stressed you are or how much you've been using your brain, you may also keep forgetting where you are in the task. Psychologist Katherine Moore at the University of Michigan has found that irrelevant cues, introduced when a person is concentrating, hijack the attention system and impair cognitive performance.[5] Similarly, Glenn Wilson of Kings College London has demonstrated that switching between different technologies, like emailing and answering the phone constantly, reduced IQ scores by 10 points.[6]

One reason we keep trying to multi-task is because of a cognitive illusion generated in part by dopamine-adrenalin activity. Facing and overcoming a difficult problem, even if we're making two simple tasks into one far more complicated one, makes us feel like we're doing well. And there is evidence that some people multi-task because it's more stimulating, interesting and challenging, and less boring than doing one thing at a time.

Another reason is that workplaces encourage us to multi-task. Many companies have rules that stipulate that emails must be answered within 15 minutes or a chat window must always be kept open. These rules, however, just mean that everyone's always checking their email or that open chat window instead of concentrating on what they're supposed to be doing.

Also, in case you're still not convinced, it turns out that the people who multi-task the most tend to be the worst at it! David Sanbonmatsu and David Strayer, Professors of Psychology at the University of Utah, had undergrads complete a series of tests to measure multi-tasking ability.[7] They found that the 25% that scored highest on the multi-tasking test tended not to multi-task at all in day-to-day work. They also discovered that the participants had an inflated view of how good they were, with 70% classifying themselves as 'pro' multi-taskers, even though the research found they were slower and less productive than the non-multi-taskers. Also, people engaged in multi-tasking not because they felt they were accomplishing more but because they were not able to block out distractions and focus on a single task.

The message, then, is this: If you want to be good at multi-tasking, don't do it.

Habit 3: Limited attention

Are there days when you miss the connection between a piece of data and a project? Like missing the impact of a decision on another department. Or does it slip your mind that two work colleagues know each other? Perhaps you sometimes fail to notice the stress in your colleague's voice when they give you a project update? Or you've found yourself reacting to things instinctively from time to time, without any real level of conscious thought and later reflected, "What was I thinking?"

Noticing these cues can make the difference between things going okay and things going really, really well.

We can think of these examples as thinking habits; they're automatic. When you make these kinds of split-second decisions or take action without considering it properly, your 'thinking' brain is closed down and that old, instinctive mammalian brain is triggered and responds unconsciously. The reaction happens in twelve milliseconds (twelve one-thousandths of a second) - faster than you can be consciously aware. This can work in your favour like when making fast decisions about danger, but it's less handy when you need to be aware of what you're doing and the information you're processing.

So why do levels of awareness change from day to day, meeting to meeting? One reason is that we get into the habit of thinking in a particular way. For example, we might find ourselves dwelling on threat and risk and what might go wrong, and overlook what's going well.

Neuroscientist Evian Gordon's analysis suggests we have five times the number of neurons that pick up threat cues as those that pick up reward cues.[8] Amy Arnstein, Professor of Neurobiology and Psychology at Yale Medical School, calls the executive brain - the prefrontal cortex - 'the Goldilocks' because it needs conditions to be 'just right' to function well.[9] When we're focused on threat, the executive brain functioning is compromised and in extreme circumstances it may even close down altogether - your mind just goes blank. When your brain is noticing threat as a habit, you're likely to make poor decisions, to focus more on the negatives than the positives and overlook important non-verbal information. You're also likely to be short-tempered, preoccupied and generally have less control over your emotional responses.

If we want to fully understand others, we need to understand more than what they say out loud. Accurate detection of these non-verbal cues is critical, especially for leaders. Emotions are the brain's automatic reaction to cues: a loud noise will set off your startle response, set your heart racing and prompt fear. A sharp decline on your profit curve can do the same. Some of these cues such as a lack of eye contact, a smirk, or a hesitant tone of voice may not even register consciously, yet all of these create a reaction.

One great habit to try to pick up is being able to examine your own unconscious reactions. These might range from picking up and eating the biscuit you promised yourself you wouldn't have to a stiffening of your body that signals to the team that there's a problem. Having a level of body awareness and the cues that create a reaction, like tensing when a person you dislike approaches or relaxing when you see your team solve a problem, is a useful skill and one that can be developed. You may be more aware of these reactions at different times and in different circumstances. Typically, people who make a point of noticing, who are less stressed and who know their own body well are better at this type of self-awareness. Look at the tools section for how to improve these skills.

Habit 4: Creating positive resilience

There seems to be a rather interesting link between being positive and being more resilient. In tough economic times and when other life challenges hit us, resilience is the difference between simply weathering the storm and actually thriving. Rather than this being an innate trait, the research points to resilience being something we can nurture, and positive emotions are a big part of doing that. Research by Barbara Fredrickson, who has studied positive emotions for many years, shows that the level of positivity in a person's life directly links to how well they will deal with personal setbacks and even global events.[10]

Her research shows too, that when people are under stress, like when they have to do a presentation that they know will be judged by peers, showing a light-hearted, amusing video afterwards relieves the build-up of those hormones associated with stress. Frederickson also found that resilient people manage negativity better than those who are less resilient. The less resilient not only react badly to challenges but also make those challenges more difficult by anticipating a worst-case scenarios. Resilient people, on the other hand, just wait until something happens and then deal with it.

It's important to point out that when people notice more positive emotions they're not denying the negative but simply keeping things in perspective. They're able to hold the positive and the negative side by side.

How to notice the positive

So what can you do to notice more positives and build resilience? Well, one thing is to understand your current positivity levels. Fredrickson has developed a quick test.[11] She says a ratio of three positive emotions to every negative one can be defined as 'thriving'.

A word of warning: It can take a bit of time to understand your pattern. Just taking the test once is not a good idea. Get a measure of yourself over time, perhaps over the course of a week. Notice the patterns that emerge. Have a think about whether you're not inclined to look on the bright side, or are you just having a particularly hard time at the moment? Once you have the trend, it's time to look at how you can tip the balance and increase the positivity.

For many people this is about noticing more positive emotions and, crucially, savouring them. Because they tend to be fleeting, we often forget the positive feelings have occurred. Also remember that the ratio isn't about finding 100% positivity in your life. The occasional negative allows us to be human and realistic about the fact that nothing is perfect all the time. Fredrickson says you can think of it like healthy eating - on the whole you want to eat the right stuff but an indulgent meal once in a while isn't a disaster.

You may also find it helps to take some practical steps to prioritise positivity. Again, this isn't about being jolly all the time or denying difficult situations. Prioritising positivity is about trying to control the feeling rather than the circumstances; it's a more authentic and sustainable approach. It means making it a definite goal to experience positive emotions. Many people do this by spending time with people they love, working on something they feel passionate about or perhaps spending more time in and around the natural world. It's about managing your time, identifying the things you know feel positive to you and making them a habit.

Finally, your expectations are also important. It can sound trite, but if you hope and expect things to turn out for the best then you'll find that they very often do.

Case study:
The benefits of adopting new work habits

We incorporate brain-savvy techniques into the broader work we do with clients, and so rather than focus on one specific case of our own, perhaps it's more illuminating to look at how we do this, how clients and participants have responded, and then look at a dedicated, third-party case study.

Our webinars that deal with brain-savvy working enable people from multiple locations to take part. Because the webinars split the topics discussed in this Principle into two sessions, we're able to ask people what they want to change about how they work and also what they've learned and what new habits they have tried to instil in order to be more brain-savvy at work.

We found that once people hear about the science their two biggest concerns are multi-tasking and emailing. Businessmen and women want to stop multi-tasking (even though this is really difficult) *when they find out* that they'll be more productive when they focus on a single task and finish it before starting another. But as we mentioned above, we get into the habit of multi-tasking and also fail to notice the impact on productivity and accuracy because of the release of dopamine and adrenaline that feels rewarding to the brain. People tell us they also want to manage when emails are dealt with. Avoiding doing emails in the morning was reported as helping people be more focused on difficult tasks and also being more creative. Following up with people a couple of months later, many had persisted with their new ways of working and were continuing to find benefits in greater productivity. They said they managed this in part by using the habit model and carefully planning around what might send them off track (see Principle 6).

An academic case study

Leslie Perlow of the Harvard Business School worked with a consulting firm to help their consultants be more productive but also reduce the levels of burnout. She wrote up this fascinating case study in her book, *Sleeping with your Smartphone: How to Change the 24/7 Habit and Change the Way You Work*.[12]

In her initial research, Perlow found that one of the main causes of stress was the unpredictability of the work day. Her clients frequently found they had to work late and this impacted on their family and personal life, interrupting holidays and social engagements. One of her first steps was to convince a team of consultants to leave the office early one night a week and to do anything but work, to turn off their phones and deliberately not check their emails.

The process she introduced was called PTO, which stands for Predictability, Teaming, and Open communications. The process works like this: Before each new client project, the team openly discusses how they will do their work and define norms for things like travel, how quickly emails require a response and how often the team will meet face-to-face. Each member also picks a different time period each week to go completely offline.

This meant that consultants found they were able to make and keep personal plans during their weekly off-line periods and, more importantly, they knew that the world will not fall apart when they turned off their phone or PC. Dedicated time off also forced them to do a better job of planning and prioritising; they spent less time on lower-value work and developed more innovative and collaborative approaches to solving problems.

Perlow and the firm found that the biggest benefit of this process was that it meant the consultants worked as a team to help each other have one night off, no matter what client issues came up. This had the positive by-product of empowering the team. The consultants found they were challenging their assumptions and changing things which they had not believed could change, and all this was being done in a collaborative way. This empowered consultants to think differently and created a growth mind-set (see Principle 3) and a sense that they could actually do something about the way they worked.

Perlow discovered that this improved teamwork also helped people to raise other issues and to improve working arrangements more generally, like dealing with a colleague who had missed a deadline or solving the demands of a difficult client who kept changing the scope of the project. The new ways of working had an enormous impact on retention and the firm was willing to invest in the methodology, assigning as they did around forty of their most talented consultants around the world to facilitate teams through the process.

Consultants in PTO teams reported being both happier and more productive. They were 21% more likely to say they were delivering high value for their clients and also 74% more likely to say that they wanted to stay at the firm for the long term. The head of People and Organisation Practice said, 'A better work-life balance, we found, is good for [name of firm]'s people and good for our clients.'

Where else do work habits matter?

The first area to look at is your wellbeing policy. How much is it based on prevention rather than cure? Do you find that your organisation is usually attempting to help employees deal with poor habits after the impact has debilitated their productivity or even their health?

Also have a think about the values and norms you set as a company, and in particular how your senior leaders exemplify good habits.

Then take a look at those more detailed policies surrounding responding to email, chat links and the like. You might also consider the informal norms about downtime and leaving the office early, and how people are expected to respond to weekend and overnight emails.

Tools

Finding your sweet spot

The sweet spot is part of the Yerkes Dobson law, also called 'the inverted U' in reference to the graph's bell curve, as discussed in Principle 1.[13] These two scientists found that if stress - which they use to mean mental stimulation rather than in the purely negative sense - is too low then we suffer from apathy. If stress is too high then we suffer from anxiety. Both of these states inhibit performance. The sweet spot is where we are in a state of what is called 'Flow', able to focus and motivated to achieve our goals.

First of all, work out where you are on the inverted U. Is stress too high, undermining your concentration and focus? Or is it too low, making you feel lethargic? If the latter:

> + Make the task more challenging

> + Perform the task in a new way or using new skills

> + Reduce the time available to complete the task

> + Challenge yourself to achieve a higher performance level than either you're accustomed to or is strictly necessary.

If stress is too high:

> + Break the task into smaller chunks.

> + Seek input from others with the necessary skills.

> + Increase your skill level.

> + Extend the time available.

The multi-tasking myth

As we've discussed, it's tempting to think we can do more than one thing at a time and our jobs often seem to demand that we do. But thanks to how the brain is wired, multi-tasking is just not effective or efficient. If you want to create a new habit, why not set yourself a goal of not multi-tasking for a week? For many people this will be quite difficult to do. Monitor the results of how you feel and how much you get done. In particular, be sure to notice the progress on important long-term tasks:

> + Fully engage yourself with the task at hand. People start multi-tasking when they think their input is not essential

+ Limit exposure to things that might distract your attention. Turn off electronic alerts

+ For a 24-hour period turn off everything with a screen - your computer, tablet and phone. Keep them out of sight. This can be a little unnerving, so prepare in advance and let people know that you'll be offline.

Being mindful

Mindfulness means being present in the moment, undistracted and accepting. According to Dan Siegel, Professor of Clinical Psychiatry at the UCLA School of Medicine and Executive Director of the Mindsight Institute, it hones our ability to pause for thought before we react, giving our minds a chance to consider our options before choosing a way forward[14].

As a leader, being skilled in mindfulness helps you notice connections, focus on important data and be more aware of others' concerns and emotions as well as being able to monitor your own moods and reactions. For example, when you listen to a gut instinct to plan your day better or to ask a colleague if they are coping with a project, you're being mindful. When you reflect on your mood and whether it will help you achieve the results you want, that's being mindful, too. Brain activity begins to change within just a few days of practicing mindfulness, decreasing stress, improving your mood and increasing your ability to step back and take a considered perspective.

To understand the difference between carrying out a task mindfully as opposed to mindlessly, you might try changing how you perform the simplest of everyday tasks, like brushing your teeth:

+ Notice every action, feeling and sound

+ Notice the difference between your normal pattern and brushing mindfully

+ Monitor how you will drift and get caught up thinking about something else. Bring your attention back to your teeth cleaning.

Now practice this with other routine tasks. Start with short time periods and build up from there. You can practice in the gym, walking to the train, on the train, eating, drinking your coffee - pretty much anywhere, any time.

Consider downloading an app like *Get Some Head Space*, which is an easy-to-learn meditation, to give yourself a head start. If you practice regularly, you'll start to notice a positive impact on your reactions and stress levels.

Principle summary

Work habits can be helpful or unhelpful.

The most common poor work habits are: being too busy to think, taxing the brain's capacity and multi-tasking.

Giving the brain downtime aids problem-solving, creativity and cognitive capacity.

Multi-tasking is a myth that actually slows down work rate and lowers productivity.

The most resilient people are positive, take time to rest and also manage their emotional reactions to events. They tip the negativity bias by noticing the positives in life.

References

1   Mary Helen Immordino-Yang, Joanna A. Christodoulou &
    Vanessa Singh, 'Rest Is Not Idleness: Implications of the Brain's
    Default Mode for Human Development and Education',
    Perspectives on Psychological Science, vol. 7(4), 2012, pp. 352-364:
    http://pps.sagepub.com/content/7/4/352

2   J Kounios & M Jung-Beeman, 'The Aha! Moment: The cognitive
    neuroscience of insight', *Current Directions in Psychological Science*,
    vol.18 2009

3   JD Creswell, J Bursley & AB Satpute, 'Neural reactivation links
    unconscious thought to improved decision making', *Social,
    Cognitive, and Affective Neuroscience*, vol.8 2013

4   Glenn Wilson [quoted], 'Emails pose threat to IQ', Martin
    Wainwright, the *Guardian*, 2005

5   Katherine Sledge Moore, Clare Porter & Daniel Weissman, 'Made
    you look! Consciously perceived, irrelevant instructional cues can
    hijack the attentional network', *Neuroimage*, 2005

6   Glenn Wilson [quoted], 'Emails pose threat to IQ', Martin
    Wainwright, the *Guardian*, 2005

7   David M Sanbonmatsu, David L Strayer, Nathan Medeiros-
    Ward & Jason M Watson, Who Multi-Tasks and Why? Multi-
    Tasking Ability, Perceived Multi-Tasking Ability, Impulsivity, and
    Sensation Seeking, Public Library of Science, 2013

8   Evian Gordon, 'NeuroLeadership and integrative Neuroscience:
    "It's about validation stupid!"', *NeuroLeadership Journal*, vol. 1,
    2008

9   Amy Arnsten, The Mental Sketchpad: Why Thinking has Limits,
    Yale Medical School, 2008

10 Barbara L Fredrickson, 'The broaden-and-build theory of
    positive emotions', *Philosophical Transactions of the Royal Society B:
    Biological Sciences*, vol. 359(1449), 2004

11 Positivity self test: http://www.positivityratio.com/single.php

12 Leslie Perlow, Sleeping With Your Smartphone: How to Change

the 24/7 Habit and Change the Way You Work, *Harvard Business Review Press*, 2012

13   Robert Yerkes & John Dodson (1908). 'The relation of strength of stimulus to rapidity of habit-formation', *Journal of Comparative Neurology and Psychology*, vol. 18, 1908

14   Daniel J Siegal. The Mindful Brain: Reflection and Attunement in the Cultivation of Well-Being. 2007 W. W. Norton & Company

Further reading and viewing

A moment of insight (animated video): http://www. headheartbrain.com/a-moment-of-insight-2/

Are your Work Habits Hindering your Brain? (webinar): http:// www.headheartbrain.com/work-habits-hindering-brain/

Managing the impact of stress on the brain: http://www. headheartbrain.com/managing-stress-the-impact-of-stress-on-the-brain/

Josh Davis, Two Awesome Hours: Science-Based Strategies to Harness Your Best Time and Get Your Most Important Work Done, *Harper One*, 2015

Amy Brann, Make Your Brain Work: How to Maximize Your Efficiency, Productivity and Effectiveness, *Kogan Page* 3, 2013

Leslie Perlow, Thriving in an over-connected world (TED Talk): https://www.ted.com/watch/ted-institute/ted-bcg/leslie-perlow-thriving-in-an-overconnected-world

Leslie Perlow, Switching off an "Always on" Culture (Big Think): http://bigthink.com/videos/switching-off-an-always-on-culture-2

Dr. Dan Siegel- On The Importance of Mindfulness. https://www. youtube.com/watch?v=FXxrJEnIboM

Dan Siegel, M.D. - Discussing the science of mindfulness. https://www.youtube.com/watch?v=yqUNtLbwoj4

Get some head space. https://www.headspace.com

Principle 8:
Manage Energy

Take a moment to ask yourself these questions before you begin:

Are you aware of your energy levels and how they fluctuate? Is it easy to identify the things that make you feel energised and those that drain you?

How much do you consciously notice the energy levels of you and your team, and do you actively try to manage them?

How would you rate the energy levels in your organisation, unit or team?

What specific things have you noticed that energise people? And what seems to drain their energy?

How well do you manage your mental energy? What about your physical energy and your emotional energy?

Would you define your role as managing and focusing the energy of your team?

The science

As we were writing this book, we were increasingly struck by the importance of organisations creating an environment that maximises the energy of employees. We began to notice more and more the difference between leaders, cultures and business practices that inspire energy in people and those that drain it.

Most of the history of management theory and practice has been about adopting a technical, analytical approach in which the role of the so-called soft factors like emotions and feelings has largely been ignored. Similarly, whilst energy is frequently talked about, it has received little attention in the curriculum of skills conventionally prescribed. That trend, however, is now being reversed, with both academics and managers recognising that soft skills have an important impact and that emotions impact behaviour in business.

It seems to us that understanding what inspires energy and what drains it is possibly the most important and least talked about role of the leader since, we'd argue, the point of leadership is to ensure that a company's purpose and strategy capture people's imagination, emotion and excitement, engage their cognitive capacities and inspire them to take action. In essence, it's all about generating an environment with a sense of genuine purpose, an environment that unleashes and focuses energy that will in turn make for maximum productivity, discretionary effort and wellbeing.

So we went in search of the science behind achieving this and what it looks like in practice.

The research suggests that leaders should first generate organisational energy and then focus it[1]. It sounds straightforward but, as one might expect, the reality is a little more complicated. Part of this means leaders being role models in terms of how they manage and direct their own personal energy. People with a lot of energy are more productive, creative and have a naturally positive influence on others.[2] High energy levels within an organisation as a whole closely resemble the state of Flow in an individual, where everything seems to happen more easily.[3] Employees stimulate each other under these circumstances by continuously giving that extra bit of effort, and productivity comes on in leaps and bounds.[4]

Although in Eastern philosophy *Qi* (life power or energy flow) is an important concept that often crops up in relation to physical and mental health and fitness, in Western philosophy it is only just beginning to be mentioned, notably in research into the impact of social networks and the role of emotions in organisations.[5] The other areas that are chiefly concerned with energy are positive psychology[6] and Flow.[7] The chapter on the importance of social connection (Principle 2) points to the positive energy generated by increased social connection both for individuals and across an organisation, and this is backed up by recent studies.[8] Yet only a few such studies have directly measured energy and its effects.[9&10] These few pieces of research, however, that have found that organisational energy is indeed measurable have enhanced people's understanding of what's meant by energy in this context and the effect it has.

What is organisational energy?

Organisational energy can be defined as the extent to which an organisation (or division or team) has mobilised its emotional, cognitive and behavioural potential to pursue its goals.[11] Energy involves the amount of interactions between people, as well as the quality. It's also contagious and malleable: it can be changed based on the context of the organisation and the style and role of the leader.

Energy can be regarded both in the short term and the long term. People can experience a long-term basic energy level as well as short-term, circumstantial changes in their energy level. Long-term energy draining can result in burnout.

Research into Flow shows that people can be completely focused and energetic in any walk of life, from sports and games to hobbies or work.[12] This complete immersion in an activity is the result of the focusing of mental energy on an activity that we find satisfying. Flow focuses attention and motivates action. However, an important reason why people often lack energy is that they have trouble determining which activities they really like and, even if they know what activities they like best, they fail frequently to seek out these activities. To remedy this and focus our energy, Csikszentmihalyi (now the Distinguished Professor of Psychology and Management at Claremont Graduate University) advises: "We must then transfer some psychic energy each day from tasks that we don't like doing, or from passive leisure, into something we never did before, or something we enjoy doing but don't do often enough because it seems too much trouble."

Three kinds of energy are often discussed in the research: mental energy (being able to focus intensely), physical energy (strength, endurance and flexibility), and emotional energy (being in touch with one's own feelings and mental state).

Mental energy

Do you find yourself creative, focused and speeding ahead in the morning but sluggish, prone to mistakes and flitting from one thing to the next later in the day? If so, it could be that your brain has run out of mental energy. The conscious, thinking, analytical part of your brain is the prefrontal cortex (PFC). It's immediately behind your forehead. We consistently over-estimate the capacity of this part of the brain to concentrate for an extended amount of time. The PFC processes something like 2,000 pieces of information each second, but while its performance is almost incredible, its endurance is actually quite limited.

Here's an analogy.[13] Think of the prefrontal cortex like your brain's bank account with a credit limit of £10,000. You start each day with the full credit in place (assuming you have had a good night's sleep). The moment you wake up, you start to spend your credit. Now, with your prefrontal cortex running full-throttle, you'd run out of credit very quickly. But the brain has developed to avoid this – much of what you do each day is run in the automatic habit system and bypasses the prefrontal cortex (see Principle 6). Things you do routinely like having a shower, brushing your teeth, eating your breakfast and even getting to work are largely run by this system. You only engage the prefrontal cortex when something goes wrong and you have to think about what needs to happen, or when you are required to do something that you need to think about and can't accomplish on 'automatic pilot'. Like when you head off to work as usual when really you should be walking in a different direction because you have a meeting with a new client before you're due in the office.

You make withdrawals on your prefrontal cortex's credit, as it were, when you start reading and responding to emails (£500), when you attend three or four meetings (£4,000), deal with employee issues (£3,000), answer more emails and handle a difficult phone call (£600). Suddenly you've used three quarters of your £10,000 credit.

At this point, if you then have to do something which is taxing for your brain, like making a complex decision with lots of data (£5,000), planning or forecasting (£4,000), brainstorming or problem-solving (£6,000) you're going to end up in the red. And that means you're mentally exhausted. The symptoms will be a lack of concentration and a limited ability to focus. You may find yourself reading something or listening to someone and then realising you have no idea what you read or what was said. Perhaps you'll be zoning out and thinking about nothing, or starting to do mindless tasks like filing emails when you should be doing that urgent report. You may simply get an urge to stand up from your desk and move around.

These facts about the brain's capacity and our lack of understanding of them lead us to work in ways that are not conductive to maximising our brain's potential. We have habits that fry our brain rather than use it in a way that's brain-savvy.

Different people work in different ways, of course, but most work norms value attention, concentration and focus. People who take a break, sit back and think or take an afternoon nap are typically seen as lazy. Companies like Google that provide facilities for this type of activity are seen by established companies as quirky, and the general feeling is that they'll 'grow out of it'. But if we think about mental energy or the rate at which it is used, we might find that these companies are adopting a much more brain-savvy approach.

Physical fitness and energy

The benefits of being physically fit when it comes to professional performance have been recognised for years and many organisations have incentive schemes to encourage gym membership and the like. There is, though, still a long way to go before this is the norm and, more importantly, before people regularly use the benefit. After all, who doesn't know someone who's got a gym membership they never use?

Picture your executive team. How would they rate on the fitness stakes? In an informal survey, most of our HR clients said about 5 out of 10. They also felt that it would be nice to have fit leaders but it was probably not going to the top of their agenda any time soon. Some recent research linking physical energy and the ability to make decisions, analyse data and retain information makes for fascinating reading - and might influence where physical fitness is on the company agenda. The article, *'Exercise, Brain and Cognition Across the Lifespan'*, was published in the online edition of the Journal of Applied Physiology.[14] The authors reviewed over one hundred studies on the impact of aerobic and strength training (that's things like running and doing weights).

The authors suggest that aerobic exercise is crucial for cognitive abilities. Throughout life, a lack of physical activity is linked to poorer academic performance and poorer results on standard psychological tests, too, whilst exercise programmes appear to improve memory, attention and decision-making. Studies involving adults also suggest that high-intensity and high-load training can improve memory. These are precisely the abilities (known as *executive functioning* - which also includes planning and regulating emotions) that leaders need, and they also relate to the levels of energy that leaders outwardly project and, because energy's infectious, pass on to others.

Emotional energy

Emotional energy is generated by our sense of purpose, our values and our motivation to achieve our goals. Emotions effectively come in two varieties - positive and negative - and produce different types of energy as a consequence.

Positive emotions like social connection, joy and hope create biochemical rewards in the brain that energise us to take action towards a goal. It's related to the activation of a person's dopamine system (more on this in a moment), which kicks in when they pursue and achieve their goals. When those goals are shared by people throughout an organisation, this builds the energy of the organisation as a whole as well. This positive energy is associated with being open to new ideas, learning and creativity.

Negative emotions, on the other hand, like anger, fear, shame and disgust are related to the way our brains respond to threat. This response diverts energy and drains motivation in favour of simply ensuring our survival and over time this will inevitably have an impact on our creativity and resilience. There's a more comprehensive look at the impact of threat in Principle 1, but for the purposes of this chapter, suffice to say that this negative energy is linked to a narrowing of perspective, being protective of the status quo and suspicion of others - especially those outside the in-group.

The importance of sleep

It's surprising how often you'll hear senior leaders referring to how little sleep they need. Margaret Thatcher claimed to need only four hours a night, and a 2012 article in *Business Insider* referred to a 'sleepless elite' who can get by with a few hours and still function well.[15] Marissa Mayer (Yahoo): four to six hours a night. Donald Trump: three to four hours a night. Indra Nooyi (PepsiCo): four hours. There's a slightly macho quality to the justification (even from women) that they 'just have too much to do to spend time on sleeping'. But what about the impact on energy and performance?

Neuroscientific research is showing that limited sleep *does* have an impact, and usually one that should concern anyone who wants to perform well. People who sacrifice sleep, from CEOs to forklift drivers, may be doing themselves and their company harm.

The physical effects of sleep deprivation

A recent study in Sweden tested a number of men who were deprived of sleep for one night. They found increases in blood concentrates similar to those associated with brain damage.[16] There were only a small number of participants in the study, so further research is needed, but researcher Christian Benedict says, "The findings of our trial indicate that a good night's sleep may be critical for maintaining brain health." Several other recent studies have linked a lack of sleep with increased risk of disease including Alzhiemers.[17]

Other studies try to give a measure of the impact of lack of sleep. Harvard Medical School researchers found that a week of sleeping four or five hours a night has an impact on performance equivalent to someone with a blood alcohol level of 0.1%. (That's twice the legal alcohol limit in many western countries.)[18] The researchers say that it's clear that the effects of moderate sleep loss on performance are similar to moderate alcohol intoxication.

"If you're not getting enough sleep before work, research shows you might as well be working drunk," says Jessica Payne of the University of Notre Dame.[19] She was not speaking metaphorically. This is ironic, considering that the workplace drinking culture has changed so drastically over the past two decades. In many organisations being drunk at work is grounds for immediate dismissal. Yet operating with inadequate sleep is still regarded as acceptable, and even as a positive trait in leaders, similar to an ability to cope well under stress.

Sleep and memory

One area of Jessica Payne's research into the impact of sleep on performance has focused on memory and the ability to make connections.[20]

Because of the metaphor of the brain as a computer we think of it as inactive during 'sleep mode'. In fact the brain is very busy, regulating and processing emotions, making decisions and accessing implicit knowledge, processing memories and learning. Using an fMRI scanner, researchers can see that the limbic areas of the brain that manage these activities are active in sleep. An area which is largely dormant is the dorsal lateral prefrontal cortex, mainly responsible for executive functioning and skills like planning, organising, strategizing, and managing time and space. It's thought this is to free up processing power for the limbic system.

Researchers believe that the sleeping brain is smart and is making decisions about what to remember and what to forget as well as sorting emotional information from background detail.[21]

Research participants studying a story with both neutral and emotionally significant information and pictures were found to have less memory of the background details of the story before or after sleep, but much more memory for emotional data after sleeping. The negative emotional information was remembered the most.

It seems the brain does not care so much about the neutral data, but in sleep sorts and retains the emotional content. As a survival adaptation this would have helped us to remember things that are important for us to learn - even - or especially - if they were negative. But if you can only remember the negative emotional impact of what happened yesterday, how are you going to make good judgements today? And if you only remember certain types of information your decisions are likely to be unbalanced.

Sleep and cognitive performance

Payne's research has also shown the negative impact on the ability to plan, think rationally and solve problems. People who lack sleep make fewer neural connections and have fewer insights.[22]

One researcher calls this sleeping process 'creative cognition', and it enhances the ability to make inferences. In an experiment aimed at getting people to form associations, it was found that if participants were given a break but remained awake they showed some improvement in performing the task. However if they slept during the break a huge increase in ability was recorded. Sleep helps us make inferential jumps. In another experiment, the researchers tested insightful problem-solving. A massive increase in insight was found after a night's sleep compared with waking rest.

Sleep and emotions

Sleep also helps to regulate emotional response. Evidence from an fMRI study shows that after sleep there is more activation of the brain's 'braking system' that helps to manage our emotions, and also reduced activity in the amygdala, which is responsible for generating those emotions[23] If we have limited or disturbed sleep there is hyper-activity in the amygdala, with none of the regulatory circuits working well.

Science is also showing that if we improve the length and quality of our sleep we reduce our stress levels and increase our energy levels.

Energy, purpose and value

Most research on values, and in particular into understanding what people value and hence dedicate their energy to, starts with the neurochemical dopamine. Dopamine is found all over the brain and determines how the brain processes reward and hence what it values. Two brain regions in particular are important to neuroscientists in this regard. One is the nucleus accumbens and the other is the ventral medial prefrontal cortex, and together they form a coherent system of value within the brain. The system is an old and all-purpose one that probably developed to provide motivation to find food and shelter and to meet other survival needs.[23] And though it developed to seek these primary rewards, it has been adapted to other, secondary things that people find rewarding such as a beautiful view, a handsome face or even money. This dopamine system comes into its own when we have to make decisions about where best to expend our energy, especially when off-setting the value of one choice against another.

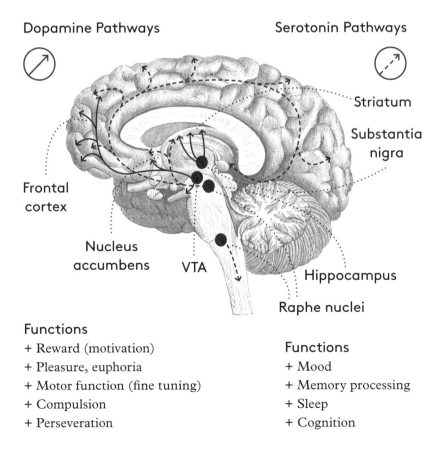

Dopamine Pathways

Serotonin Pathways

Striatum

Substantia nigra

Frontal cortex

Nucleus accumbens   VTA

Hippocampus

Raphe nuclei

Functions
+ Reward (motivation)
+ Pleasure, euphoria
+ Motor function (fine tuning)
+ Compulsion
+ Perseveration

Functions
+ Mood
+ Memory processing
+ Sleep
+ Cognition

These types of decisions are more complex than a coldly calculated, purely rational choice where one alternative is clearly valued more than the other. In situations where we have to choose between qualitatively different things, dopamine helps where rational analysis does not. In these situations the value we assign feels different to us; chocolate feels different to being given a hug or a hug feels different to getting a bonus. But because these are all processed in the same reward system, we're able to measure the relative value we place on these choices and hence the reward received. Neuroscientists think of this as a common neuro-currency of value.

Context is key

This does not mean there is only one *type* of value - the reward system may be attuned to different things in a different context. What is of value to one person may not be valuable to another, and what is important in one context may not be so important in another. So knowing precisely what will produce energetic behaviour will depend on the specific context and vary from person to person.

For example, social context can change what people turn their energies to. When they're in a positive group, people generally work energetically based on the norms of that group. They may not value these norms in a different context, such as when they're on their own or with their family.

It's not just about the company we keep either, that dictates what we value. Take fashion choices, for example. Black shirts, very high heels, long hair - these all go in and out of style, and so it may be that at one period in their life a person may energetically have pursued these and then found that their ardour for these things waned as the sartorial tide changed.

The 3 value variables

Jamil Zaki, a neuroscientist in the department of Psychology at Stanford, has a very useful three dimensional model that describes the contexts that influence an individual's values and hence their energy.[24]

> 1. The first dimension or axis is the continuum between risk and safety. This continuum is not just important to humans - animals balance this too, thinking about the need to search for food or other primary drivers versus staying safe from

predators.

As discussed in the section on temporal discounting in Principle 4, we are generally quite risk averse and so tend to take a reward now rather than a greater, though less certain one in the future. In experiments, scientists see the same dopamine value system active in these kinds of decisions as when we're assessing what's important to us. Also, when subjects took a risk and chose an unknown value, it engaged their anterior cingular cortex, which is known for controlling conflicts, suggesting that they were clamping down and deliberately ignoring risk alerts.[25]

2. The second dimension or axis is social connection versus social disconnection. We've seen already that liking what others like is in itself rewarding, as is being liked by others. In other words, people tend to value what their group values. In his research, Zaki looked at whether people shift their sense of value superficially to conform, to fit in and create a social connection, or whether the way people process what they perceive as of value fundamentally changes when they adopt the values of the group. His subjects were asked to rate pictures of faces as attractive, neutral or unattractive. They were then shown the ratings of their peer group for the same faces. Later, they were again shown the faces and asked to re-rate them. The research looked at whether the re-rating was nudged by the peer rating. They found that indeed people were nudged by peer views. People were scanned during the research and the same pattern showed in brain activity. People were not just claiming to like the faces their peers liked more, their brain placed greater value on those higher rated faces. They took on the values of the group. This research suggests when the group ascribes a certain value to something, this will actually change the individual's values too. In the same experiment, disagreement with the group showed no activity in the brain region for reward and later those people tried harder to engage with the group, to be more like them and to establish a social connection.[26]

Scientists found a similar result in an experiment that we covered back in Principle 2, where people had an opportunity to make money for themselves. In some cases making money was fair to others and in other cases it wasn't. Getting money usually shows a positive activity in the brain's reward networks but in cases where obtaining the money put at risk their social connections, participants showed less activity in these regions. The value of money was overridden by the risk to social connection.[27]

3. Social comparison is the third dimension that influences values. We draw value from being good at something, but also from being better than others. Studies of Olympic medal winners have found that bronze medallists were happier than silver medallists because bronze winners compare themselves with the person who came in fourth place, whereas silver medal winners compare themselves with the person who won gold. In a study investigating this phenomenon, researchers gave people money and simultaneously showed them others getting more money than them. This completely eliminated the reward response. This suggests money is only of value if it gives us positive information about our social status.[28]

These dimensions or variables interrelate, of course. Our values may be impacted by more than one at the same time, so although someone may want to be connected to their colleagues they may also simultaneously want to get a promotion. This means they may be required to be better than others on the team and this will generate a values conflict between being better than others and being socially connected, and the resulting behaviour will be driven by whichever values win out.

Understanding what people value and why they value it is therefore essential to our understanding of what's going to energise them and what's going to dishearten them.

Energy in organisations

Whilst different types of energy can be perceived in each of us individually, it's probably emotional energy that organisational leaders should concern themselves with most, although setting themselves as a good role model for managing other types of energy is also arguably part of a leader's role.

Energy varies in intensity as well as quality. Intensity is a measure of the strength of personal or organisational energy as evidenced by the level of activity, the amount of interaction, the levels of alertness and the extent of emotional arousal. For example, if intensity is low then you're likely to sense apathy and inertia, tiredness, inflexibility and cynicism. Heike Bruch of the University of St. Gallen in Switzerland and the late Sumantra Ghoshal say that it is the combination of intensity and quality that determines the total energy in an organisation.[29] Their model has four categories that can be used to diagnose energy levels and to determine whether the right energy is available for a particular task or strategy to be executed.

In the **Passion Zone** (high-intensity positive energy), people experience high emotional involvement, mental alertness and high activity levels. They have the stamina to work hard on projects and this results in high levels of productivity, particularly when there are clearly defined shared goals.

In the **Comfort Zone** (low-intensity positive energy), people experience high satisfaction and good relationships but with lower activity levels, so they go about their business more slowly. Spending some time in the Comfort Zone is important for rest and recovery and results in greater resilience. But when people and organisations spend too long in this zone it can hamper creativity, agility and, over time, performance. This is often the case where other energy zones have dominated for too long or where that vital sense of purpose has become unclear and people have lost sight of their shared goals.

When the Passion Zone energy is combined with Comfort Zone energy people get a chance to rest and recuperate, and this results in resilient individuals and a sustainable organisation, both of which have the ability to deliver, innovate and achieve long-term success.

The **Resignation Zone** (low-intensity negative energy) is characterised by high levels of frustration, mental withdrawal, detachment, and low drive to achieve goals. This may be the result of a lack of resilience brought about by too many change programmes or extended periods of stress.

The Aggression Zone (high-intensity negative energy) is characterised by collective aggression, destructive thinking and behaviour, high levels of anger, politics and the intention to weaken others through self-interest. This energy state undermines collaboration, trust and connections between people and groups. Organisations in this zone find it hard to pursue their purpose and opportunities - people are in survival mode. This might be brought about by a negative leader who pits groups against each other or there could be external threats that haven't been well managed. Negative emotions direct energy towards survival and protection with little time, inclination or energy for establishing social connections. Goals related to self-interest are pursued over the goals of the group.

Brain-savvy energy model

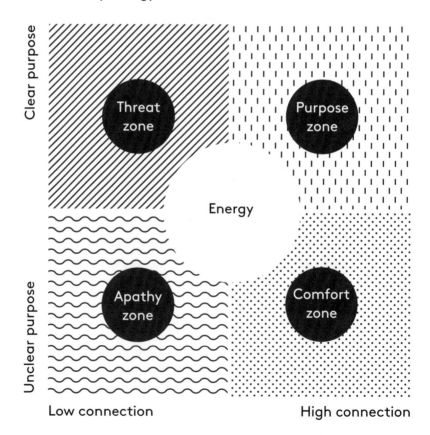

We have created a model similar to Bruch's and Ghoshal's that takes into account the brain and what may be going on in each energy zone:

In the Purpose Zone:

The prevailing emotions are positive like social connection, passion and excitement. There is deep commitment to the purpose and goals of the company and team as well as the motivation to achieve the purpose or activity and to give discretionary effort. Because of the positive emotions, there's support for others in achieving their goals and people are also happy to challenge ways of working and to suggest alternatives thanks to the strong bonds and commitment to the company and the team. In the Passion Zone the brain is activated by positive emotions, a valued purpose and clear goals, all of which combine to produce energy. Expectations are met and dopamine provides the rewards.

In the Comfort Zone:

The prevailing emotion is social connection, especially with the in-group. There are strong supportive behaviours, too. But there is also limited drive towards a purpose and goals. People are focused on a desire to maintain the status quo rather than to make things better.

Energy is low and undirected and there is a sense that people may be taking their foot off the gas after a challenging time or have become complacent.

In the Apathy Zone:

The prevailing emotion is a cynicism, which results in a sense of frustration and emotional withdrawal. People seem not to care. This results in resistance to change and possibly also fatigue and burnout. There are low levels of communication or desire to achieve goals. The brain is either diverting energy to protect itself from potential or perceived threats or has overextended its capacity and needs a chance to recuperate.

In the Threat Zone:

The prevailing emotions are, as the name suggests, threat based and include anger and suspicion. There are also likely to be high levels of stress along with self-serving behaviours. People are using their energy for their own protection, are often suspicious of leaders and restrict social connection to a very small and trusted in-group.

Using the model to manage energy

Companies may well experience all four energy states simultaneously in different contexts and different areas of the business. For instance, although there might be people in the Threat Zone at board level, others working in customer service might still be busy trying to keep sales coming in.

There are therefore a number of questions for leaders to consider:

> What are the prevailing energy states in the company or team?
>
> How intense is each energy state?
>
> Which state is dominant at any given time in any given area?'
>
> What triggers different states?
>
> What can I do to make sure the energy state is in line with what needs to be achieved?'

Leaders need to be able to assess the energy state of a team or organisation and to stay alert to changes. More specifically, understanding the four different energy states helps put our gut feelings about energy into a common language that can be shared with others. Being able to discuss energy states and what creates them is the first step to making change and proactively managing energy. (See Tools)

The application

Energisers and de-energisers

Many leaders may feel that energy is a tricky subject to tackle. It's mercurial and it can be hard to identify. It can also be hard, for these very reasons, to see the effect it has, though we intuitively know the impact it has on us personally and on our teams.

There has been research that links energy levels and the creation of positive energy with the social connection of people in the organisation. Rob Cross, Wayne Baker and Andrew Parker, writing in the *MIT Sloan Management Review* in 2004, report research that matched work performance information collected about people with the person's position within the network of people they interacted with.[30] The data showed links between energy levels and positive performance as measured by annual performance management ratings.

The same research also linked those who energise others with higher performance.

These energisers are more likely to have their ideas considered and put into action. They motivate others to collaborate better within an organisation and also with clients, who as often as not make the decisions about who to work with or what products to purchase based on the levels of energy they perceive.

The researchers found that people will also engage more fully with an energiser, giving undivided attention in a meeting or problem-solving session. People are also more likely to give discretionary time to an energiser's ideas or projects. For example, people working with an energiser will spend time reflecting on a problem outside of office hours and they'll make additional efforts to solve issues and / or work with others to do this.

Energisers also attract the commitment of other high performers; people deliberately position themselves to work for them. And not only are energisers better performers themselves, people who are well connected to an energiser are also better performers. Thus a single energiser can cause positive networks or clusters of energisers to spring up quite naturally.

Interestingly, Cross and his colleagues also found that energisers affect what individuals and networks as a whole learn over time.

People rely on their networks for information to get their work done, and they are much more likely to seek information and learn from energisers than from de-energisers. The flip side of this is that the expertise of de-energisers is underused, no matter how relevant it is. De-energisers, who may have exceptional and wide-ranging expertise but find it difficult to modify their behaviour to keep the organisation running smoothly, tend to persist in unconstructive approaches when they're bypassed like this. For example, they might cause more problems because they don't feel they're being listened to or perhaps they'll keep pushing the same advice (only more forcefully) rather than trying different ways to engage their colleagues constructively.

Energy has a substantial and predictable effect on performance and innovation in organisations.

Energy creation

Two themes emerged from the research as a whole. First of all, energy is not just about the observable behaviour between people in an isolated context. It also depends on the characteristics of the individuals involved and the relationship between them. In identical discussions with different people, a person may very well be energised by the vision of someone known for their integrity but de-energised by the other, who is inconsistent or sends conflicting signals about their trustworthiness.

Second, energy is created in conversations that balance several dimensions, as listed below. This is backed up by Sandy Pentland's research that we mentioned in Principle 2. According to Pentland, the best teams have people who are high energy and fully engaged as well as people who connect outside the group and bring in new ideas.[31]

A compelling purpose: People are energised by conversations with others when a clear, shared purpose is created, such as when people define why they will pursue certain actions, the way the team will work, the goals they will pursue and how any difficulties will be handled. Energy is not usually generated and may even dissipate in conversations about current or past problems.

The purpose needs also to be well defined and the direction to achieve it clear. Clients we talk to say consistently that conversations about unrealistic projects or where goals are unclear were draining and that they left these meetings either annoyed that they had wasted their time or concerned about how to do the work. What people are indicating here is a concern about certainty in the CORE model (Principle 1). A clear purpose and steps to achieve it provides certainty for people and a good dose of dopamine in the brain.

A person's ability to create a clear purpose is a consistent differentiator between energisers and de-energisers. Energisers see realistic possibilities; de-energisers see roadblocks and obstacles.

Making a contribution: People are energised by interactions in which they can make a meaningful contribution. Energisers create these kinds of conversation, getting others involved in finding a solution no matter how expert they are. De-energisers either don't create the space for others to contribute or signal that they don't value their contributions. Effective contributions need to be acknowledged and ineffective ones handled in a way that doesn't threaten the person's sense of options and reputation as described in the CORE model. This can be a particular problem for people with a great deal of expertise and who may find it hard to hold back and allow others to contribute.

Emotional engagement: People are energised when they're emotionally engaged. Body language plays an important role in this. If people display a lack of attention (like looking at their phone) or attempt to do more than one thing at a time, it can send signals that dissipate energy. Equally subtle cues can increase energy, however, such as being animated and giving undivided attention. Full engagement like this can be tiring, though, so energisers are also good at using humour and mental breaks to help others stay energised.

Progress towards goals: People are energised when they get recognition for progress towards their goals.[32] The Cross, Baker and Parker research already cited found that energisers are goal driven but also open and flexible about how they attain those goals.

In contrast, de-energisers may have a goal in mind but a preconceived plan of how to get there that they attempt to impose on everyone else. We see this happen more frequently than many leaders might think. Often overloaded with problems, they come into meetings with a 'fix it' mentality and think they are putting out a fire. What they miss is the devastating effect on energy that the exclusive focus on problems and their own favoured solutions can have.

De-energisers can also wipe out a sense of progress by being too un-focused - by constantly bringing up problems to the extent that no one understands which direction to take. People feel more certain when they know what steps they need to take and the options they have, and both of these activate the brain's reward networks.

Positive emotions: People are energised by positive emotions such as hope and excitement.[33] Hope, for instance, reflects the fact that people believe that the objective is worthwhile and can be attained; they get excited about the possibilities and stop looking for the pit-falls.

Energisers have two characteristics that influence people's will-ingness to hope. They are direct and straightforward in how they speak, even when the message is not good, and they display integ-rity - there's no mismatch between their words and their actions. Cross *et al* said they frequently heard in the course of their inter-views about de-energisers who dashed hopes; energy was depleted because people did not meet their commitments.

One practical action suggested by this research is to look at the com-pany's policies and practices whilst asking whether the organisation needs to energise or de-energise. Even apparently minor changes to things like hiring criteria or performance evaluation processes can have a big impact. For example, one organisation included items on enthusiasm and energy in the criteria to assess potential hires. An-other included dimensions of energy and trust (an important factor in social connection) in 360-degree performance feedback. A third embedded ideas about increasing energy in leadership development training.

Managing energy to implement the strategy

Some leaders can drive a business unit or team towards the more negative emotions and energy quadrants. Constant change programmes, particularly when past projects have not been completed or celebrated, can sap energy in a big way, as can leaders that drive people so hard they have no time for recuperation in the Comfort Zone.

Leaders should bear in mind the impact of their own energy, their style and their demands on the energy levels in the company. Energy usage needs to be paced and periods of recovery factored in as well as celebration and a focus on positive emotions.[34] Managing organisational energy well means that it becomes self-reinforcing, creating a robust and resilient organisation. Adopting a rhythm of intense periods in the Purpose Zone and then recuperation in the Comfort Zone can work well and mirrors the pattern of high-performing athletes and performance artists.[35]

Changing the energy in organisations

When leaders realise they need to change the energy status of their organisation to achieve their goals, we typically see one of two approaches used.

Many turn to the Threat Zone. Indeed, management theory often encourages this with the emphasis on creating a 'burning platform' to motivate people. The Threat Zone uses negative emotions like anger, fear, hate and shame, all of which effectively shock people into action by activating their survival instincts.

This focus on a threat will, it's true, create energy and focus people's attention. The issue with this strategy is that in this state people lack creativity; energy will burn out quickly and there's a high risk of unintended side effects such as excessive stress and reduced wellbeing as well as reduced social connection because people are putting their energy into self-preservation at the expense of working together.

This strategy is particularly unsustainable in the long term and results in untold potential damage for future change projects. People show resistance to change and won't buy into new ways of working. Also, because of the impact negative energy has, once the immediate threat is reduced people will tend to move to the Apathy Zone, further reducing growth and creativity. In these zones - Apathy and Threat - leaders will require more discipline, time and energy expenditure to keep people focused because there won't be the mental energy reserves available that people draw on when thinking for themselves.

This strategy may work, but only for a limited time, if people are made to feel personally the negative emotions so long as it is quickly followed by a more positive energy release prompted by setting a clear purpose.

The alternative strategy, one that is less often seen, is to harness the positive energy of the Purpose Zone. Companies like Zappos have adopted this approach. The strategy builds enthusiasm for an exciting vision and involves people in co-creating the future. It taps into positive emotions and the connections between people, and gets them concentrating on the *purpose*. In this context, purpose relates specifically to *why* the strategy is important rather than what is to be done or how it is to be done. This understanding activates the brain regions responsible for thinking about ourselves and others, so has a natural link to maximising personal and team efforts when the purpose is co-created.

Crafting a clear purpose

According to recent research by Andrew Carton at the University of Pennsylvania's Wharton School, it's often initially difficult to get people to buy in to a purpose, especially when it has not been created jointly.[36] He looked at formal statements of purpose, both good and bad, and in particular he looked at what type of language actually works when writing these statements. He found that the most effective statements include very few recognisably corporate 'values' and rather used less vague words, and instead used words that describe concrete images for employees. That is, the good statements tend to focus on specific images.

Carton gives examples of good and poor statements. Here's an example of the latter from a hospital that says that the hospital will 'distinguish itself for its achievement of excellence in quality outcomes'. It's hard to know what that means or why anyone would like to be treated at that hospital in particular! A good example, because of the concrete image it creates, was another hospital that said their purpose would be realised 'when donors tell friends and neighbours that gifts to [hospital name] are the best decision they have ever made'.

The researchers point out that jargon and abstract language is difficult, if not impossible, to visualize. They use the example of 'sustainability'. People have a general understanding of what the word means, but it's not something that anyone can actually see. When you hear about 'environmental sustainability', it's hard to summon a concrete image to mind. But if someone says 'a city full of hybrid cars' you know immediately what they mean. It's these types of images that get people aligned behind a purpose statement.

Another thing that doesn't translate well into images is a number. Leaders often think a clearer purpose means that it is more quantifiable since numbers are more specific than general notions such as 'maximising shareholder value' and instead refer to 'a 10% increase in revenue', for example. But numbers are actually abstract concepts that are difficult to visualise.

To understand why, briefly consider the anatomy of the brain. We have two cognitive systems - one that thinks logically (the analytical system, or our 'rational brain') and another that encodes sensory information coming from the external environment (the experiential system, or our 'mind's eye'). Numbers are processed in the analytical system. They do not trigger a mental image. Image-based words are processed in the experiential system. When we read or hear image-based words, they are instantly converted to pictures in our mind's eye.

So leaders should try to formulate purpose statements that are meaningful to their teams as individuals and relevant to their roles. They should help individuals see the specific benefits. All of this helps to create greater certainty. Symbolic actions can also be very powerful in this respect, such as leaders changing their own behaviour and habits.

Managing mental energy

Let's consider the case of Helen. She works for ten hours pretty much without stopping, she's head down at her desk most of the day when she isn't running to and from meetings. She even eats lunch at her desk whilst scanning her emails. Let's say she begins work at about 80% effectiveness, instinctively pacing herself because she knows she's got a long day ahead. By lunchtime she's dropped to 60% and is feeling fatigued. After 4pm she's working about 40%. As a result, her thinking is uncreative, she makes errors and has to rework them, all of which means her energy is low and she's not enjoying her work.

Nick works in an entirely different way. He works intensely for around an hour or an hour and a half, and then takes a fifteen-minute break before working again. At lunchtime he goes out either for a walk, to the gym or to have lunch with friends. At around 3pm he closes his eyes at his desk and takes a rest. Sometimes he just lets his mind wander, at other times he has a nap for quarter of an hour. Finally, between 4:30 pm and 5pm, Nick takes a fifteen-minute walk outside. At the end of the day he sits back for another quarter of an hour to reflect on his day and then makes a list of what he has achieved and what he's got planned for tomorrow.

If we run the numbers for Helen and Nick we see some interesting results. Nick takes off a total of two hours during his ten hours at work, but when he *is* engaged he's working at around of 80% of his capacity, so he's delivering just under six and a half hours of full-capacity work.

Helen's average work capacity over ten hours is 60%, which means she effectively delivers six hours of full-capacity work. Nick is actually more productive than Helen because the breaks enable him to work at closer to full capacity. Because Nick is more focused and alert than Helen, he also makes fewer mistakes, is more creative, has more energy and enjoys the work, and at the end of the day he still has energy to pursue his own interests.

This rhythmic pattern, switching between focus and down time, between effort and renewal, has been found to be the most effective way to work by – amongst others - psychologist K. Anders Ericsson, who studies expert performers such as musicians. His subjects work hard but take planned rest periods[37]. This method also contributes to learning and helps embed skills properly.

Many people tell us there just aren't enough hours in the day. Perhaps they need to work smarter, not longer or harder. Doing more may mean doing less. Companies who adopt this work style include the likes of Google, Apple, Facebook, Coca-Cola, and Genentech. There is evidence that when they do, people like their job more and are willing to go above and beyond their basic duties, leading to higher performance and greater productivity.[38]

One way to help manage physical and mental energy has been devised by David Rock and Daniel Segal. It's called the *Healthy Mind Platter*.[39] The Mind Platter uses the metaphor of a plate of food, each 'food' representing an activity such as rest, play or exercise that promotes energy. By making sure we're getting our five-a-day, as it were, they claim we'll be mentally fitter and able to perform better. (See Tools)

Managing energy through sleep

Many senior leaders believe that it's the responsibility of their team to make life a bit easier for them, and that they should pick up the slack (or steer clear!) when they're under a lot of pressure or as is so often the case, they're short on sleep.

Even if that is the accepted corporate culture, Jessica Payne's research (above) demonstrates that lack of sleep affects leadership performance in more significant ways than simply making the team's life difficult. Sleep plays an important role in emotional regulation, so it's about more than simply avoiding Grumpy Boss Syndrome.

Energy and focus

Everyone loses energy to focus at times, and this is where someone who is sleep deprived can easily fall into a trap. If we start to lose energy to focus but have had enough sleep then the brain is able to compensate and increase attention. If we are sleep deprived, however, it can't.[40] "The main finding is that the brain of the sleep-deprived individual is working normally sometimes, but intermittently suffers from something akin to power failure," says Harvard neuroscientist Clifford Saper.

Sleep-deprived people have limited brainpower to steer themselves back to focus once they lose attention. But even more significantly, they don't notice their decrease in performance and may have a false sense of competency.

How much sleep is enough?

Jessica Payne's research findings show that the formula for optimum performance is mild stress, good sleep and a good mood. But how much sleep is enough to maintain the levels of energy needed at work? The answer is that no one really knows. What is right for one person may not be enough for another, or excessive for someone else. People need to monitor their own sleep needs and performance. But for those who really want an objective measure, Daniel Kripke of the UC San Diego School of Medicine claims, "People who sleep between six and a half and seven and a half hours a night live the longest, are happier and most productive."[41]

It's also worth considering introducing exercise or a meditative practice into your daily regime because there's evidence that these things not only boost your performance but also encourage deeper, more restful sleep. And why not review your daily habits whilst you're at it? How late do you work? Do you always put the TV on for an hour or so before going to bed? Is your tablet or phone always on the bedside table, ready to interrupt your sleep?

Organisations demand a lot from their leaders and the neuroscience research clearly demonstrates that macho all-nighters cannot deliver best performance. We owe it not only to ourselves to get adequate sleep for our health and wellbeing, but also to the company's bottom line.

Case study: Creating energy to implement a new strategy

We worked with a major UK bank's operations and IT functions to help shift them from the Apathy Zone to the Purpose Zone. These functions had some 1,300 leaders and provided services to the revenue producing areas of the bank. These areas were described as 'customers', although the customer wasn't always right; in fact, these so-called customers had pretty much to accept what they were given.

The leadership team within the functions, however, were optimistic. They had worked on a strategy that would make them more effective and efficient, that would help them provide a more commercial and responsive service that was better value for money and also delivered services in a timelier manner to the bank. They recognised that the current attitude meant that key areas of the bank had begun lobbying to have their services provided by third-party suppliers and that, unless the functions dramatically improved how they responded to the internal customers, they risked becoming figuratively - and literally - redundant. But the leadership team could envisage a future that not only involved happy internal customers but also the possibility of providing a great service to third party companies as well.

Whilst work had been done to cascade the strategy, employees remained unconvinced. Their behaviour remained the same and their performance unchanged. In essence people were in the Apathy Zone and many of the leadership were in the Comfort Zone about the strategy.

We were asked to design an event to improve energy levels and boost employees' sense of purpose. Having talked with a number of key stakeholders we felt it was essential that the leadership team didn't just talk about their commitment to the programme of events but actively took part.

The event mirrored the positive energy of the Purpose Zone and inspired the leaders across all the functions not only to change their own beliefs about the strategy but to inspire their teams to do so, too.

Articulating the purpose and strategy

The first steps involved doing two things. First, we had to convince the senior leadership team that they should be part of the programme. Second, we needed to get them to articulate more clearly the strategy and to get people involved in laying out what it would be like to work in the respective functions in the future. Having achieved the first, we set about the second by running an event with the leadership team where they worked through the strategy articulating it at a number of levels:

When and where? - The work environment of the future.

What? - The specific roles and behaviours that people would undertake.

How? - The capabilities and mind-set they would have.

Why? - The beliefs and values that would drive their decisions and lead to their actions.

Who? - Their sense of identity and purpose in the future.

Whilst we now had a clearer picture that provided more certainty to people, we needed to ensure that people had a personal, emotional commitment and had worked through what the change meant to their role.

One of the challenges we faced in doing this was that there was a strong reliance and emphasis on process, which had the effect of being de-energising. For the type of functions we were working with, process was an important element in successfully carrying out the work, but it sapped energy when applied relentlessly to interactions between people and their customers. It could also be used as an excuse to resist change, innovation and being more responsive to the customer.

Since one of the key aspects of the strategy was to focus on being responsive to customers, we had to stop process getting in the way whilst at the same time not abandoning it completely, thereby allowing the functions to slip into chaos. So people needed to uphold processes so far as they were necessary to maintain effective control over IT software, for example, but not adhere to them so dogmatically that these same processes became simply a way of controlling people. This meant there needed to be both more understanding of the functions' fundamental aims and a greater freedom to allow people to make judgement calls.

Getting leaders to exemplify purpose

This reliance on process had created a culture where the focus was on seeing roadblocks and things that might go wrong rather than inspiring action and transforming the future organisation. Transformational leaders are energising - they're able to inspire others and change the way people work towards a common goal.[41] We wanted leaders to be promoting the positive aims of our programme and individual judgement rather than negative, essentially preventative approach of process-heavy risk aversion. We believed that if we could create enough leaders who understood this and were emotionally engaged and actively working at it, the levels of energy in the organisation would shift and with it the ability to work in a way that matched the organisation's strategy. Leaders needed to be positively promoting initiatives to help the customer and to focus on what could be achieved - not what couldn't.

Although we are unaware of any research explicitly investigating the role of (positive) promotion versus (negative) prevention focus in enhancing or diminishing energy levels, that people with a promotion focus may be more goal oriented and less distracted by thoughts of what they ought to do. We do know people with a prevention focus, on the other hand, will be more inclined to ruminate on possible negatives and to spend their time thinking about potential down-sides, which is fine in moderation, but isn't conducive to change - especially a change in energy. Consequently, people with a promotion focus will be better able to focus their energy on the goal and be more productive. The research mentioned above on energizers and de-energizers suggests this will impact overall energy in the company and people's willingness to engage in the strategy.

In order to shift energy, we designed a three-day leadership programme based on our brain-savvy methodology (see Principle 5) that gave people the opportunity to understand the strategy, to get a 'felt sense' of what it would be like to work in the organisation they were trying to mould and to translate the strategy into their day-to-day work and that of their teams.

We introduced a variety of interesting ways of doing this. We set up rooms which modelled the company in the future, for example, where people would go to undertake activities like interacting with a customer in a more responsive way, solving hypothetical problems that customers might bring and working with their equally hypothetical team in a more responsive way. We also gave people an opportunity to test and challenge the strategy, ask questions, make suggestions and generally work through the implications for them personally - a way of turning critics into designers and builders of the detailed steps that would need to be taken to realise the strategy in their job role. In addition, guided visualisation helped to prepare people for the future as it gave them a detailed image of themselves working in the new way.

Alongside this, we helped people to develop skills in making judgements, in challenging the reliance of process with customers and in energising their staff.

Part of the design meant the most senior leadership team took part and experienced the learning and insights for themselves. They also got to see first-hand the shift in energy of the other leaders as they experienced energising behaviours versus de-energising ones.

The results

The culture of the organisation and IT functions began to shift almost immediately, and as more and more people went through the programme they reached a tipping point where there were more Purpose Zone behaviours and energy than not. The workshops also created a common language that allowed people to talk about energising and de-energising behaviour and to challenge the latter when they experienced it.

Tools

Measuring energy

When you consider the energy matrix as laid out in the brain energy model, how do you view your organisation? Which energy states dominate the experience of people in your organisation, department or team? It can be helpful to distinguish the energy state by hierarchical levels as sometimes senior leaders experience a different energy state to, say, the front line employees who are dealing with customers, which can lead to a mismatch between policy and practice that the leadership fail to understand.

Consider these questions to help you assess the energy state in relevant areas of the business or across the business as a whole. You can also use these questions to assess your energy personally, or as a team on a particular project.

People (in the company/ team/business unit)	Strongly disagree	Disagree	Neither agree nor disagree	Agree	Strongly agree
Score	0	25	50	75	100
1 ...feel positive about their role					
2 ...lack drive					
3 ...like what they do					
4 ...are stressed and fearful					
5 ...like to make things happen					
6 ...are reluctant to try new things					
7 ...are suspicious of the leadership's intensions					
8 ...are committed to success personally / of the company/ business unit / team					
9 ...seek to be effective and efficient					

10 ...often behave in a destructive or defensive manner					
11 ....go out of their way to help others					
12 ...feel discouraged in their role					

(Adapted from Bruch and Vogal)

How to score the questions

Answer the questions as objectively as possible. You may wish to ask others to complete the questions as well and then compare your results. Be aware that leaders' self evaluations are often more optimistic than other employees, which means you may have a positive bias.

Add up the numbers as follows:

Purpose Zone: Questions 5, 8 and 11, then divide by 3

Comfort Zone: Questions 1, 3 and 9, then divide by 3

Apathy Zone: Questions 2, 6 and 12, then divide by 3

Threat Zone: Questions 4, 7 and 10, then divide by 3

Plot your scores onto the figure opposite. Connect the lines to form a 'spider web diagram'. This is your energy profile.

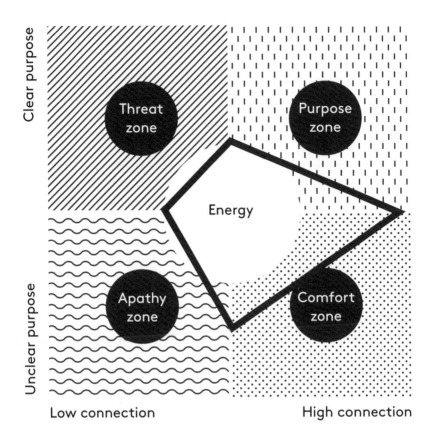

Clear purpose

Unclear purpose

Threat zone

Purpose zone

Energy

Apathy zone

Comfort zone

Low connection

High connection

Interpreting your results:

Identify the dominant energy state or states. If you have asked others to answer the questions as well, compare their results by plotting them on the graph in a different colour.

What are the areas of agreement and disagreement?

Purpose Zone: 75% and upwards is great. If this is the case you're in a strong position, especially if Comfort Zone energy is slightly lower than Purpose Zone energy and both negative states are low (below 25%). Your core challenge is how to maintain this energy level. Maximise energisers' behaviours and ways of working (described above) and ensure you monitor and minimise de-energisers.

Comfort Zone: This shouldn't be the highest, ideally. If the score is around 70% and the Purpose Zone is too then that's good. If the Comfort Zone dominates then you need to increase a sense of purpose.

Apathy Zone: You're looking for a score below 25%. If it's above that, then take a look back at the questions that scored high in this area. What does this tell you about the behaviours and culture?

Threat Zone: This should not be higher than 25%, either. Pay close attention to this area in particular if it's above or close to this figure.

Once you've worked out the scores, write down what you feel are the energisers and de-energisers. Discuss your views with others. Go back to the questions and make notes of typical behaviours or examples, especially for the negative energy states. What's the root cause of these behaviours? What's their frequency? Are they organisational habits or individual ones (see Principle 6)?

Also consider if your assessment holds true throughout the company hierarchy. Is your organisation highly connected and purpose driven at the top while disenfranchised in the frontline services or amongst middle managers? Alternatively, has the top team begun to show signs of corrosion that's trickling down though your organisation?

Eight everyday habits that increase energy

These eight habits are useful when you want to enhance energy levels, perhaps to move you and your team from the Comfort Zone to the Purpose Zone. We've explicitly listed them in order to emphasise that people can and do choose their habits - many times in most days - that have a striking effect on others' energy.

+ Do you take the opportunity to enhance relationships in day-to-day work? Concern for others and connections outside of work-based roles allow trust to develop

+ Do you honour your commitments? Do you do what you say you're going to do? People are de-energised by lack of follow-through

+ Do you have a clear purpose? Do you talk about your own purpose and how it relates to the business? People are energised when others stand for something larger than themselves and set high standards

+ Do you look for possibilities or do you just identify problems? De-energisers keep ideas from ever getting off the ground by seeing only obstacles to success

+ When you disagree with someone, do you focus attention on the issue at hand rather than allowing the disagreement to become personal? Energisers are able to disagree with an idea while not marginalising the person who presented it

+ Are you focused during meetings and conversations? Rather than going through the motions of being engaged, energisers physically and mentally show their interest in the person and the topic of conversation

+ Are you open to others' ideas and new ways of solving an issue or do you like others to do what you suggest? Energisers draw people into conversations and projects by finding opportunities for them to contribute

+ Do you facilitate the buy-in of others, even when you know the answer (or think you know the answer)? Experts or leaders can easily and accidentally destroy energy in their haste to find a solution or demonstrate their knowledge.

Managing energy

According to David Rock, a consultant who specialises in neuroscience, we can significantly improve the quality of our thinking (and therefore our value to the business) by understanding the biological limitations of our brain and then tailoring our work style to accommodate those limitations. Here are some ways to manage your brain more efficiently:

+ Start the day with planning and prioritising a to-do list. Better still, do it the night before. Work on the most important and challenging tasks first since they need the most energy and focus

+ Turn off distractions before they take over. Close down your email, switch your phone to silent, turn off alerts and ask not to be disturbed unless it's an emergency

+ Avoid scheduling meetings at a time of day when you know you'll be tired

+ Take regular breaks. Take a stretch or walk round the office. Even pausing to grab a glass of water helps.

The energy prescription

Below are some ideas for generating energy. Make a prescription of the ideas and techniques that appeal to you or work with your team to do this. Apply these ideas at work

+ Adopt a high energy state of mind
+ Develop new skills on the job
+ Avoid sweet foods and drink
+ Eat more fruit and drink water
+ Create a bond with the team
+ Ask for people's help
+ Add colour to the work environment
+ Move around
+ Create fun and laughter
+ Create goals and tract progress
+ Celebrate success
+ Do things for others
+ Take mental breaks
+ Create a sense of meaning in your work
+ Notice what's working
+ Savour positive events

Load up a healthy mind platter

The platter is a metaphor for the activities we should undertake each day to ensure sustained mental and physical energy. Some of the activities may surprise you whilst others are pretty obvious, but the question is this: Do you consistently undertake each of the activities and keep them in balance?

Rock's and Segal's Healthy Mind Platter

Focused attention - focusing on our goals and accepting challenges.

Play time - being spontaneous and enjoying new experiences.

Connecting time - connecting with other people and / or the natural world.

Physical time - exercise and bodily movement.

Time in - reflecting and focusing on our own thoughts and ideas.

Down time - letting our minds wander, relax and refresh themselves.

Sleep time - important for learning and recovery.

Rate yourself on each of these or keep a journal to monitor them over a period of time - a week, perhaps. Note also how you feel, both physically and mentally. Then, based on your rating or journal observations, plan how you will achieve a balance of activity, assuming you don't have it already!

Look at the section on habits (Principle 6) for ideas about how to develop the habit of a balanced Mind Platter.

Working in Flow

Most of the work on Flow has been carried out by Csikszentmihalyi, who has found that once people know how to get into Flow they find it easier to achieve the state repeatedly.[42] Flow, to re-cap, refers to a balance between the difficulty of a challenge and your self-perceived ability to meet it. If either is too low then you coast. If they're too high, you panic.

So try to limit stress but only to the point of Flow. You could try taking a quick walk to activate another area of the brain or write ideas down to get them out of your head. If you're feeling overwhelmed, divide the task into smaller, more manageable chunks.

When you need to do the opposite and bring your arousal level up, try visualising a mild fear - fear brings on an immediate alertness. Or you could challenge yourself to carry out the task in a new way, using new skills for example.

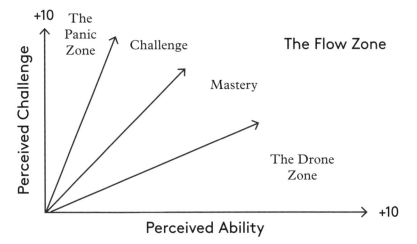

Physical energy

The Centre for Creative Leadership researched the link between fitness and executive performance using a number of essential leadership criteria. The research concluded there was a strong correlation between regular exercise and executive performance.

For example, exercising in the morning before going to work:

+ Spikes brain activity

+ Prepares you for mental stress for the rest of the day

+ Aids retention of new information

+ Produces greater tolerance of complex or challenging situations

+ Is linked to greater creativity and clearer thinking.

One of the issues that gets in the way of drawing up and sticking to a regular exercise programme is the way in which many people label and think about exercise. How do you think about it? Is it:

+ Something you should do rather than something you want to do?

+ A chore rather than a pleasure?

+ Hard rather than easy?

+ Painful rather than beneficial?

+ Taking time away from pleasurable things rather than a pleasure in itself?

+ Associated with negative self-talk rather than encouraging self-talk?

How can you change the way you think about and label exercise?

Getting enough sleep

Jessica Payne, whose research we mentioned earlier in this chapter, has made in-depth studies into how disturbance in sleep influences memory consolidation and how this in turn influences cognitive functioning.

To ensure you sleep well and wake up with all the energy you might need the following day:

+ Make sleep a priority even if you're tempted to stay up late

+ Create a ritual or habit that optimises your ability to sleep. If you've been working all day and you're a bit frazzled then have some wind-down time. Disengage and calm your mind for at least an hour before you get into bed

+ If you have trouble getting to sleep, try slow, deep breathing or relaxation techniques like stretching or meditation to calm your mind

Principle summary

Energy can be felt and also measured.

Energy determines – amongst other things - wellbeing, productivity and discretionary effort.

There are three types of energy - physical, mental and emotional.

Energy varies in quality and also intensity. Understanding the base levels of energy in yourself, your team and your organisation helps to manage it.

Circumstantial triggers may impact short-term energy, e.g. in a meeting.

There are identifiable behaviours that enhance or decrease energy.

References

1 M Tushman & CA O'Reilly III, 'The Ambidextrous Organization: Managing Evolutionary and Revolutionary Change', California *Management Review*, vol. 38, 1996, pp. 8–30

2 H Busch & B Vogal, Fully charged: How great leaders boost their organisations energy and ignite high performance, Harvard Business Review Press, 2004

3 Mihaly Csikszentmihalyi Finding Flow: The psychology of engagement with everyday life, Basic Books, 1997

4 Isaac Emery Ash, 'What Makes a People Lethargic or Energetic?', *American Journal of Sociology*, vol. 19(3), 1913, pp. 370-379

5 Andrew Parker & Rob Cross, The Hidden Power of Social Networks Understanding How Work Really Gets Done in Organizations, Harvard Business School Press, 2004

6 Martin Seligman, Authentic Happiness: Using the New Positive Psychology to Realise Your Potential for Lasting Fulfilment, Nicholas Brealey Publishing, 2003

7 Mihaly Csikszentmihalyi, Good Business: Leadership, Flow, and the Making of Meaning, Hodder Paperbacks, 2004

8 Emily D Heaphy & Jane E Dutton, 'Positive social interactions and the human body at work: linking organizations and physiology', *Academy of Management Review*, vol. 33(1), 2008, pp. 137–162

9 Heike Bruch & Sumantra Ghoshal, 'Unleashing Organizational Energy', *Sloan Management Review*, October 2003

10 R Cross, W Baker & A Parker, 'What Creates Energy in Organisations?' *Sloan Management Review*, July 2003, pp. 51–56

11 H Busch & B Vogal, Fully Charged: How Great Leaders Boost their Organisation's Energy and Ignite High Performance, Harvard Business Review Press, 2004

12 Mihaly Csikzentmihalyi Finding Flow: The Psychology of Engagement with Everyday Life, Basic Books, 1997.

13 Thanks to Sylvia Vorhauser-Smith of Pages Up for this idea

14   Michelle W Voss, Lindsay S Nagamatsu, Teresa Liu-Ambrose
      & Arthur F Kramer, 'Exercise, Brain, and Cognition Across the
      Lifespan', *Journal of Applied Physiology*, April 2011

15   Carolyn Cutrone & Max Nisen, '19 Successful People Who Barely
      Sleep', businessinsider.com, 2012

16   Christian Benedict (2013). Acute sleep deprivation increases
      serum levels of neuron-specific enolase (NSE) and S100 calcium
      binding protein B (S-100B) in healthy young men. Sleep. 2014 Jan
      1; 37(1)

17   Adam P Spira PhD, Alyssa A Gamaldo PhD, Yang An MS
      et al, 'Self-Reported Sleep and Beta-Amyloid Deposition in
      Community-Dwelling Older Adults' and 'Modification of the
      Relationship of the Apolipoprotein E E4 Allele to the Risk of
      Alzheimer Disease and Neurofibrillary Tangle Density by Sleep',
      JAMA Neurology October 21, 2013.

18   Drew Dawson & Kathryn Reid, 'Fatigue, alcohol and performance
      impairment', *Nature* vol. 388, 1997

19   Jessica Payne, Neuroleadership Summit, London 2013

20   JD Payne, R Stickgold, K Swanberg & EA Kensinger, 'Sleep
      Preferentially Enhances Memory for Emotional Components of
      Scenes', *Psychological Science*, vol. 19(8), 2008, pp. 781-788 and
      Jessica Payne, 'Sleep on it: Stabilizing and transforming memories
      during sleep', *Nature Neuroscience*, vol. 14(3), 2011

21   J Tamminen, JD Payne, R Stickgold, EM Wamsley & M Gaskell,
      'Sleep spindle activity is associated with the integration of new
      memories and existing knowledge', *Journal of Neuroscience*, vol.
      30(43), 2010.

22   JD Payne & L Nadel, 'Sleep, dreams and memory consolidation:
      The role of the stress hormone cortisol', *Learning & Memory*,
      vol.11, 2004, pp. 671-678

23   Nils Kolling, Timothy EJ Behrens, Rogier B Mars & Matthew
      FS Rushworth, 'Neural Mechanisms of Foraging', *Science*, vol.
      336(6077), 2012, pp. 95-98

24   Nook & Zaki, cited at the NeuroLeadership Summit, 2014

25   J Zaki & J Mitchell, 'Equitable decision making is associated with

neural markers of subjective value', *PNAS*, vol. 108(49), 2011

26 Falk et al., 'Social comparison affects reward-related brain activity in the human ventral striatum', *Science*, 2007

27 Peter Sokol-Hessner, Colin F Camerer, & Elizabeth A Phelps, 'Emotion regulation reduces loss aversion and decreases amygdala responses to losses', *Social Cognitive and Affective Neuroscience Advance Access*, February 15, 2012

28 Falk et al., 'Social comparison affects reward-related brain activity in the human ventral striatum', *Science*, 2007

29 Heike Bruch & Sumantra Ghoshal, 'Unleashing Organizational Energy', *MIT Sloan Magazine*, October 2003

30 R Cross, W Baker & A Parker, 'What creates energy in organisations?' *Sloan Management Review*, July 2003, pp. 51–56

31 Alex Pentland, Honest Signals: How They Shape our World, MIT Press, 2010

32 Teresa Amabile, Steven Kramer & Sharon Williams, The Progress Principle: Using Small Wins to Ignite Joy, Engagement, and Creativity at Work, Harvard Business Review Press, 2011

33 Barbara L Fredrickson, 'The broaden-and-build theory of positive emotions', *Philosophical Transactions of the Royal Society B: Biological Sciences*, vol. 359(1449), 2004

34 Jim Loehr, Building Resilience: The new Business imperative, The Human Performance Institute, 2010

35 KA Ericsson, 'Creative genius: A view from the expert-performance approach', from DK Simonton (ed.), *The Wiley-Blackwell Handbook of Genius*, Wiley 2014, pp. 321-349

36 Andrew M Carton, Chad Murphy & Jonathan R Clark 'A (Blurry) Vision of the Future: How Leader Rhetoric about Ultimate Goals Influences Performance', *Academy of Management Journal*, vol. 57(6), 2014

37 KA Ericsson, 'Creative genius: A view from the expert-performance approach', from DK Simonton (ed.), *The Wiley-Blackwell Handbook of Genius*, Wiley 2014

38 Osman M Karatepe, 'High-performance work practices and hotel

employee performance: The mediation of work engagement',
International Journal of Hospitality Management, vol. 32, 2013

39 David Rock & Daniel Segal, The Healthy Mind Platter: http://
www.healthymindplatter.com/

40 Clifford Saper and Thomas Scammell (2013). Emerging
therapeutics in sleep. Annals of Neurology 74(3).

41 Daniel Kripke, Lawrence Garfinkel, Deborah Wingard, Melville
Klauber & Matthew Marler, 'Mortality associated with sleep
duration and insomnia', Archive of General Psychiatry, vol.59,
2002

42 Ronit Kark & Dina Van Dijk, 'Motivation to Lead, Motivation
to Follow: The Role of the Self-regulatory Focus in Leadership
Processes', *Academy of Management Review*, vol. 32, 2007

43 Mihaly Csikszentmihalyi Finding Flow: The Psychology of
Engagement with Everyday Life, Basic Books, 1997

Further reading and viewing

Angela Ahrendts, The Power of Human Energy
(TEDxHollywood): https://www.youtube.com/
watch?v=mZNlN31hS78

Jack L Groppel, PhD & Ben Wiegand, PhD, Biology of Business
Performance: https://www.hpinstitute.com/sites/default/files/
Biology%20of%20Business%20Performance.pdf

Alex (Sandy) Pentland, 'The New Science of Building Great
Teams' Harvard Business Review April 2012

Tony Schwartz & Catherine McCarthy, 'Manage Your Energy Not
Your Time', *Harvard Business Review*, October 2007

Barry Schwartz, 'The way we think about work is broken', (TED
Talk) 2014: Http://www.ted.com/talks/barry_schwartz_the_way_
we_think_about_work_is_broken?language=en

Barry Schwartz, 'Rethinking work', New York Times, August
2015: http://www.nytimes.com/2015/08/30/opinion/sunday/
rethinking-work.html?_r=0

The Brain-Savvy Leader

All of our work leads us to believe that understanding how the brain works is an excellent way of helping leaders become more effective. There are, of course, a number of elements that are important, all encapsulated to the Principles that we've covered over the course of this book.

Every one of these ideas will have an effect on how you lead and how successfully you do it. Though some of the effects may be small, cumulatively they'll make a big difference. They could make *all* the difference.

But even with all this neuroscience, all this research and information at your disposal, there's one more vital characteristic of all the most successful leaders we've encountered. It's one that's often overlooked and that we've left until last. It sounds simple enough, but then many of the most difficult challenges we face do, don't they?

Know thyself

It's tempting to think that, as a leader, your job is easy enough to define. It's about working out what you need to do, figuring out how to do it and then doing it. The right ideas and the right tools for the job. It's about strategy and tasks.

But there's a wealth of evidence that leaders need to do more than this. Unfortunately, this thinking has never really caught on in the majority of businesses.

A study by management consultants Green Peak Partners with John Hausknecht of Cornell University found that executives who drive hard for results may actually destroy value in a firm, while leaders who have high levels of self-awareness are able to build teams that are high-performing.[1]

Their findings directly challenge the conventional view that 'drive for results' is the primary skill that leaders need. The research found that the leaders most likely to deliver good bottom-line results were self-aware leaders who are especially good at working with individuals and in teams.

That's why, self-awareness should be seen as one of the Holy Grails of leadership. Self-aware people are able to do a number of things that those who remain blind to their inner self can't do.

Self-awareness gives you that ability to notice and understand other people's reactions and to anticipate how someone you know will react in a given circumstance too.

You'll also be more sensitive to how you feel in any given situation, able to inhibit unwanted reactions as they occur and you probably know what will trigger them in the first place and make sure you avoid those situations.

In short, you'll know your strengths and weaknesses not just intellectually but in a practical way that enables you to do something about them and to manage them effectively.

The self-awareness part of the brain

Numerous neuroimaging research projects have shown that thinking about ourselves, recognising images of ourselves and reflecting on our thoughts and feelings are all forms of self-awareness.[2]

But self-awareness is more than just seeing yourself in the mirror or recognising your picture, of course. It's a lot more complex. It's about *how* we see ourselves.

A Dartmouth College study showed participants words such as 'polite' and 'talkative', and then asked them if the word described themselves or the President of the United States. The researchers recorded the subjects' brain activity and saw similar patterns as when we see ourselves in a mirror as was expected, but also activity in the medial prefrontal cortex and the precuneus when the participants thought that the word applied to themselves. This, to put the technical details to one side for a moment, means that thinking about ourselves engages more areas of the brain than straightforward self-recognition would.[3]

Building self-awareness

We tend to believe that the self we are aware of and think about is composed of personal beliefs, goals, and values. But how do we gain our self-awareness? Nietzsche believed it was cumulative - our beliefs and memories build up over time, a consequence of the people in our life and our interactions with them.

Other similar theories include one called the social construction of reality, which posits that over time we create mental representations of our actions called 'mental maps' that determine the way we interact with the world and each other.[4] We tend not to question our own beliefs and assumptions and in turn they determine what we notice and what we don't notice. These beliefs and actions become a habit. When these unconscious assumptions are brought to the surface and questioned, new alternatives can be considered, more choices are on the table, and movement from one way of seeing an issue to another becomes possible. It's this awareness that provides insights that enable us to learn and change.

How the group affects us

One question it's well worth considering in the context is this: Are our ideas our own?

Think, for example, about our response to fashion. We like to think we look at a trend and decide for ourselves whether it's right for us. It might be the fashion for ties the same colour as business shirts, or for women a fashion in ultra-high heels. To start with, we often resist. We tell ourselves that we're not going to go along with the herd. That's not our look, we say. But how often does it happen that after a few weeks or months of seeing everyone else wearing those ties, or those shoes, you find yourself buying into the trend? It turns out it *was* our look, after all.

Having our beliefs and values unconsciously influenced by those around us is, UCLA's Matt Lieberman argues, a way of creating harmony in a group.[5] He suggests that our sense of self is created by our interactions with those who matter to us. We adopt their beliefs and values to be more like them and to strengthen our bonds with them. Over time this social interaction implants a collection of beliefs about ourselves and what constitutes a worthwhile life, and we measure ourselves and our lives against them.

In a professional context, this would mean we adopt the norms and values of the business we're in rather than the other way round - we don't just find a business that has the same values as our own.

Matt Lieberman and Jennifer Pfeifer studied adolescents to test their theory that we create our self-knowledge by adopting the views of others. They worked on the assumption that adolescents would have more need to think about the views of others to be sure about their own view of themselves.[6]

If you have teenage children, you have no doubt despaired at how easily they seem to be influenced by their peers in everything from fashion sense to study habits, but up until this time no one had looked at 13 year-olds' brains to understand how they formed their sense of self.

The neuroscientists asked adolescents and adults to report on both a direct appraisal of themselves ('I am smart') and a reflected appraisal ('My friends think I'm smart').

They expected to see activity in the medial prefrontal cortex when asking the direct appraisal question 'Are you smart?' and this was the case for both adults and adolescents. With reflective appraisal 'Do your friends thing you're smart?' they expected to see activity in the default or mentalizing system and this was also the case. (The mentalizing system is associated with thinking about the mental states of others.)

The adolescents showed strong activity throughout the mentalizing system, including when they were making direct appraisals of themselves. The adults, on the other hand, did *not* mentalize when thinking about themselves; their mentalizing system activated only when thinking about how others viewed them.

These results suggest adolescents brought to mind the reflected views of others rather than their own internalised views. Adults had internalised their self-awareness whereas adolescents had to draw on the views of others to know themselves.

These activities - being self-aware and wondering about how others see us - are generally seen as different processes, and in business we tend to build development programmes based on this psychological assumption. But when we're learning to understand ourselves as adolescents they're actually intertwined.

Looking inwards or outwards

So what are the implications of this for leaders' self-awareness?

We often characterise leaders as embodying unique, authentic characteristics. The late Steve Jobs advised graduates to avoid letting the 'noise of others' override their own voice[7]- the data would suggest this is poor advice. Rather than battle for a more profound self-awareness, we would be better off integrating successfully into our respective groups and to let the 'self' work through others.

Not only can this approach have a bigger impact on an organisation's bottom line, but in terms of self-reflection it can be especially fruitful in the early days of leadership when feedback from others is helping an emerging leader form their own awareness.

The point, then, is this: Instead of trying to know and understand ourselves by examining our innermost thoughts, we might find it more useful to pay attention to what other people tell us about ourselves, both directly and non-verbally. Perhaps there's something to be learned from teenagers, and we should be defining our identity less by thinking about how we see ourselves and more by considering how those who are important to us think about us.

As the philosopher Alain de Botton says, *"Living for others is such a relief from the impossible task of trying to satisfy oneself."*[8]

Self-awareness isn't about assigning blame. It's about being open to your reactions and emotions, accepting them and resolving to change or control them if they're counterproductive. Everyone's snapped at a colleague at one time or another. Everyone gets the feeling from time to time that others aren't pulling their weight. Everyone has times when they should avoid a situation or it will make matters worse. Everyone has occasionally let a personal disagreement cloud their professional judgement.

Self-awareness is simply about recognising these things when they happen, taking responsibility for them, and resolving to get them under control without judging yourself too harshly. It's a practice that can become second nature, leaving you calmer and free to concentrate on implementing the changes you want to see and getting the best out of yourself and your organisation.

What next?

When you're done with this book. Pass it on! Give someone a leg up on their own brain-savvy journey. But don't forget those CORE principles: You don't want them to think you're criticising them and that they need to change - you want them to feel reward not threat, so try to inspire in them an image of their future self - a more fulfilled, more effective self both at work and at home.

Or, if you're not quite ready to part with this book and you're still reflecting on the contents, resist the old habit of putting a freshly finished book back on the shelf. Leave it somewhere where you'll see it. Dip in and out from time to time. Take on board an idea and test it out tomorrow. Share it with others. Then try another.

Then another...

References

1 J P Flaum, When it comes to business leadership, nice guys finish first, Green Peak Partners, 2010

2 Bud Craig, 'How do you feel — now? The anterior insula and human awareness', *Nature Reviews Neuroscience* vol.10, 2009

3 William Kelley, Todd Heatherton & Neil Macrae, 'Finding self? An event-related fMRI study', *Journal of Cognitive Neuroscience*, vol. 14(5), 2002

4 Peter Berger & Thomas Luckmann, The Social Construction of Reality: A Treatise in the Sociology of Knowledge, Anchor, 1967

5 Matthew Lieberman, Social: Why our brains are wired to connect, Oxford University Press, 2013

6 Jennifer Pfeifer, Carrie Masten, Larissa Borofsky, Mirella Dapretto, Andrew Fuligni & Matt Lieberman, 'Neural correlates of direct and reflected self-appraisals in adolescents and adults: When social perspective-taking informs self-perception', *Child Development, vol.80,* 2009

7 Steve Jobs (2005). *Stanford Commencement speech.*

8 Alain de Botton (2012). *@alaindebotton.*

Further reading and viewing

Brain-savvy leaders: http://www.headheartbrain.com/brain-savvy-leaders/

Know yourself better: succeed at your goals: http://www.headheartbrain.com/know-thy-self/

Gremlins: http://www.headheartbrain.com/gremlins/

Brain-savvy leading: http://www.headheartbrain.com/brain-savvy-leading-webinar-2/

Daniel Goldstein, The battle between your present and future self (TED Talk): https://www.ted.com/talks/daniel_goldstein_the_battle_between_your_present_and_future_self?language=en

Index

inverted 'U' stress model, 24, 324
see also stress

Jennings, C., 271

Jenson, E., 256

Jobs, S., 392

Johnson, M. K., 220

Journal of Applied Psychology, 339

Kahneman, D., 180
    Thinking Fast and Slow, 171, 98, 186

Kim, K., 220

Kolb, D., Experiential Learning Theory, 246-8

Kripke, D., 363

Leader's Change Charter, 64-5
    see also change; leaders

leaders
    see also leadership
    approach to teams, 106-9
    encouraging dialogue in teams, 95-6
    experience survey, 243
    general, 388
    impact on organisational energy levels, 368
    Leader's Change Charter, 64-5
    self-awareness, 389-93

leadership
    see also leaders
    case study: Creating leadership habits, 286-933
    developing, 7-8

learning myths
    70/20/10 strategy, 242-50
    learning styles theory, 245-8
    use of webinars, 244